A CHOICE OVER OUR HEADS

"Well, if you don't like it you don't have to look at it."

A CHOICE OVER
OUR HEADS

A guide to architecture
and design since 1830

Lawrence Burton

EASTVIEW EDITIONS, INC.
Westfield, New Jersey

Published in the United States of America
in 1979 by:

EASTVIEW EDITIONS, INC.
P.O. Box 783
Westfield, New Jersey, 07091
(201) 233-0474

Library of Congress Catalog Card Number: 78-78288
ISBN 0-89860-000-6

Printed in Great Britain

Contents

Acknowledgements

I am very grateful for the help given by John Thole, and Donald and Eve Gillies, who started me off on this book, and to Jack Lambert for many useful suggestions. None of these are in any way responsible for the opinions expressed in the book. I am also grateful to the Principal of Royal Holloway College and to Miss Jeannie Chapel for information about W.H. Crossland. Photographs nos. 3, 6, 7, 8, 9, 10, 13, 14, 15, 18, 19, 21, 22, 25, 27, 28, 29, 30 are reproduced by kind permission of David Cutting.
Photographs nos. 2 and 17 are reproduced by kind permission of Kerry Kennedy.
The cartoon (drawing no. 1) is reproduced by kind permission of *Punch*.

8   A CHOICE OVER OUR HEADS

Abbreviations

V. and A.	Victoria and Albert Museum, London.
M.O.M.A.	Museum of Modern Art, New York.
L.C.C.	London County Council, the local authority which ran London in the first half of the 20th century, being controlled by the Labour Party from 1933 until a Conservative Goverment abolished the L.C.C. and replaced it with a larger, but weaker, 'Metropolitan' authority, called —
G.L.C.	Greater London Council; it has inherited much of the L.C.C.'s building programmes.

List of Illustrations

22 An American example of a typical "Italian Renascence" pair of villas of the mid 19th century.

23 A Shaker chair.

24 A Utility chair.

25 A Utility table.

Photographs

1 Scandinavian apartments: Frederiksvej, Copenhagen (2nd half of the 19th century).

2 European apartments: apartment block with shops in the square opposite St. Vincent de Paul, Paris.

3 Apartments for the well-to-do: Albert Hall Mansions (R. N. Shaw, 1885).

4 Apartments for artisans: Peabody Trust dwellings, Wild St., off Kingsway, London (Darbyshire, 1881).

5 Gates to the Frogner Park, Oslo (Gustav Viegeland, c.1930).

6 Arts and Crafts: 14 South Parade (Voysey, 1891).

7 "Queen Anne": The Tabard Inn (R. N. Shaw, 1875).

8 Contrast in architectural fashions in London: the "Brutalist" Queen Elizabeth Hall of the 1960's alongside the Festival Hall of the 1950's. Behind and above, the Shell Tower of 1958-9.

9 Roehampton Housing Estate: the "Corbusier" blocks.

10 National Theatre (Denys Lasdun, 1976).

11 The Eigen Haard Estate (Michael de Klerk, 1917).

12 The De Dageraad Estate (P. L. Kramer, 1921-3).

13 French Renascence: Whitehall Court apartments alongside the Thames Embankment, London (Archer and Green, 1884).

14 Decorative ironwork in New Orleans, mid 19th century.

15 International Modern: Kensal Rise apartment block, London (Maxwell Fry and others, 1936).

16 "Swedish Modern": Vällingby, outside Stockholm. Town Centre. (Backström and other, c.1950).

17 The "New Louvre": north wing of the Louvre, Paris (Visconti and Lefuel, 1852-71). Now the *Musée des Arts Décoratifs.*

18 Remote "Second Empire" influence in Rhode Island, USA, c.1880.

20 National Provincial Bank, Bishopsgate, London (Gibson, 1865).

19 "Edwardian Baroque": Admiralty Arch, London (Aston Webb, 1911).

PART ONE   Introduction

1. General introduction to the ideas which have dominated architecture and design since 1830.

(i)

During the last 150 years architecture and design have been taken over by professionals. Before 1830, people who could afford new houses and furnishings knew what they wanted and expected the craftsmen they employed to carry out their wishes. It is significant that at this time there was still a vagueness over the use of the terms 'builder' and 'architect', and the term 'designer' was hardly used at all. It is all different now. Backed by professional institutions, architects and designers tell their 'clients' what they should be glad to pay for, and there are critics ready to applaud.

In 1830 there were very few clients who could afford to decide what buildings or furniture they wanted. However, as the years passed, more people (in Western societies at least) have been able to afford to choose what they want; indeed economists are always assuring us that 'the consumer is king'. Nevertheless, as much as there has been more money available to make choice possible, so, also, step for step, there have been a number of developments which have frustrated choice:

1. During the 19th century the idea spread that all building, and not merely expensive public and aristocratic commissions, should be considered as Architecture, and therefore as Art. The same process happened with other fields of design in the 20th century. Critics had as much interest as architects and designers in establishing design as Art, because Art by its nature should be free from lay supervision, and in need of critical explanation.

2. The growth of mass production, and the success of fewer, larger firms, creates a need to control markets.

3. The 'revolution' that happened in the arts around the year 1900 has made the developments more difficult for laymen to understand or influence. Revolution can be resisted, even countered. It was here that critics came to its aid with the historicist theory of 'our time', so that hostility to the new revolutionary styles of architecture and design, and perhaps even a rejection of them in favour of some other styles (not necessarily from 'the past'), could be met with talk of a 'style of our time', an unsound concept.

These three developments are discussed in this introduction. They have led to an increased denial of choice which became complete in most public architecture and design, including municipal housing, although some authorities, especially in Britain, have made some changes in their programmes in response to public dislike of, for example, tall blocks of flats. This denial of choice is also an underlying motif in the history of architecture and design since 1830.

(ii)

The dividing line between art and technique is difficult, perhaps impossible, to define. The term 'creative art' emphasizes one aspect of art without doing much towards defining its boundaries; There have been times when people were so impatient with the line drawn between art and technique that they announced that it does not exist. 'Architecture is fine building', wrote Lethaby at a time when most people would have wanted a clear distinction between architecture (art) and building (technique). This attempt to solve the problem by dissolving it was characteristic of the ARTS AND CRAFTS Movement (to which Lethaby belonged) which flourished from about 1870 to 1914. They did not succeed in establishing their views.

The trouble was that by 1870 'art' had become a prestige activity; painters, sculptors and architects either had become or were becoming professionals, like physicians and lawyers, and like all professionals felt the need to make distinctions. These distinctions last. Physicians and surgeons have their own professional institutions, nurses and pharmacists have theirs, and they are educated separately. Architects and industrial designers now also have their professional bodies and special art schools; bricklayers and plumbers go to trade schools. A line has been drawn between art and technique by including within art a generous number of those trades which would have been left out a hundred years ago.

An essential aspect of this professionalism is that the opinions of a professional on his own subject cannot be challenged by the layman. Only the very rich can shop around for medical opinions, and even they are not qualified to argue on points of detail in a diagnosis. With the arts, professionalism is allied to the mystique that art has gained in modern times: the artist's judgement is in fact what the patron is paying for, and in some of the arts patrons will even pay for something that is technically weak, if the artistic spirit is thought to be valuable.

How important it has been then, for the 'useful' arts—architecture and design—to make sure that they are included amongst the professional arts and not relegated to the ranks of plumbers and plasterers!

In the process, however, the layman has found himself being told that he is not qualified to understand the design of his own surroundings any more than to understand the chemistry of his own body. Both must be left to professionals. His interests will be safeguarded, not by his own taste, but by institutions which were set up to protect the interests of their members.

Prominent in this transition from 'tradesman' to 'artist' has been the propaganda of writers on architecture and design. During the 19th century the growth of a large, prosperous reading public provided an audience for a number of critics of not only books, but also paintings, sculpture and buildings. A critic can gain esteem by 'discovering' artists whom no-one else has noticed, or by championing artists hitherto derided, and reversing opinion with critical eloquence. Such a critic was John Ruskin, whose defence of the Pre-Raphaelites was a vital early help to them, and whose advocacy of 'Venetian Gothic' brought a style into English architecture, for a few years, which had not been seen in England before.

The success of Ruskin and his colleagues helped to undermine the confidence that laymen had in their own judgements on art and design, especially if they were now being persuaded to use criteria that they had not even heard of before. However, the belief that works of art should be judged by ordinary standards died hard.

It is not surprising then, that words like 'truthful', 'honest' and 'false' caught on. These words seemed to carry into the criticism of art and design concepts which the lay public could gratefully recognize. What they do not seem to have recognized is how far the decisions about what was true and what was false were being left to designers and critics, because the whole idea of truth and falsity in buildings is a fantasy (as David Watkin has shown in *Morality and architecture*). It is this misuse of the meanings of words that makes one have doubts about even William Morris.

Morris (1834-1896) saw around him a world which he deemed ugly in many ways; the bulk of the population bound to a dreary life by a system which, not surprisingly to him, supported an ugly art. As a rich man with a talent for designing, the immediate thing for him to do was to design well—and 'honestly'. This he did with such success that his work still appeals today. However, this was not enough for Morris. He was not so naive as to suppose that he could reform society through his designs, but he did believe that good art could flourish only in a good society, and he devoted many of his last years to socialism which he saw as the best hope for the future. The trouble is that there is no evidence that the bulk of that downtrodden society would have wanted to surround themselves with anything at all like Morris's designs, even if a social revolution had suddenly released them from their drudgery and filth. Such evidence as there is for popular taste in the 19th century suggests that it favoured something like a baroque style — music hall, Trade Union banners, canal barges. It would be a false step to assume that this taste was the product of deprivation; Morris would not have agreed that his work was the product of a *rentier* class. The inadequate part of Morris's legacy was the encouragement it gave to the belief that an artist had a contribution to make to the reform of society *through his art*. In cruder and more ambitious hands this idea has become overpowering.

The French-Swiss architect Jeanneret who called himself 'Le Corbusier' published a number of manifestos before he had designed many buildings. In *Vers une architecture*, published in 1922, he not only put forward architecture as the alternative to revolution (he ended the book: 'Architecture or Revolution. Revolution can be avoided.'), but launched attacks on traditional home comforts which most people might have supposed an architect would encourage and even enhance. He wrote:

Houses have not changed. But the cult of the house has remained the same for centuries. The house will also fall to the dust . . . We are to be pitied. Our houses disgust us; we fly from them and frequent restaurants and night clubs; or we gather together in our houses gloomily and secretly like wretched animals. . .

Corbusier's work is the classic modern example of architecture where everything is sacrificed to the artisitic vision of the architect. When his supporters deign to answer criticisms of his work, they always do so in terms of his greatness as an artist.

Although Corbusier began to build a number of houses in the 1920's and his books began to be translated into English, he made little impact in Britain and America. Nor did the work of the BAUHAUS, the German art school founded in 1919, where the doctrine was worked out that designers tackle 'design problems' rather than merely design artifacts, and that every 'solution' must be a fresh one, unhampered by any memories of previous 'solutions'. When Nikolaus Pevsner, an admirer of Bauhaus ideas, conducted his *Enquiry into industrial art in England* in 1937, he was dismayed to find that most manufacturers were still producing designs that their customers wanted to buy. However, help was at hand. In 1934 the art critic Herbert Read, already committed to abstract painting and sculpture, published *Art and industry*, and there were several editions in the '30s. It became a 'bible' for a certain type of progressive art-lover, and for designers themselves. Read claimed a role for designers as abstract artists with a functional justification to add to the artistic. The scope of this role has an extravagance which even Corbusier had not matched:

> An artist must plan the distribution of cities within a region; an artist must plan the distribution of buildings within a city; an artist must plan the houses themselves, the halls and factories and all that makes up the city; an artist must plan the interiors of such buildings — the shapes of rooms and the lighting and colour; an artist must plan the furniture of these rooms, down to the smallest detail, the knives and forks, the cups and saucers and door-handles.

Since 1945 'artists' in many countries, democracies and tyrannies alike have been given a free hand in most public and in some semi-private buildings. Where there have been rumbles of complaints about having such comprehensive decisions taken out of the hands of those who have to use these buildings, critics have come to the defence of their artists. Two examples will serve from recent buildings in Oxford. In his section on the city of Oxford in *Oxfordshire* in the *Buildings of England* series, Pevsner describes St. Catherine's College at some length. The college was designed by the Danish architect Arne Jacobsen and built in 1960-64 ('a perfect piece of architecture', Pevsner calls it). Jacobsen was one of those artists who fulfilled Herbert Read's vision; he did indeed design everything in St. Catherine's, down to the knives and forks. Pevsner comments: 'if young people don't like it, that may be an argument against them rather than against the college'. The whole article is well worth perusing, because this extraordinary statement is a defence of a *great* architect's right to override the possible preferences of his clients. But, as if realising the enormity of this claim, Pevsner adds something about Denmark being a 'relaxed, untotalitarian country'. The article is a mare's nest of *non-sequiturs*, but, interestingly, it does hint that Pevsner might be prepared to admit that Corbusier, for example, carried things too far.

The second example is James Stirling's Florey Building for Queen's College, built in 1968-70, but about a mile away from the main college buildings. Nicholas Taylor, otherwise one of the foremost critics of inhumane concrete housing, dismissed student complaints about the Florey on the grounds that they must not expect to find it like a traditional college building.

Art historians hold that architecture and design, if they are to form part of art history, must be considered as art, like painting and sculpture, and be judged in terms of the originality of creative artists. They have tended to write their histories of architecture or furniture entirely from the viewpoint of such original creative talents as they can identify. However, there are other viewpoints. One can distinguish between what one might call 'fashionable' architecture and design, and 'polite' architecture and design. The term 'polite' comes from R.W. Brunskill's *Illustrated handbook of vernacular architecture*. He uses it to describe all that surviving building which is influenced by some architectural ideas rather than following local and traditional practices. A further distinction can be drawn, within Brunskill's 'polite' category, to identify architecture and design created by 'artists' who are part of one fashionable movement or another.

Histories of architecture and design tend to relate the fortunes of these fashionable movements. Any 'polite' building or piece of furniture which does not fit into the already outlined sequence of fashions is ignored. If challenged over a particular item from what is a vast store of 'polite' buildings and furnishings, the art historian would reply that it was not an *original* work; that its prototype dates from years before it was made, when the design was an original idea, and that anything which follows that is merely a 'copy' — any modifications being due to the incompetence of craftsmen, not the ideas of a creative mind. The historicist idea of 'a style of a time' is an important part of the art historian's critical apparatus here.

This treatment results in a great deal of 19th and 20th century design and architecture being written off as 'derivative'. To read architectural histories, even many of the good ones, it takes a long time to realise some simple facts: for example, the GOTHIC REVIVAL was a movement confined to a small part of society and lasted as an important style for only a short time; the prevailing style of the years 1830 to 1930 was classical, as it had been in Europe and America for two hundred years before, and in the 1920's there were new classical buildings as interesting and original in their way as any in the past; most 19th century furniture was plain, solid stuff, so that practically every piece illustrated in the histories of furniture is an exceptional, uncharacteristic specimen.

This art-historical habit obscures a much more interesting question than 'who were the original artists?' That question is, what is the relationship between 'polite' architecture and design, and 'fashionable'? Which of the many fashions that are recorded in the histories could be taken up by 'polite' designers and manufacturers? Instead of writing off minor Georgian streets as being of no special artistic value, we should perhaps consider what qualities there are in the Palladian 'originals' which could be adapted to such good use in 'polite' building.

'Polite' building and design, like folk art, which also borrows from grander styles, can flourish only when the decisions about what to take from fashion are left to a co-operation between client and craftsman. It is this partnership which has suffered from both art criticism and propaganda and even more severely, perhaps, from the growth of professionalism in architecture and design. A typical example of this development can be traced in the history of the Royal Institute of British Architects. Starting as something like a club, the R.I.B.A. has gradually come to embrace the whole architectural profession in Britain, promoting Acts of Parliament (against much opposition) to secure the exclusive right of people licensed by themselves to design buildings. Barrington Ward, in his *Growth of the architectural profession in Britain*, has an interesting quotation from the *R.I.B.A. Journal* in 1948:

> The ultimate objective is naturally to prevent anyone performing the duties of an architect unless he is registered — a legal enactment found in some American states.

The cause of their unease was the builder who followed a popular design, or interpreted his client's idea. Soundness of construction is covered by other Acts of Parliament and inspectors.

We can go to art galleries and enjoy paintings and sculpture. It is one thing to admire an artist's mind, but another to have to live in it. Deciding on the surroundings that please us is something which we cannot often carry out thoroughly, but it is certainly a major part of that *pursuit* of happiness which Jefferson put only after life and liberty as an *inalienable* right. Many of these rights have been undermined by tradesmen claiming to be artists; but they are inalienable rights, we cannot give them away. Other people, however expert, even if they are William Morris, cannot pursue our happiness for us.

(iii)

The development of industrial production from the late 18th century onwards made great changes in some, but not all, building and design. During the 19th century the characteristic industrial firm could satisfy only a small part of the potential demand by itself, and had to compete with a large number of firms, mostly of the same size. Competition became tougher in the middle of the century when transport improved enough to move goods around and abroad easily. These firms formed the basis for the 'market' which early economists set up as a model in their theories of economic activity. Some of these firms, for example in the ceramic industry, were among those which helped to create the industrial revolution in the 18th century; many of them carried on almost unchanged through the further revolutions in industry in the late 19th and early 20th centuries.

Many more firms did go through a further revolution, in methods — developments in the chemical industry and the use of oil and electricity in place of coal and water for power — and in business organisation. Whereas the characteristic firm in the 19th century was too small to have much influence on the market (real or theoretical), the characteristic firm of the 20th century is big enough to control markets (real, but not yet theoretical) either alone, or more often in consort — tacit rather than open — with its 'rivals'. The effect of these changes on architecture and design has been uneven. Many industries have remained surprisingly unchanged over 150 years; notably the furniture makers, especially in countries like Denmark, where the Copenhagen cabinet makers' guild played a large part in the development of modern Danish furniture design. Crafts like hand-thrown pottery, which might well have died out in the face of industrial production, have stirred into life again.

The conflict between 'industry' and 'craft' was a burning issue in the design world of the 19th century, and it still smoulders. An aspect of this is the nature of factory work. One of the main driving forces behind William Morris's philosophy was the conviction that factory work dehumanises people; there is a lot of modern research to support him. Some firms, like the Swedish car manufacturers SAAB and Volvo, have tried team production instead of assembly-line production and have found that this encourages workers to stay longer with their firms. This is not to suggest, though, that Morris would have given his blessing to even Swedish car works.

The trouble for Morris was that he realised that his work, and all designs produced by hand, were expensive, probably always had been, and, because of the cost of materials and the time spent by craftsmen, always would be. His frustration was expressed in strange outbursts, like the remark that all he was doing was 'to pander to the swinish luxury of the rich'. Most of the histories tell us that Morris's dilemma was resolved only through Gropius and the Bauhaus, when they translated Morris's ideals into mass-production. Morris himself, they write, could not solve them because of his opposition to 'the machine'. 'To resolve his conflict', the Penguin *Dictionary of the decorative arts* says: 'he retreated into poetic dreams of a future in which machinery would be abandoned and the medieval guild system restored.' It adds, however, that the essentials of his message were taken up on the continent, notably by Van der Velde, through whom he exerted a vital influence on the early C20 development of industrial design'.

Morris is a powerful and attractive figure in arguments about design as well as being a designer of genius himself. It is important, therefore, to use him on one's side if possible, something which was realised long ago by the International Modern Movement; by Gropius and after him by Nikolaus Pevsner in his 1936 book *Pioneers of the Modern Movement*. But the evidence is against this appropriation. On few matters can Morris be shown to be in sympathy with the Bauhaus and its heirs, least of all with the whole practice of 'industrial design'. The one concept which the Bauhaus and Morris share is the shaky idea of honesty — no-one, surely, would publicize his designs and ideas as 'dishonest'. The Penguin *Dictionary*, too, is deceptive about Van der Velde. He was indeed inspired by Morris, and continued to practise and preach his principles, most publicly at the debate held at the *Deutsche Werkbund* exhibition in Cologne in 1914, where Van der Velde defended craftsmanship against Muthesius, who argued for mass-production.

There is also much confusion over the word 'machine'. It became almost an article of faith in the Arts and Crafts movements and their admirers, followers of Morris all of them, that the 'machine' should be resisted. When in 1910 C. R. Ashbee, leader of the Guild and School of Handicraft, said 'modern civilization rests on machinery, and no system for the encouragement and endowment of the teaching of the arts can be sound that does not recognize this', it seems to have been taken as a body-blow to the whole Arts and Crafts Movement in Britain — if not in Scandinavia. All civilizations have depended on machinery of some sort. What was, or should have been, at issue was mass-production, where the 'enemy' is not so much the 'machine' as the economic system which uses machines and humans alike. That is what Morris realized.

There was considerable excitement in the early years of the 20th century among some people for the achievements of industrial machinery; the enthusiasm even survived the war of 1914-18. Some art movements, particularly Futurism and the Dutch group DE STIJL, made a cult of the machine, believing that human spirituality could be achieved only by a divorce from the randomness of Nature. After 1923 De Stijl became the leading influence in the Bauhaus; enthusiasm for 'the machine' made mass-production, and industrial design, potentially respectable.

This 'resolution' of Morris's dilemma seemed to give the designer immense power, as Herbert Read was soon to recommend in *Art and industry*. But mass-production industry is not interested in art, but in selling goods. Art can sometimes help sell goods, when it will be used; and sometimes not help at all, when it will be ignored. J. K. Galbraith has a chapter in his *Economics and the public purpose*, called 'The market system and the arts', in which he differentiates between the kinds of design which can be standardised and absorbed by the mass-production system, and those which depend on individual, creative qualities which the system cannot absorb. Amongst the creative arts which the system cannot absorb are personal services like hairdressing, and fine arts generally where it is the unusual which has a value. Quite clearly, when Morris was talking about 'everyone' being able to enjoy art, he was not thinking of those goods whose suitability for mass-production is decided by committees of marketing experts, advertising executives and sales-managers. And equally clearly, our present economic system cannot afford to allow creative designers, however well-trained in Bauhaus principles, to decide on the shapes of products for which millions must be committed, unless they are firmly guided towards their 'solutions' by teams of managers.

Mass-production depends on turnover; what is produced in the mass has to be expendable and therefore short-lived, no matter how good a design it may be. And 'good' in this context must not mean 'long-lasting'. If we were able to use our old, beautifully designed gadgets for years, the gadget factory would have to close down. This is the production 'world' that the Bauhaus claimed as its kingdom; a world where good designs as much as bad ones have to give way to the new season's designs.

The Bauhaus ideal, then, can be seen as an illusion. With its 'abstract' ethic, it is a dull illusion too. In that same book, *Art and industry*, Herbert Read sneered at ornament, comparing it to tattooing, the delight of primitive peoples and childish minds. This view was often repeated in the '30's and for a couple of decades afterwards. Although ornament has now come back in clothes fashions, and fabrics are unashamedly decorative, the products of industry remain drearily plain. Industrial design may not have succeeded in its Herbert Read, platonic ambitions, but its one achievment has been the banishing of ornament. The aesthetic subtleties of abstract art, whether painting, sculpture, or the selected, unornamented industrial goods one sees in the pages of *Design* magazine, have never been enjoyed by more than a few people, who constitute a quite self-conscious élite. It is ironic that a 'movement' which started out with the aim of making the world a more beautiful place for everyone should have ended by making the world undoubtedly much drabber for most people, and producing a design cult which appeals only to a narrow range of them. This has, though, been the fate of most movements that have consisted in a few high-minded, earnest people who know what is good for other people better than they do themselves.

One cannot seriously claim that modern mass-production has provided people with a significant choice. Between the efforts of advertisers and market research men, engineers and accountants, there is, at best, only a narrow range of choices. This may be one reason for the steady revival of handmade crafts, whether in the developed countries or in the underdeveloped ones, where they are encouraged by relief organisations. In the face of heavily advertised synthetic carpets, Oxfam, as well as helping peasants to survive, may be doing a great deal for individual choice.

(iv)

Most of us have been appalled by the wholesale destruction of British cities since 1945. It is ironic that people fought to save these cities from the Nazis during the 1939-45 war, only to lose them to town-planners, architects and developers in the years of peace that followed. In Britain a careful restoration was forbidden by the ideology of 'our time', so that Hitler won over Exeter, but not over Warsaw.

This phrase, 'the style of our time', recurs in many books and pamphlets about modern architecture. It is meaningless, because the phrase 'our time' is a theoretical concept, and concepts do not have styles. It is as misguided to talk about 'the style of our time' as it would be to talk about 'bad-tempered gravity'.

The concept of a 'time' has been used by some writers during the last 200 years to analyse the culture of societies. More fruitful methods of analysis have related art, buildings and customs to concepts of social class, or economic power, though there are problems with these methods, too. It is always difficult to know how 'our time' writers decide when one 'time' has ended and another begun, and even more difficult to know what criteria they are using to distinguish between which buildings, etc., are 'of a time' and which are not. Anything built in a given period, one would suppose, must be a manifestation of some aspect of 'that time', and therefore the characteristics which might qualify Corbusier's *Citrohan* house project as 'in the style of the time', but would reject Lutyens's Midland Bank in Piccadilly, cannot have anything to do with *actual* time, since they date from the same year, 1922.

Some 19th century writers demanded a new style, but it was not until the 20th century that anyone could identify any style which could plausibly be called 'new'. The only way this could be done, in fact, was to design buildings (and later on furniture) with no style at all, relying on either the textures of the materials used, or on the residual geometric shapes. It was the shapes that were taken up first which became the International Modern style, as used by Corbusier and the architects of the Bauhaus. This is usually called 'the style of our time'. Designers in other styles today wisely tend not to use that concept at all. Corbusier himself was anxious to establish that his architecture was part of the continuing tradition of all that was best in architectural design — he called his book *Vers une architecture;* it was the English translator who made it *Towards a new architecture*. Nevertheless it is true, in a trivial sense, that it has been only in the 20th century that the various elements of the International Style have been brought together. However, what was 'our time' in 1922 or even in 1930 may not be 'our time' in the late 1970's.

So there is a tendency among many architects, designers and critics to write as though we are still living in the same 'time' as the architects of the 1920's, in a sense that we are not living in the same 'time' as the architects of, say, the 1910's. The Smithsons, for example, talk about the 'Heroic Period of modern architecture' (the 1920's) as 'the rock upon which we stand'. (see INTERNATIONAL MODERN). Such sentiments do give the impression that these architects are, as it were, defending a revolution of some kind; that the style they practise is more than merely one style among many possible styles, indeed the only permissible style. The atmosphere of a none-too-successful revolution seems to have crept into the argument.

It is certainly evident in much historical writing. Many of the historians who believe, like the Smithsons, that the International Modern is a rock on which they stand, have defended it by re-writing history, in the way that political revolutionaries do. To take two examples of books written for a popular readership (many others could be found, too): J.M. Richards's *Introduction to modern architecture* spends considerable space on describing the 'in-adequacies' of earlier architecture, as a justification for the International Modern. R. Furneaux Jordan gives a very strange account of *Victorian architecture* in his efforts to present it as the pre-revolutionary muddle for which the International Modern provided the only answer.

There is an amusing example of the tangle that this mistake over the concept of 'our time' can produce. In *Experiencing architecture*, Steen-Eiler Rasmussen has a photograph of an actor dressed up as King Christian IV of Denmark, trying to ride a bicycle. Rasmussen uses this picture to clinch an argument that the costume and the bicycle, though both excellent, 'simply do not go together. In the same way, it is impossible to take over the beautiful architecture of a past era . . .' But if we look at paintings from King Christian's lifetime — the early 17th century — we can see ordinary people dressed in clothes which would be quite suitable for cycling. On the other hand, there are many costumes of 'our time' — deep-sea divers' or space suits for moon-walking — which would be as unsuitable for cycling as King Christian's costume.

(v)

In spite of the strong institutional position of architects and designers, it does seem possible that they are not going to be allowed to get away indefinitely with the kind of control over our lives that they have been claiming during the last century. The dogmas of the International Modern Movement have not become a part of general ideas; we are still Jeffersonians. The 'revolution' that was defended has not succeeded entirely in the field and is failing in its educational propaganda missions. As Mark Girouard writes in *Sweetness and light*, 'The Modern Movement, as doctrinaire and intolerant in its day as the Gothic Revival, has fallen even more heavily out of favour'. The Modern Movement has done infinitely more damage to the environment than the Gothic Revival, but the critical reaction to *Sweetness and light* shows that the old guard of the Modern Movement cannot give up the idea that art matters more than choice.

Then there is the resources and energy crisis. One thing that many of the high buildings of the Modern Movement share with the world of industrial design is an extravagant waste of resources. High buildings are expensive to build and expensive to maintain. Without a large supply of energy, these buildings are unusable; we remember accounts of New York City during the strike of 1977.

If we are to look at the real world, and the ways in which designers can help a free society to make the most of its resources for a visually interesting life, we must, for a start, jettison a great deal of the 'artistic' theory of the past century, and return to a state of affairs where the clients have the major say in the design of the buildings and chattels they buy. In the 1970's we ought to have more people free to choose than in the 1830's. The International Modern Movement in particular has been a disaster, not only for the extreme and brutal quality of many of its buildings, but for the arrogant attitude to its clients, to the whole world of existing designs and to the environment. It is always worth recalling that the owners of two of the most publicised buildings of the Modern Movement, both still quoted as classic designs, Corbusier's Villa Savoye of 1929 and Mies's Farnsworth House of 1950, found them too expensive to maintain; the Savoye family had abandoned their villa before the war.

Houses could now be built without any of the clichés of the Bauhaus from the most suitable materials available — brick, wood or even stone — with windows which let in only enough light for normal purposes (see Steen-Eiler Rasmussen's chapter in *Towns and buildings* on the use of shutters to vary the light in a room). The craze for blinding one's rooms with light from plate-glass windows, which overheat the room in summer, and waste heat in winter, is an example of the kind of 'Modern' cliché that should be discouraged.

As for public buildings, there ought to be discussions on whether the public actually wants monuments. Apart from showing off, there is no reason why buildings should as a rule be more than two storeys high, built with local materials and local labour. Town halls, hospitals, schools, shops and offices would be cheaper, friendlier and less intrusive if on a smaller scale.

In the 18th century in England and eastern America, architects and designers published books of plans and elevations and furniture designs. These were then copied, simplified or adapted by local craftsmen, usually to commissions. It was not unlike the way suits are sometimes ordered from tailors, or how knitting patterns are adapted. In America today, developers show prospective buyers a variety of house styles — colonial, Spanish, etc. — as well as sizes to choose from before they are built. It ought not to be impossible for even local authorities to do much the same service for their future tenants, chosen from the housing lists before the estates are built, rather than after. In London, the G.L.C. is attempting to meet prospective tenants' choices in its 'PSHAK' housing in Adelaide Road, by offering them at least a choice of interior arrangements. One cannot predict the tastes of future tenants, of course, but neither could the private developers between the end of the 19th century and 1939, when estates were built for letting rather than selling. (Individual choice is, of course, much more limited by blocks of flats than by houses.) There is also the idea of architects and designers providing 'kits' from which clients can build up something individual — it happens already in Finland. The work of some younger architects, particularly the housing estates of Darbourne and Darke in London, shows a new awareness of the need to create human-scale and pleasant environments.

Books like Turner and Fichter's *Freedom to build* and Brolin's *The failure of modern architecture* are impressive in that they show that many young architects are turning away from the dogmas of their teachers — and the arguments in these books are compelling in themselves. It is true that the kinds of buildings they praise may not have the excitement or the 'layers of meaning' that a critic like Charles Jencks looks for, but in any society which claims to be both liberal and democratic, we are long overdue for a chance to develop our own meanings and no longer have to live as part of the meanings of someone else. An appreciation of the arguments of the past 150 years could be a help towards this aim, and an unbiased study of the buildings and designs can be a very useful guide to action.

2. An outline of architecture since 1830.

2a. An Historical Chart.

	1830	1840	1850	1860	1870	188
Neo-Classical ('Greek Revival' in U.S.A.)	World-wide	U.S.A. British Colonies	U.S.A. British Colonies	U.K.		
Romanesque ('Rundbogenstil' in Germany until 1850)	Germany U.S.A.	Germany U.K. U.S.A.	U.K. U.S.A.	France U.K. Scandinavia	France U.K. U.S.A.	U.S
Gothic Revival	U.K.	U.K.	Canada Germany France Britain Austria	Germany France U.K. U.S.A. Austria	U.K. U.S.A.	Neth U.K U.S
Italian Renascence	U.K.	U.K. France	U.S.A. U.K. France			
Elizabethan Scottish Renascence etc.	U.K.	U.K.	U.K.	U.K.		U.K U.S
French Renascence	France	U.K.			U.K. U.S.A.	U.K U.S
Neo-Baroque ('Second Empire' in France 1850-1870)			U.K. U.S.A. France	World-wide	World-wide	Worl
Queen Anne/Shingle		U.K.		U.K.	U.K. U.S.A.	U.K U.S
Arts & Crafts						
Art Nouveau						
Expressionism						
International Modern			U.K.			
Scandinavian Modern						
Brutalism						

1900	1910	1920	1930	1940	1950	1960	1970
Scandinavia U.S.A. Germany	Scandinavia U.S.A. Germany (until c.1914)	Scandinavia (until c.1925)					
Netherlands U.K. Germany							
U.K. U.S.A.							
World-wide	World-wide	World-wide	U.S.A.				
U.K. Scandinavia	Scandinavia						
Belgium France Austria Spain							
Spain Germany	Netherlands Germany	Netherlands Germany		Latin America			
		Germany France Netherlands	Scandinavia France Czechoslovakia	Scandinavia U.S.A.	World-wide	World-wide	
			Scandinavia	Scandinavia U.K.	Scandinavia U.K.		
				France	France U.K.	World-wide	

2b. Notes on the Origins of 'Modern' Architecture.

There are two main 'streams' which have run together to make modern architecture. One is a modest, comfortable, lack-of-style associated with Philip Webb and W. R. Lethaby, suited to houses but also to any building which does not need to be large — local branches of libraries, clinics or shops. The obvious materials for such buildings are whatever comes to hand: brick in clay districts, stone where it is easy to quarry, wood where there are forests. There are modern wood-frame and clapboard houses erected in America in a 'polite' style, now, as they have been for 300 years. A more self-consciously artistic aspect of this 'non-style' can be seen in the work of many Scandinavian architects, especially Aalto, and there is also wooden furniture by him. The prevailing life-style of the western managerial classes is self-indulgent and much more informal than it was in the 19th century, so that a class which might have responded to the 'artistic' architecture of the International Modern Movement prefers something much more flexible, almost do-it-yourself, with 'eclectic' borrowings, if they please. Moderately well-to-do people are still free to have 'Georgian' fireplaces installed in Canadian 'log-cabin' villas, if that is what they want.

The other stream is traceable to the wool and cotton mills built in northern England at the end of the 18th century (see IRON ARCHITECTURE). These iron-frame buildings have been hailed by some 20th century writers as 'the style of the 19th century', but this historicist interpretation prevents us from seeing their real position in the development of architecture. These mills were usually designed in a classical style, excellent examples of 'polite' architecture. To write about a *Functional tradition,* as J. M. Richards did, is to ignore the actual style of these buildings. Iron-frame is anonymous; so the same classical style was used for mills and warehouses as had been used for dockyard storehouses in the 18th century before iron-frame had been thought about, and indeed the same style as many 18th century row-houses — plain brick with a mainly vertical emphasis to counteract the horizontality brought about by repetition along the street, with classical trimmings where appropriate on doorcases and windows. In Richards's book there are some photographs of later 19th century buildings which are almost devoid of any classical styling, but the pre-International Modern buildings have nevertheless differences which must be noted. The boathouse at Sheerness dockyard which was 'discovered' by the photographer Eric de Maré is a four-storey, fourteen-bay frame building with horizontal strip windows; from a distance it looks like a building of a hundred years later, one of those exceptional 'previsions' in architecture. Close-to, a contrast between '1861' and '1961' becomes clear. Each bay of the horizontal windows is divided into five distinct windows, each with glazing bars and six panes. A classical quality of detail sits easily in a 'modern' frame.

In the years after 1910 the revolutionary architects took the structure of these iron-frame buildings and anathematized the external visual style (in the alleged cause of 'honesty'). They were not the first to experiment with facades; the architects of the CHICAGO SCHOOL had already tackled the problems in designing tall buildings. They found that even the minimal classical element of 'polite' architecture was not suitable (which may be a strong argument against tall buildings: classical architecture is a great humane yardstick). The Chicago architects drew instead on the ROMANESQUE, the other main style of the 19th century to be used for large buildings, and created some impressive blocks. The revolutionary architects of C.I.A.M. and the BAUHAUS seem to have been unaware of these buildings. They certainly put forward a completely different 'solution' from that of Chicago. Their facade design could be one of two types: either completely smooth — windows flush to the wall, stucco surfaces, cubic shapes — or 'announcing' the structure. Both have tended to monotony, because even a 'structure' building tends to be repetitive. The fondness for a glass 'skin' over the outside of these high frame buildings satisfies both these possibilities: it gives the whole block a smooth shiny surface — like a 'precise machine', to take a favourite simile of theirs — and, being transparent, it shows the structure.

It might have been better if these two 'streams' had kept to their own beds, but the International Modern, being a revolutionary movement, needed to absorb or destroy any rival philosophy, so the 'suitability', 'no-nonsense' part of modern architecture was claimed by the propagandists of International Modern, however far-fetched this claim might seem. In practice, iron-frame, or reinforced concrete (the other main new structural method of the 19th century, used until recently as little more than an alternative to iron-frame), was used for buildings where they had no place. Corbusier's 'Domino' house, where roof, floor and basement would be held apart by a few steel columns, has always been hailed by propagandists as a brilliant 'solution' to the 'problems' of The House, as though Philip Webb would have given a million dollars to have thought of it, and as though people had not been building, experimenting and testing techniques for thousands of years. It is in fact really an unsuitable 'non-solution' because it entails elaborate construction methods and technical back-up where none are needed, and is in fact much more rigid that a conventionally built house (it may be possible to shuffle screens round on each floor — if noise and smell insulation do not matter — but the main structure cannot be changed). What the 'Domino' house would be, of course, is a work of art.

The most spectacular way in which the International Modern Movement has asserted the 'artistic' over the 'suitable' stream has been in encouraging local authorities to commission huge apartment blocks. Factory construction methods masterminded by 'artists' are necessary for these. A reaction to this nowadays may draw attention back to the much more fruitful 'suitable' tradition, and remind us why the mills and factories were made with iron frames in the first place: for a very practical purpose, to cut down fire risk in continuous shift-work factories, not in the pursuit of technological ideology, and not in order to give 'artists' their head. It may remind us too that an internal iron frame did not make the designers think that they should give up the traditions of 'polite' architecture.

2c.   The Influence of Architectural Fashions on 'Polite' Architecture.
'Polite' architecture between 1830 and 1930 was classical, and so what
determined how far, if at all, fashionable styles would have any influence was
whether they could be fitted in to the classical framework already there. Thus
the GOTHIC REVIVAL had very little influence outside high fashion; some
details of gables, porches and occasionally windows were picked up in the
middle years of the 19th century, but no more. The various fashions within the
classical style, on the other hand, had a much greater influence: 'Second
Empire' with its high-pitched roofs with their ornamental ridges had a lasting
influence on houses in America and Europe, and to a lesser extent in Britain.
In England and America, the revival of interest in wooden glazing bars that
came with the QUEEN ANNE fashion affected 'polite' architecture so that in
many developments after 1870 glazing bars were used in preference to the
plate glass windows which the mid-Victorians had favoured.

Of other possibly influential styles, ROMANESQUE was effective only on a
large scale, and remained a high fashion style. ART NOUVEAU had a wide
influence in its special fields — stained glass, ornamental woodwork, wrought
iron, and so on. Mid-Victorian classical houses had stained glass windows,
even if only in plain panels; Art Nouveau provided more exciting patterns and
colours which were taken up and mass-produced. In England this particular
feature lasted well into the 1930's, no longer anywhere near original art and
high fashion, but unmistakably a 'polite' version of Art Nouveau. In the
1930's lattice windows finally ousted the mauve and orange flower shapes
from the top windows of suburban drawing rooms.

One of the difficulties of the International Modern style is that it is a totality
of design and has little that can be comfortably taken up by 'polite'
architecture; in fact, the whole idea of a separate building tradition outside
high fashion is contrary to the aims not only of the INTERNATIONAL MODERN
Movement, but also to those of professional associations like the R.I.B.A.
Nevertheless some of the clichés of C.I.A.M. have been picked up by 'polite'
architecture. In the 1930's, the horizontal obsession of the Modern Movement
was early noticed and copied — windows were lengthened and lowered and
sometimes wrapped round the corner of the house. 'Streamlining' generally,
without going wholly ART DECO, became a quite common stylistic habit. All
this was scorned by the critics. After about 1960, large plate-glass window
walls became fashionable, and even 'polite'. It was at a time when some of the
Moderns were advocating 'breaking down' the distinctions between the inside
of a house and its garden, so that the tiles of the terrace would be used through
into the living-room, underneath a plate-glass wall, some of which would be a
sliding door. Plants would be grown inside the house as well as outside. This
'indoor/outdoor space flow' ethic still survives in favourable climates like
California. Similar plate-glass walls/doors were used in shops and public
buildings in the early 1960's, until a number of accidents caused by people
walking into them, made them uneconomic. Huge plate-glass windows do not
fit into traditional house shapes, but such ill-advised insertions can be seen
from many railway-lines in the suburbs.

2d. The Problems of Scale.

Modern engineering has given designers the opportunity to design very big objects. Until the 20th century only the cathedrals in Europe and some temples and pyramids elsewhere were large, and they took many years to build. The great years of sensational 'bigness' were the 1920's and '30's. There were books with titles like *The wonder book of ships* which had drawings of the *Queen Mary* resting across Trafalgar Square with steam coming out of her funnels, her bows into Whitehall, her stern into St. Martin's Lane, and Nelson's column reaching up only as far as the bridge deck. We could see how thrillingly enormous she was.

In buildings the Americans had led with the tall Chicago blocks of the 1890's and the spectacular development of Manhattan in the years up to 1930 (the Empire State Building, the tallest in the world at the time, was built in 1930-32). It was about this time that architects like Corbusier, noticing how many people could be lodged in such blocks, toyed with the amusing idea of 'villages in the sky'. The blocks in America had been designed as offices or hotels.

It was not until the 'reconstruction' period after 1945 that tall buildings began to rise in European cities. Just as skyscrapers had transformed New York, dwarfing buildings like St. Patrick's cathedral, which had stood out before, so the tall European buildings transformed their cities. Even Paris, where the authorities put up the longest fight against these intruders, now has towers at Montparnasse and beyond the Arc de Triomphe.

As with the cathedrals, 'bigness' is meant to make us gasp, though there are now so many tall buildings that our gasps have turned to yawns. Whatever the merits of individual designs, a tall building which is completely out of scale with its surroundings changes its neighbourhood altogether, Aylesbury in Buckinghamshire is an example of a small country town suddenly brought down to being no more than the podium for a tall tower-block built to house the county council's offices. One has to choose one's viewpoint to avoid it.

John Stuart Mill discerned two types of action — self-regarding action, upon which society should put no restraints, and other-regarding action, which should be subject to restraint. There is some difficulty in deciding what actions are purely self-regarding, but there can be no doubt that a tall building is other-regarding. In so far as visual standards matter at all, any tall building is an infringement on the freedom of other people.

3. An outline of design since 1830.

3a. An Historical Chart.

	1830	1840	1850	1860	1870	1880
Neo-Classical (1830-1860 'Biedermeyer' in Germany & Scandinavia) (1830-1850 'Louis-Philippe' in France)	Germany Scandinavia U.K. France	Germany Scandinavia U.K. France	Germany Scandinavia			
Rococo		Most of Europe & America	Most of Europe & America	Most of Europe & America		
Second Empire			France: then World-wide	World-wide	World-wide	World-wide
Art Furniture				U.K. U.S.A.	U.K. U.S.A.	
Aesthetic Japan				U.K.	U.K.	U.K.
Morris/Arts-Crafts		Scandinavia	Scandinavia	U.K. Scandinavia	U.K. Scandinavia	U.K. Scandinavia
Art Nouveau						U.K.
System Furniture Deutschewerkbund						
Art Deco						
Bauhaus						
Scandinavian Modern						
Pop Art						
Ethnic						

00	1910	1920	1930	1940	1950	1960	1970
K. S.A.	U.S.A. Germany	France U.S.A.	France U.S.A.				
orld-wide	World-wide						
K. S.A., Europe andinavia	Scandinavia	Scandinavia	Scandinavia	Scandinavia	Scandinavia	Scandinavia	Scandinavia
rope, S.A.	U.S.A.					England, U.S.A., Europe	U.K. U.S.A. Europe
ermany	Germany				World-wide	World-wide	World-wide
S.A.	U.S.A.	France 1925: then World-wide	World-wide	World-wide	World-wide	World-wide	World-wide
		Germany 1923	Germany (ends 1933) U.S.A.	U.S.A.	World-wide	World-wide	World-wide
		Denmark	Denmark Sweden Finland	Denmark Sweden Finland	U.K. Denmark Sweden Finland U.S.A.	U.K. Denmark Sweden Finland U.S.A.	U.K. Denmark Sweden Finland U.S.A.
					U.S.A.	U.S.A.: then World-wide	World-wide
						World-wide	World-wide

2 *A room design from Garrett's* Home decoration *(1879). The furniture
is 'Georgian' and the décor quite plain.*

3b. The Aims of Victorian Designers and Critics.

There are some questions that should be considered about design. What were
Victorian designers and writers about design trying to do?

In Britain, Henry Cole and others (including Prince Albert) worked
tirelessly from the 1830's onwards to promote 'good design' (not always for
purely aesthetic reasons). Certainly the designs which won prizes at the Great
Exhibition in 1851 (Cole's enterprise) were by and large a failure; but what
exactly were they failing to do, or be? It is easy to be misled by the many pleas
for 'fitness of purpose', 'honest workmanship', or 'straightforward design'
which ring out down the years, and have been so often quoted since. The early
Victorians (and their neighbours overseas) were surrounded by good design
on those terms. Not only were there streets of excellent plain 18th century
houses, but there was a vast quantity of sober 18th century furniture,
silverware, glass, and china. Much of it survives now, and there must have
been even more of it then. If they really wanted good, honest design, there it

3 A 'cosy corner' typical of late Victorian décor. This comes from the magazine Furniture and decoration *for 1st March 1893.*

was. And in America, there were the Shakers, even simpler and even more honest. All this seems to have been ignored. Perhaps it was due to a silly hatred for everything to do with '18th century' culture — allegedly immoral and therefore incapable of 'honest' design — but this is, one hopes, an unconvincing explanation, in spite of the rantings of the GOTHIC REVIVALISTS.

It may be that until at least the late 19th century, everyone assumed that good design meant *rich* design. Even William Morris, whatever he may have said about preferring whitewashed walls, designed some of the most elaborately intricate wallpapers and furnishing fabrics ever sold. A great deal of even 18th century furniture, especially that made for the very rich in the last quarter of the 18th century, is on the edge of vulgarity, held back (for us) by the very rigid rules of NEO-CLASSICISM, without which all that inlaid gold and enamel would overstep the bounds of good taste. But whereas the 'Louis XVI' style was held in check by neo-classical taste, fashion in the 19th century favoured baroque and rococo, and found neo-classical tame.

4 *A fireplace and overmantel from C. L. Eastlake,* Household hints.*The overmantel was meant to be a family 'museum'.*

So the problem that 19th century designers were tackling may have been how to produce good, highly ornamental design. This is difficult. Even more difficult is how to produce richly ornamented pieces *cheaply*. Cole never succeeded, neither did Morris ever manage to produce his designs, which were by far the best of the richly ornamented designs in the century, cheaply. A few designers did come near to succeeding later on in the century. But Eastlake's highly eclectic designs were in the end not such good *models* for 'polite' design, as, for example, Chippendale's had been. It is not surprising that Eastlake disowned many of the products that were made by manufacturers claiming to be inspired by his books, especially in America.

Art Nouveau designers also came close to succeeding, reaching a kind of rococo elegance. The weakness of the style — from the point of view of 'polite' design — was that when manufactured cheaply, it could easily be debased.

3c. The Influence of Fashionable Design on 'Polite' Design.

How far have any of the fashionable design movements affected 'polite' design?

Cost is the chief factor. Designs which depend for their effect on expensive materials or expensive processes are always a bad model for 'polite' design. Modern design is particularly vulnerable in this way. Any chair which is originally designed to be made with chrome-plated steel frame and upholstery in real hide is going to look unsatisfactory in painted iron and plastic upholstery. So some designers have split their work: Charles Eames has designed a much imitated chair with a moulded body and iron legs; and also an expensive reclining chair with moulded rosewood and real leather. But the drawback of good, cheap plastic furniture is that, for most people, plastic and painted iron do not go well in the home, and many would rather have crude 'kitchen' chairs in wood. The Eames chair may be more comfortable, but it looks like furniture in the Post Office.

None of the 19th or 20th century design movements ever achieved anything like the influence of 'polite' design which the classical designs had, and this may be one of the reasons for the now steady revivial of appetite for Georgian, Regency or Colonial furniture. The greatest achievment of any design movement has been that of the BAUHAUS, but it is strictly confined to 'new' designs — mostly electrical goods, sewing machines, cookers. Apart from them, only isolated designs caught on — Thonet's bentwood chairs; swivel library or desk chairs, and the wooden arm chair called a 'captain's chair'; and Morris wallpapers.

5 A Victorian office swivel chair.   *6 A "captain's chair".*

3d. Interior Design and Individual Choice.

The idea itself of interior design is a bold claim on the part of the 'artist' to oversee the whole environment of his client, and it has been a recurring theme throughout the history of design since the mid-18th century. One of the most famous of interior designers was the architect Robert Adam, who remodelled two country houses near London in the 1760's — Osterley Park for Robert Child and Syon House for the Duke of Northumberland. Adam's style was one which would accommodate no other; there was no place for cherished old pieces in his rooms. The suites of rooms he decorated at Osterley and Syon are *parade* rooms, where the artistic authority is acceptable. At Kedleston Hall in Derbyshire, where Adam was also called in to design interiors in the 1760's, the central 'parade' block was built after the two smaller wings which contain the comfortable family rooms. This marks the difference between the use of the 'artistic' designer, and the use of 'polite' designs for living in.

On the whole this kind of comprehensive designing was in abeyance in the 19th century, in spite of the pronouncements of designers like Pugin and Morris. The fact that there was indeed no 'style of the 19th century' helped to make newly designed interiors, however grandiose, more varied.

The designers of the 1920's reacted against this ECLECTICISM as against everything else in Victorian design, and the idea was revived that someone — preferably the architect (as at St. Catherine's College in Oxford) — should design interiors in one uniform style, and should design everything, or at worst, choose the furnishings himself. Architects like Mies van der Rohe, Philip Johnson, and their many followers and imitators, leave little room for personal creative expression in their interiors. This probably works well enough in places where one does not have time to notice the decoration — airports and banks, for example, but becomes tedious in hotels and would be intolerable in a home. In Mies's rooms, as much as in Adam's, there is no place for Grandma's old rocking-chair.

4. Town planning since 1830.

4a. Notes on the Main Ideas.

Town planning is architecture and design on the grandest scale. There has been town planning of some kind since the beginning of civilization, but until modern times not many 'artistic' plans. In the Renascence and in the 18th century, artists made plans for 'ideal cities', based on geometric figures, often a circle with identical segments. One or two were actually built. It is characteristic of these and many subsequent 'artists' ' plans that no consideration was given to the experience of centuries, and that a 'perfect' geometrical figure was assumed to be the perfect shape for a town. Some kind of plan is essential when an existing city is about to expand. An orderly plan for expansion was drawn up by the burghers of Amsterdam — the *Great Plan of 1600*. The main feature of this is a set of three more-or-less concentric canals which fold round the western two-thirds of the old city. It is interesting that although there is a general impression of three concentric circles, they are not rigidly drawn, and walking through the city, one is aware of as much irregularity as of regularity. This is in contrast to such plans as that for Palma Nova in the 16th century, or Ledoux's plan for the town to service the salt works at Arc-et-Senans, built during 1775-79. The adaptable orderly plans are interestingly discussed by Steen-Eiler Rasmussen in *Towns and buildings*.

One plan which did become standard for new cities was the grid plan, which also dates from ancient times — Miletus and Priene were famous examples — and which needs only a surveyor, not an artist to draw it out. William Penn chose a grid plan for Philadelphia in the 1680's. To a certain extent it is a 'populist' plan, since all quarters of the city are in a sense undifferentiated. Not all new cities in the 17th and 18th centuries were laid out in grids: Quebec (1605), Nieuw Amsterdam, later New York (1626), Boston (1630), St. Petersburg, later Leningrad (1706) and Sydney (1788) all began with a non-grid plan, but all of them were extended onwards from the 19th century as grids, the old quarter of New York being replanned into a grid in the early 19th century.

The 'populist' grid can be contrasted with 'autocratic' plans like that for Karlsruhe in western Germany (1748 onwards), where all the streets radiate from the royal palace. The taste for long straight avenues grew during the 18th century; they were good for military parades. Berlin was built round just such a long parade-ground; Paris too had its Champs Elysées and after the revolution there was the Artists' Plan of 1797 which called for wide boulevards sweeping through the narrow streets of the old city, with monuments (Arc de Triomphe, Madeleine, etc.) as eye-catchers at the ends of vistas. However the Artists' Plan echoes that of another French designer, L'Enfant, who in 1791 drew up the plan for the new Federal Capital of the United States of America, Washington, which combined a general grid plan with wide intersecting boulevards leading towards monuments.

Though all these plans (even one put forward by Leonardo da Vinci) made allowances for water-supplies, drainage, transport, cattle markets, and so on, their purpose was mainly visual and ceremonial — republican parades in Paris and Washington, autocratic parades in Berlin and St. Petersburg. In this, artistic, sense the grid plan was almost a non-plan, since it allowed for indefinite extension, as far as the terrain allowed, and provided for changes in the location of the town's central buildings. None of these plans took into consideration the effect of winds blowing down long avenues, or of the dangers of monotony — grid plans on flat country can be uninteresting. San Francisco is a famous example of a grid plan acting as a contrast to the terrain, and so producing varied effects; perhaps flat country needs curving streets — or curving canals.

From the early 19th century onwards, city populations grew very suddenly and then steadily in most of Europe and America and, later in the century, in Asia and Africa too. Anyone's 'ideal' city plan would soon become inadequate, since ideal cities were planned for static populations. It is interesting (and depressing) to contrast the urban quality of the city of Paris with the untidy mess of its 20th century suburbs which seem not to have been in any plans, artists' or anyone else's. However, few cities have come out well from the elephantiasis which has struck them in the last hundred years.

Town planning from the early 19th century onwards divides into two kinds: the ceremonial, artistic variety (accepting in the 20th century that these have to cater for much larger populations than the earlier plans did), and the hygienic variety, a desperate attempt to keep up with the unhealthy, dangerous and growing industrial sprawls.

4b. Ceremonial Artistic Planning.

In Paris and London in the the first years of the 19th century there were two formal developments that in many ways mark the differences between the two cities. Starting in 1802, Percier and Fontaine laid out and built the Rue de Rivoli, grand apartment blocks with impressive classical shopping arcades at street level. These faced the Louvre Palace. To a certain extent in emulation of Paris, John Nash, the Prince Regent's favourite architect, laid out the Regent Street sequence, also connected with a palace — Carlton House, the Regent's London home — and leading from this to Regent's Park. Whereas the Rue de Rivoli is a grand frontage to a grand quarter of the city, and is quite straight, Regent Street is laid out on several axes, because the Prince Regent could not buy up a straight line of properties. Nash made use of this difficulty by ensuring that Regent Street divides smart Mayfair from unsmart Soho. A full description of this can be found in Rasmussen's *London, the unique city.*

In Paris, the Artists' Plan had to wait until the Second Empire; it was Baron

Haussmann, appointed by Napoleon III as Prefect of the Seine Department, who carried the plan out. Leonardo Benevolo has pointed out in *Origins of modern town planning* that the great cities of Europe were reorganised after 1848, that is after the defeat of the liberal movements which had inherited the ideals of the French Revolution, and which for the first half of the century had been the originators of most ideas about planning, city organisation, and so on. Thus the necessary replanning of these cities to cope with the new industrialised society and its larger populations was carried out by authoritarian governments, sometimes paternalists, sometimes merely repressive, but always bureaucratic. The monuments include Haussmann's Paris and the Ringstrasse in Vienna, laid out from 1858 in the area occupied before by the city's fortifications. The coda to these grandiose plans came with the rulers of Nazi Germany, their parade grounds and sports stadiums. One of the characteristics of 'ideal' cities is that people tend to be part of the décor, like plants in a terraced garden — Versailles had human plants as well as real, that could be regrouped from time to time. There is an interesting parallel in the transition in dancing from elegant people forming patterns as they dance, to a disciplined *corps-de-ballet*. Even a popular entertainment, like the line of chorus girls in a musical, can be seen as part of this process. It is a curious fancy to want to see a hundred legs all moving in unison. However, in the 1930's, this urge to assign people to the role of garden ornaments reached the level of art. The Nazis had their Nuremburg rallies where the scene looks like a formal garden, until one realises that the bedding plants are soldiers. Even in America, Busby Berkeley movies like *42nd street* or *Gold-diggers of 1933* had dancers making patterns like flowers opening and shutting. Both the Nazis and the Peoples' Republics that came after them have had their troops goose-stepping, like a chorus-line.

Architects' plans for the 'Heroic Age' of the 1920's, and especially Corbusier's, entailed sweeping away cities altogether, and enlarging the scale of the new work to give space for airfields in the city-centres, and tower blocks standing above a landscape. Corbusier's and similar 20th century plans always seem to envisage a society which lives its meaningful life in public, far more so than even the Mediterranean café society has ever done, because that traditional society was strictly divided between men and women, with home the women's territory. The C.I.A.M. sees us all dropping the children in a crèche while we go on to a political meeting in the Sports Palace.

4c. Remedial Hygienic Planning.

Behind the glamorous boulevards of even the Imperial cities, and even more in those cities where political power was to a certain extent shared, as in Britain and America, the huge increases in population and in the building to cope with, or exploit them, went on for at least the first half of the 19th century almost entirely unchecked by any government regulations. The few self-conscious attempts at ceremonial planning in Britain (like Regent Street) point up the difference between a liberal and a totalitarian society, when contrasted with the developments in Paris.

England suffered first and worst from the sudden and unexpected effects of the Industrial Revolution; there were more people and more factories all at once. The upper classes did well out of the growth of industry and saw little reason to interfere with the freedom of entrepreneurs who were proving such a good investment for their money. It took the cholera epidemic of 1847, which killed rich and poor alike, to convince the British Parliament that something must be done to save themselves, even if it meant doing something for the poor at the same time. However, their reluctance is shown by the fact that the first Health Act (1848) was seen as a temporary measure only. Fresh epidemics produced more grudging measures, and in the 1870's all the Local Government functions — drainage,house regulations, roads — were gathered under the wing of the Poor Law Administration, which had a forty-year-old tradition of *saving* money.

Meanwhile, private charities were building 'flatted dwellings' (see APARTMENTS). New building regulations in the latter half of the 19th century laid down minimum rules for housing ('by-law housing') but the old slums were mostly still there. The East End of London, the 'Jago', had many large areas where the police did not go. The London County Council, set up in 1889, began the slow process of clearing some of the slums — finding who were the owners of the property and of the land, buying it from them, and so on. They made a special attack on those areas which were uncomfortably close to the smarter districts — Kingsway and Aldwych were laid out in the first years of the 20th century after a large area of slums had been cleared away.

Two possible 'solutions' to this problem of the dreadful city offered themselves: 'escape' (much the easier), and rehabilitation. Rehabilitation of the centres of cities unfortunately had to wait until after the 1939-45 war, by which time the ideas of Corbusier and his admirers had captured the planning departments of the cities, and not merely rehabilitation, but re-creation in an altogether different mould was carried out. War also wrecked many of the city centres of Europe. Some have been rebuilt, some re-created. In America, which did not suffer any war damage, the centres of cities have been largely rebuilt to take advantage of business firms and (e.g. in midtown Manhattan and in Chicago) well-to-do tenants who are willing to pay high rents for central property. The inner rings, however, have decayed as badly as the eastern part of London's inner ring decayed in the 19th century. This has been aggravated in America (and since about 1960 in Britain and France too) by racial problems, since only the poorest will live in these areas.

'Escape' has seemed to most middle-class families in this century the obvious answer, and it seemed so too to enlightened planners at the end of the last century (see GARDEN CITIES). After the 1939-45 war, the same motive was behind the creation of the New Towns in Britain and elsewhere. The danger of the New Towns, and even of Garden Cities, is that where one architect, or even a team of architects, are planning a city, there is obviously a much more restricted choice for individuals. This is marked in the latest New Towns in Britain, such as Cumbernauld in Scotland, where dwellings are interlocked, or Milton Keynes in England, where the dwellings are more traditional, but designed by few architects (though more than in other New Towns). For the 'philosophy' behind these 'totally designed' New Towns, the best book is that published by the Greater London Council on the aborted plan for a New Town at Hook in Hampshire.

4d. A Chronological Outline of the Main Achievements of Planning.

1802	Rue de Rivoli begun in Paris (completed 1855).
1812-27	Regent Street — Regent's Park layout in London.
1828-52	Calverley Estate at Tunbridge Wells.
1835-47	The town of Fleetwood in Lancashire.
1845-59	St. Leonards, an extension of Hastings in Sussex.
	These last three by Decimus Burton.
1834	The layout of a new centre, above and north of the old, of Newcastle-upon-Tyne, much of it designed by Dobson.
c1835	The layout of Belgrave Square, and 'Belgravia'; a continuation of the Georgian estate development of Mayfair in the 18th century.
1849	Sir Titus Salt begins Saltaire, near Bradford in Yorkshire.
1859	Colonel Ackroyd begins Ackroyden, near Halifax, Yorkshire.
	These last two are among the earliest wholly new planned towns for workers.
1853	Haussmann appointed Prefect of the Seine Dpt. and begins to carry out the 'Artists' ' Plan for Paris.
1855	The beginning of part of Shaftesbury Avenue, London; part of an intended road from Trafalgar Square to the British Museum, which has never been finished.
c1855	Olmstead begins the layout of Central Park, New York.
1858	The start of laying out of the Ringstrasse in Vienna on the site of the former fortifications and firing lines.
1859	Similar developments with the old fortifications of Copenhagen, although the Tivoli pleasure grounds had been laid out in part of the fortifications a decade earlier.
1860	Olmstead plans Riverside, Illinois, one of the earliest 'garden suburbs'.
1864-70	The Embankment from Westminster to Blackfriars built.
1867-71	Queen Victoria Street, from Blackfriars to the Mansion House; both the new roads were also the routes for the Inner Circle Line underground.
1875	Bedford Park, in west London, the first London garden suburb.
1877-86	Shaftesbury Avenue (which broke up Piccadilly Circus), part of London's traffic improvements (which also included at this time New Oxford Street and the Seven Dials).

1879	Port Sunlight — model town for workers in the Lever Brothers soap factory, in Cheshire across the Mersey from Liverpool.
1885,etc.	Bournville; villagy New Town for workers in Cadbury's chocolate factory, on the southern outskirts (then) of Birmingham, England.
1889	Publication of Camillo Sitté's *Der Stadtbau*, usually translated into English as *City planning according to artistic principles*: it was the first to set out the ideas of a picturesque development of existing cities — buildings as well as parks.
c1890	Several German model workers' villages on the lines of Bournville, etc. — some of them for Krupp's Essen.
1898	Publication of Ebenezer Howard's *Tomorrow*; see GARDEN CITIES.
1903	Letchworth Garden City started.
1906	Hampstead Garden suburb.
before 1914	Housing estates on the edges of the suburbs of London, built by the L.C.C. to garden suburb designs. The various plans for Canberra, the federal capital of Australia.
1920	Corbusier's *Urbanisme*: setting out his sweeping plans for a new kind of city; owing much to the futuristic ideas of the Italian architect St. Elia, who was killed in the 1914-18 war.
1933	Radburn — the development of traffic free housing principles by Clarence Stein in the New Jersey town of Radburn.
1950's	Vällingby, first complete satellite town of Stockholm built. The New Towns in Britain, mostly in the 1950's on GARDEN CITY principles; in the 1960's on 'Hook' principles.
1951 onwards:	Corbusier's plan for Chandigarh, in India, and designs for the government buildings there.
1956	Lucio Costa's winning plan for the new city of Brasilia; carved out of the wilderness in the shape of a giant bird; huge open spaces and symbolic buildings; undifferentiated housing can be understood only as material for the overall effect.
1960's	Experiments in Britain with different types of New Town: Cumbernauld on the 'Hook' pattern; Thamesmead, Milton Keynes, Washington, all with mixed developments.

PART TWO

A guide to movements and ideas.

Aesthetic Movement English art and design movement in the last quarter of the 19th century, popularly associated with the slogan 'art for art's sake'. It was, in part, a reaction against the heavy seriousness of mid-19th century taste (the 'moral' Gothic Revival, for example). As a movement, it was very loosely organised, depending as much on personalities as on a number of sympathetic magazines. The painter Whistler was one of the central figures, and perhaps the most characteristic artifact was the famous 'Peacock Room', a dining-room designed by Thomas Jekyll for 49, Princes Gate in London. The room had two large paintings by Whistler (one of them of a peacock). The room is now reassembled in the Freer Gallery of the Smithsonian Institute in Washington, D.C., together with the Whistler paintings, but without the oriental porcelain which was an important part of the décor. The arts of Japan were as important to the Aesthetic Movement as the arts of China had been to English rococo in the 18th century; Japan had been opened up to trade in the 1850's. Some furniture design in England — by E.W. Godwin, for example — was influenced by Japanese design (see ART FURNITURE). The 'movement' included poets (like Swinburne) and essayists (like Whistler's friend Oscar Wilde), and was a major subject for cartoons in *Punch* and a Gilbert and Sullivan opera (*Patience*). Contemporary figures like Philip Webb and William Morris (who also wrote poetry, etc., as well as painting and designing) are influential outsiders rather than participants. The Arts & Crafts Movement — though almost as unorganized as the Aesthetic — carried on the 'moral' tradition, although there were many links between all these movements (whose clients were mostly the same groups of well-to-do upper-middle-class families); see also QUEEN ANNE.

READING:
Robin Spencer, *The Aesthetic Movement.*
Mark Girouard, *Sweetness and light.*
Elizabeth Aslin, *The Aesthetic Movement: prelude to Art Nouveau.*

Alternative Design One of the terms for design and architecture planned to be suitable for the poor in both the overdeveloped and underdeveloped worlds, and — as the word suggests — a possibly more wholesome alternative for everyone. Closely allied to this is what is now called Appropriate Technology: appropriate to the economy and life style of those for whom buildings and machines are being designed. Like Intermediate Technology, an earlier term, it means using mangles rather than spin driers or clothes-lines. If those who are to use the building or machine play a larger part in the design, the importance of the professional designer will be lessened. Local materials, too, will be used unless quite unsuitable. This kind of designing is in contrast to, say, Buckminster Fuller's proposals for 'solving' the problem of housing shortages in poor countries by means of his 'Wichita' house, mass-produced like jeeps in the '39-45 war, light and easily moved by air, but still part of an industrial system which would not have fitted the societies the houses were meant for. In the end, his scheme came to nothing.

READING:
There are many books now in this field:
J. F. C. Turner and R. Fichter, *Freedom to build* has papers by a number of young architects, and discusses building in America and the 'third world'.
Barbara Ward, *Home of man,* connected with the U.N. conference 'Habitat'.
Kurt Schumacher, *Small is beautiful*; the book that first made the idea of Intermediate Technology popular.
A. Boericke and B. Shapiro, *Handmade houses* — wooden houses in northern California.
Bernard Rudolfsky, *Architecture without architects*; an historical survey through photographs and commentary.

Apartments Purpose-built lodgings in blocks of two or more storeys, with the accommodation on one floor (maisonettes if on two floors). The British word 'flats' comes from 'flatted dwellings', the 1840's term for the first housing in London designed for artisan families. Few were housed in this way, though; most went on living in rooms or parts of rooms in run-down houses abandoned by better-off families.

Blocks of flatted dwellings were built either by charitable trusts (like Peabody) or as an investment (like Waterlow). Sometimes charitably-minded people could put their money into companies building such flats, and expect only a small return on their investment. H.A. Darbyshire began designing blocks for the Peabody Trust in the 1860's. Some of his later estates are impressive, grey brick barracks, which can still be seen in London, with good examples in the streets behind the Strand near St. Martin's Lane, and near Kingsway. Many of these charitable dwellings were built well — one cannot hear much of the neighbour's noise inside the apartments.

In the wake of the GARDEN CITY movement, flats were, for a while, out of architectural fashion in England as a means of artisan housing. Although Local Authorities had been given powers by Parliament (in Shaftesbury's Act of 1851) to build dwellings, they had mostly kept themselves to making regulations. The Housing of the Working Classes Act of 1890 encouraged Local Authorities to build, and many of the early estates were of cottages rather than apartment blocks. The London County Council built some estates of red-brick cottages on the edges of the suburbs, although they did also build an estate of flats behind the Tate Gallery in Pimlico, in 1897-1902.

Until about 1880, hardly anyone in England and America, except artisans, dwelt in apartments. The better-off preferred houses; row-houses for the most part, though semi-detached houses (America: duplexes) were built from the 1840's onwards. Those who could afford them, naturally preferred detached houses — more so in America. Although a house, detached or not, has continued to be the most popular form of dwelling for anyone who could afford it in England and America, apartments began to be fashionable with some groups of people — for example, those without young families — in the last years of the 19th century. In Europe, however, apartments were the usual housing in cities for all except the rich. Typical developments in Paris in the 1820's had shops on street level and apartments above. A. J. Pellechet designed a block in 1834 at 10, Place de la Bourse; it had four storeys over the ground floor. These 19th century boulevard flats are unlike 20th century blocks, in that they are attached to their neighbours.

Over forty years after Pellechet's block, flats began to be fashionable in London. Amongst the earliest blocks for well-to-do tenants are R. N. Shaw's Albert Hall Mansions of 1879; Archer and Green's Whitehall Court, facing the Thames a few streets down river from Parliament (1884), and the 'mansion flats' behind Victoria Street (e.g. Artillery Mansions of 1895). All these are in one or another of the classical styles of the 19th century, except that Whitehall Court also has a roofload of turrets, like the 16th century Loire châteaux.

With the coming of the International Modern Movement, apartment blocks were back in architectural fashion. A tower or a slab of flats is a much more emphatic 'statement' than an estate of houses, and also a block of flats — the bigger the better — is a convincing excuse for industrialised designing, which a group of small houses is not. Thomas Sharp, in his influential Town planning, first published in 1936, advocated demolishing country houses in their parks and replacing them with a block of flats per park. Not only would one creation replace another, but, as he argued, a wide range of facilities could be gathered under one roof: shops, restaurants, day-nurseries and swimming pools (if one were living in the middle of a landscape park, it would be useful to have these services on the premises). Here would be the 'village in the sky' that Corbusier and others were writing about, though Corbusier's own sky-villages were not built until after 1945; he called them 'dwelling unities'. Before 1945 there were some 'luxury' flats built with many facilities on hand, as in Dolphin Square in Pimlico, London (designed by Gordon Jeeves in 1937). It is only a step from flats like these to hostels or service flats and from them to hotels. The advantage of not getting wet going out shopping has to be weighed against the institutional atmosphere of such buildings. a 'Unitè type block, inspired by Corbusier, was put up in Moscow as early as 1928-9 (designed by Milinis), but proved to be unsuitable for the style of life of the people it was built for.

During the '39-45 war, Swedish architects experimented with several types of apartment block. Their best-known innovation was the *point block (punkthus)*. In these blocks there could be either four apartments on each floor opening off a 'core' of lifts, staircases and services; or three apartments, arranged in three wings to give better views and sunlight. These three-winged blocks could be linked as at Örebro by Backström and Reinius. The two plans are:

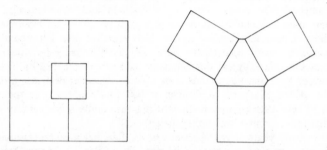

7 *Layout of apartments on each floor of two kinds of Swedish housing block: the* 'punkthus'–*point block, with four apartments, and the* 'star' *with three. The stairs, etc. are in the middle of each layout.*

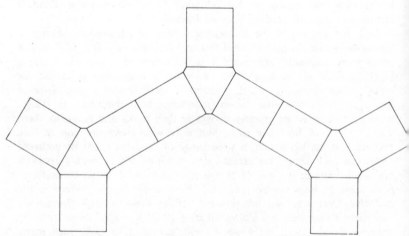

8 *The* 'star' *plan could be linked to make a varied contour, as at Örebro, in Sweden.*

Swedes also pioneered the idea of mixed developments: some very tall four-apartment-per-floor towers (ten or more storeys); some four-storey slabs (perhaps two rows of maisonettes, one on top of the other, as copied later at Roehampton near London) and even some houses. An estate could then be shaped into a landscape so that the whole thing would look like a big sculpture — at least from the air or when looking at the architect's model.

The heyday of this kind of apartment block was 1950-70, when it was assumed by architects and planners that all modern city-dwellers — and suburban-dwellers too — would want to live in such apartments. Throughout the developed world there are blocks of apartments for all income-groups scattered through the suburbs of big cities, and some are still being built, even if without the confidence of heretofore. But if cities become dangerous at night, an apartment block is easier to guard. A point block, too, is much easier for the police to surround than the old warrens and yards ever were.

As a method of public housing, however, the apartment block has no advantage over traditional housing, except for ideological reasons and except where inner-city crowding is thought desirable. An apartment block houses no more people than would two-storey houses on the same site, because of the need for daylighting (and for space to show the block off). It costs a great deal more to build; it is difficult and expensive to maintain; it is extravagant to run — the costs of power for heating, lifts and other services are going up every year. The fashion for plate-glass windows, all the way up, also adds to fuel costs as well as the tenants' vertigo. For a number of reasons, among them that the police could not get a good firing line, some public housing blocks in the U.S.A. have been demolished (blowing up seems to be the safest way). In England, government ministers are still begging people to live in them. This is just, because the central government civil servants brought pressure on local authorities to build large blocks rather than houses in the 1950's and '60's.

BUILDINGS TO BE SEEN:
Apartment blocks are everywhere; those mentioned in this note are still to be seen.
For 'sculpture': the best examples are the SATELLITE TOWNS around Stockholm, Vällingby, Farsta, etc.
Roehampton in south-west London is a good example of the sculptural effect, but only in part copied from Sweden — see BRUTALISM.
The 'Parisian' type of apartment house can be seen in most of those European cities where large parts of the city were developed in the late 19th and early 20th centuries.

READING:
G. E. Kidder-Smith, Sweden builds.
Brent C. Brolin, The failure of modern architecture; particularly good on the unsuitability of the 'European' (i.e. INTERNATIONAL MODERN) type of apartment block for other cultures.

W. Ashworth, *The genesis of modern British town-planning* for the 'housing question' in 19th century England.

Appropriate Technology — see ALTERNATIVE DESIGN.

Art Deco The term comes from the *Exposition des arts décoratifs* held in Paris in 1925. This exhibition also had on its fringe Corbusier's pavilion *'de l'ésprit nouveau'* (the title of his magazine) hardly noticed then, but much illustrated since. Art Deco is Art Nouveau gone Egyptian and angular. The 'exotic' elements came from various sources: the ballet *Cléopatra* with its décor and costumes by Bakst; the exhibitions of colonial art, especially from Africa and Indo-China (Negro art had influenced painters like Picasso and sculptors like Epstein in the decade before the First World War). A cinema in a streamlined, sunburst style (like many in Britain) can be rescued from contempt and called Art Deco. A cinema which looks as though it is a copy of a Gothic cathedral, however, still hovers in the limbo of KITSCH. One of the brightest buildings in this style was the Carreras factory in Hampstead Road, London, of 1926 ('abominable', as the *Buildings of England* described it) which had columns along the front painted with an Egyptian leaf pattern (alas now painted out) on the otherwise glass and white painted building. The 'sunburst' pattern was used for any suitable surface: doors, front gates, the fronts of wireless loudspeakers, and inverted for hanging lamps. Art Deco is an interesting example of a fashionable style that was almost immediately

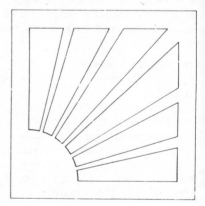

9 Art Deco 'sun burst' pattern–used on gates, wireless cabinets etc.

taken up by 'polite' design, but this may have been because there was already a kind of 'polite' Art Nouveau, which had begun to look not unlike Art Deco.

Why did the style arouse so much hostility? The hostility of the

cal 19th century Continental Apartments

andinavian apartments: Frederiksvej, Copenhagen (2nd half of the 19th century).

ropean apartments: apartment block with shops in the square

site St. Vincent de Paul, Paris.

Apartments in London
3 Apartments for the well-to-do: Albert Hall Mansions (R. N. Shaw, 1885).

4 Apartments for artisans: Peabody Trust dwellings, Wild St., off Kingsway, London (Darbyshire, 1881).

Ironwork in the Art Nouveau Mood
5 Gates to the Frogner Park, Oslo
(Gustav Viegeland, c.1930).

ord Park, London
ts and Crafts: 14 South Parade
sey, 1891).

7 "Queen Anne": The Tabard Inn
(R. N. Shaw, 1875).

'Brutalism' in London
8 Contrast in architectural fashions in London: the "Brutalist" Queen
Elizabeth Hall of the 1960's alongside the Festival hall of the 1950's.
Behind and above, the Shell Tower of 1958-9.

9 (opposite page, top) Roehampton Housing Estate: the "Corbusier" blocks.

10 (opposite page, bottom) National Theatre (Denys Lasdun, 1976).

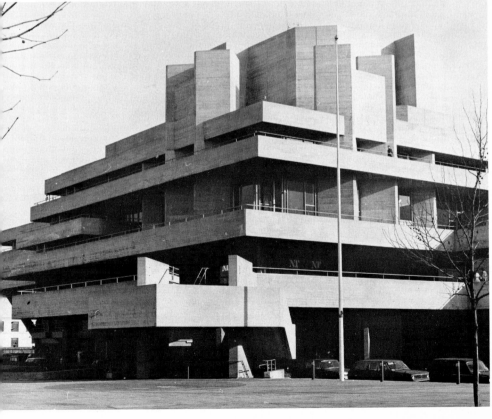

Expressionism: Amsterdam Apartments
11 (above) The Eigen Haard Estate
(Michael de Klerk, 1917).

12 (above) The De Dageraad Estate
(P. L. Kramer, 1921-23).

13 French Renascence: Whitehall Court apartments alongside the Thames Embankment, Lon
(Archer and Green, 1884).

Iron Architecture
14 Decorative ironwork in New Orleans, mid-19th century.

15 International Modern: Kensal Rise apartment block, London
(Maxwell Fry and others, 1936).

16 "Swedish Modern": Vällingby, outside Stockholm. Town Centre
(Backström and others, c.1950).

BAUHAUS camp is clear: Art Deco was seen as an alluring and meretricious rival. It was a mass-production style, and those who were preaching that an *abstract*, unornamented style was the only fit style for mass-production, knew that Art Deco cut the ground from under them: lively designs like those of Art Deco can as easily be turned out in the mass as plain ones like the Bauhaus work.

A kind of Art Deco erupted again after the '39-45 war, especially in the styling of large American automobiles. The use of chrome to give a shiny finish to bumpers and other parts of cars could be thought of as the longest surviving legacy of Art Deco. Then, in the 1960's, Pop Art influenced design.

DESIGNS TO BE SEEN:

Museum directors have been rather more cautious displaying their Art Deco treasures, if any, than in showing Art Nouveau. The Milwaukee Gallery, however, had a major exhibition in 1971, and Bevis Hillier's catalogue for it is one of the best introductions to the subject.

READING:

Giulia Veronesie, *Into the twenties*; good illustrations.
Don Vlack, *Art Deco architecture in New York.*
Bevis Hillier, *The world of Art Deco.*

Art Furniture A term for expensive furniture designed in the last third of the 19th century: the term is British. Most 19th century furniture was plain, much like provincial furniture of the 18th century, only with 'line' sacrificed to comfort, with heavier padding. Some designers (mainly architects), among them William Burges, E.W. Godwin and Charles Eastlake, designed elaborately ornamental furniture which became fashionable. Elizabeth Aslin writes (in *Nineteenth-century English furniture*) that 'by the mid '70's, "Art Furniture Manufacturers" (were) listed in the London Telephone Directory quite separately from ordinary cabinet makers and furnishers'. The term 'Art Furniture' was Eastlake's in 1868, and Godwin had a firm called the Art Furniture Co. Some of Godwin's own furniture is angular and perhaps influenced by the then current Japanese vogue; there is a sideboard by him dating from 1867 in the Victoria and Albert Museum. There is not a great deal of difference between the Art Furniture of the late '60's and '70's and the work of cabinet makers like Charles Baudouine and John Henry Belter in New York in the 1850's; their work was more consistently in a rococo style popular in mid-century, whereas Art Furniture styles were from various sources. Art Furniture began as something of a campaign for well-designed pieces. Influence on general furniture was through books (like Eastlake's), or through exhibitions, especially the international shows.

FURNITURE TO BE SEEN:

By its very nature, Art Furniture was expensive, self-consciously artistic, and something to be collected; many of these collections have now found their way into museums, and Art Furniture is the type most likely to be found in the 19th century galleries of most major museums. The Metropolitan in New York and the V. and A. in London have examples.

READING:
Elizabeth Aslin, *Nineteenth-century English furniture.*
N. Pevsner, 'Art Furniture in the 1870's in *Studies in art, architecture & design,* Vol. 2.

Art Nouveau This term comes from the name of a shop opened in Paris in 1895 by Samuel Bing; the German term for Art Nouveau is *Jugendstil* (from the title of a magazine, *Jugend* — 'youth'), and the Italian is *Stile Liberty* after the London shop which then, as now, imported and sold oriental wares and 'artistic' designs. Thus two of the terms came from fashionable shops, and the movement had an air of high fashion from the start, which stayed with it even when the style became popularised and perhaps debased. There is no separate English term for the movement. This may be due to the strong dislike of it in English critical circles, although it had its roots in England. 'New art' in the 1890's would have suggested the New English Art Club, founded in 1885 by painters.

It was called Art Nouveau because the designers claimed that it had no dependence on past styles. People had been calling for a genuine new style for 'the 19th century', so here at last it was, even if a bit late. However, when things are marketed as 'nouveau', they run the risk of something even more 'nouveau' coming along before long and replacing them in fashion. In Paris, for example, it was the Russian Ballet, brought over by Diaghilev in 1909. The heyday of Art Nouveau as a fashionable style lasted about 15-20 years; as a 'polite' style, somewhat longer — until it merged with Art Deco after 1925.

It was 'nouveau' at least in presentation, for Art Nouveau, whatever the designers said, had debts to earlier designs. It can be seen as an offspring of Gothic and Rococo, both of which enjoyed good revivals in the 19th century. A development has been traced (by Tschudi Madsen, in *Sources of Art Nouveau*) from the graphic work of William Blake, through the Gothic Revival, to William Morris, Macmurdo and Voysey (especially their wallpapers), and so to Art Nouveau. With three-dimensional designs the link seems to be more with Rococo than Gothic; with some Meissen pastoral figures and even with 'Chinese Rococo', the most extravagant of the Rococo styles used in England in the 18th century (there are examples in Claydon House in Buckinghamshire). Much Art Nouveau furniture could easily fit into rooms of the Louis XV Rococo style, and as that was succeeded by the Louis XVI neo-classical reaction, so Art Nouveau was succeeded in many countries (especially Germany and Scandinavia) by a neo-classical revival.

Perhaps it is the two-dimensional work which is the most characteristic of Art Nouveau: graphics, including posters and book designs; the jewellery that is two-dimensional: silver brooches and buckles with flowing

10 *Gothic Revival.*

11 *Rococo.*

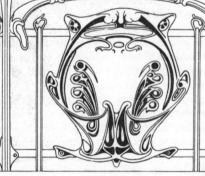

12 *Art Nouveau.*

13 *Art Deco.*

lines derived from plants, water or women's hair (a Leonardo influence, perhaps).

The architectural side of Art Nouveau is almost entirely in ornamental ironwork. A good (though in a sense posthumous) example is the set of eight wrought iron gates designed by Gustav Viegeland to surround his central monolith in the Frogner Park in Oslo. These gates date from the 1930's. They have the face-on appearance of a Walter Crane drawing roughened up a bit and translated into drawing in air; move a little to the side and the figures become a solid mass, just when they become lost in an Art-Nouveau swirl of iron.

Hoffman's Palais Stoclét in Brussels (1905-11) is thought of as a good example of Art Nouveau, but the building itself is cubic and white. Only the decoration is Art Nouveau, especially inside — the mural by Gustav Klimt is famous. Two other architects have been put forward as Art Nouveau: Mackintosh in Glasgow (his School of Art, which is still there, and the tea rooms for Miss Cranston, which are not) and Gaudi's in Barcelona (his apartment blocks). Most of those who admire these architects do not agree that their work is Art Nouveau, pointing out that Mackintosh has many affinities with Scottish architecture of the 15th and 16th centuries and with Celtic art, and that Gaudí has affinities with traditional Catalan Gothic architecture and decoration. These other sources — Celtic and Gothic — are not unlike Art Nouveau, for which they may be remote sources. Certainly Mackintosh's graphic work, much of it done in collaboration with his wife Margaret Macdonald, is closer to Art Nouveau, and so is Gaudí's ironwork. Their buildings, however, have more in common with the architects usually called EXPRESSIONIST.

Mackintosh had no success in London, where the Arts and Crafts designers in particular were disgusted with his work ('unhealthy'), as they were with Art Nouveau generally. This is a curious reaction, since so much of the Arts and Crafts work looks now, nearly a century afterwards, to have some of the same shapes and motifs as Art Nouveau. Mackintosh and his friend George Walton had more success in Vienna where they exhibited at the eighth Vienna Secession exhibition in November 1900, and thereafter had a considerable influence on Austrian and German design. The reason for this may have been that the 'Glasgow' design was sufficiently Art Nouveau to fit in with *Jugendstil,* but severe enough to attract those designers who were beginning to find *Jugendstil* too florid.

Otto Wagner's underground station entrances — like that for the Karlsplatz Station (1898) — in Vienna are in the same vein as Guimard's slightly later Paris Métro stations. Guimard's buildings are perhaps the most familiar Art Nouveau architecture left, now that the facade of Samaritaine, the Paris department store, has been altered, and a similar store in Brussels, L'Innovation, burnt down. Guimard's Métro stations (1899-1904) are little more than iron and glass shelters over access stairs to the underground railway, and his Castel Béranger apartments of 1894-98 are also Art Nouveau only in their ironwork. This is not surprising. Iron and glass screens and roofs do not need to have a prescribed 'functional' pattern so long as they shelter us from wind and rain, and let in light. An otherwise uniform building can be humanized by decorative ironwork. A good example of this is Louis Sullivan's Carson Pirie Scott store in Chicago (at State and Madison; finished 1904. its roofline has been altered since). The shop part of the building has an attractive, rich decoration not unlike Art Nouveau; the office floors above have minimal repetitive ceramic trimming. (Sullivan's decoration generally is another of those contemporary examples which are like Art Nouveau but not formally part of the movement.)

Art Nouveau ceased to be high fashion after about 1909, but by then it had become generally popular, especially for the decoration of restaurants, theatres and shops, where a loose, pre-1914 Baroque-cum-Rococo-cum-Art Nouveau established itself. Thonet bentwood chairs with their curves lent themselves very well to this kind of restaurant setting. Thus a general trend had set in which could support Art Deco after 1925.

In the 1960's there was a revival of interest in Art Nouveau, to the despair of International Modernists. It was in part a reaction to the ban on all ornament which had been orthodoxy since the BAUHAUS. The Art Nouveau revival has been mostly in graphics, especially advertising. There have also been some Italian buildings which could be said to lean towards a NEO-LIBERTY, and they have been censured for this.

DESIGN AND BUILDINGS TO SEE:
As well as the buildings mentioned in this note, most museums now have some Art Nouveau work, even if only a Beardsley drawing; the 1960's revival prompted many curators to bring out their Art Nouveau collections.

READING:
Nikolaus Pevsner and J. M. Richards (editors), *The anti-rationalists*. In spite of its irritating title, it is a useful collection of essays on Art Nouveau and Expressionism.
Tschudi Madsen, *Art Nouveau.*
Robert Schmutzler, *Art Nouveau;* a large book, but more serious than coffee-table.
P. Selz (editor), *Art Nouveau;* a collection of essays.

Art Schools Until the mid-18th century, drawing and painting were taught by painters in studios, either private or in academies. Everyone else in the art world served an apprenticeship, in cabinet making, engraving, pottery and even in architecture. Reviving this practice was one of the ideas Gropius toyed with in the early years of the BAUHAUS, though it proved unworkable in an art school. In France, the royal system of *Ecoles* ('schools', e.g. for engineering) was strengthened by the Directory in the.1790's with the creation of an *Ecole Polytechnique.* The many crafts assembled here were those taught in the *Ecoles* of the *ancien régime.* J.N.L. Durand was a professor there and the text of his lectures on architecture *(Précis de leçons)* was published in 1802-5 and had a great influence on early 19th century architecture; there is a full account of this in Hitchcock's *Architecture, 19th and 20th centuries.*

During the 19th century, several art schools were set up in Europe with the purpose of teaching students to design for industry: 'Schools of Arts and Crafts' was the usual title. There were many of them in the Germanies. In England, there was a Parliamentary Select Committee in 1836 to look into the teaching of design. There was alarm about British trade not doing as well as its competitors', particularly the French — even in the home market. It was thought that this disparity would be remedied by training. The long struggle over the ensuing Government Schools of Design is chronicled by Quentin Bell in *Schools of design.* What was produced in the end was not so much a supply of designers as of art-teachers for schools. However, in spite of the unforgettable excellence of 18th century English design — and of course of 18th century European design — the constant drone throughout the 19th and indeed the 20th century discussions about the state of design was the need to get *artists* to design for industry. More and more artists were trained in more and more art schools and design got worse and worse.

In 19th century schools of arts and crafts, most of the instruction was in copying standard types of ornament or, occasionally, drawing from nature. The intention was to produce designers who could make suitable patterns and shapes within a more or less accepted group of styles. *Originality* was not yet something that was encouraged in future designers.

The Arts and Crafts Movement was cool about art schools. With its emphasis on craft, a direct master-pupil relationship nearer to apprenticeship was favoured, and Morris went to no art school. What he did do, was work for a time in the office of an architect, G.E. Street, and the leaders of the Arts and Crafts Movement after Morris were also trained in architects' offices. Some change in their attitude came about with the setting up by Lethaby of the Central School of Arts and Crafts in London in 1896. It had a great influence in Europe, especially in Germany, which suggests that the London school was closer to a craft revival than its German namesakes. The Arts and Crafts bias to craftsmanship-above-all-else led them away from copying designs for industry's benefit, but Lethaby's characteristic 'non-style' was negatively, not positively, in favour of originality.

The BAUHAUS, however, changed all that, being committed to the policy of re-thinking every 'design-problem' afresh, both in its 'expressionist' and in its 'de Stijl' phases. Herbert Read's propaganda in England in the 1930's encouraged industrial designers to think of themselves as functional abstract artists. Originality was now fashionable and, since 1945, it seems to be understood as an essential ingredient which distinguishes the *design* student from, say, the engineer.

Many industries have not welcomed art school trained designers over the last 100 years, and have not been waiting for the kind of 'originality' fostered by the schools. *Novelty* is what sells and novelty means something like, perhaps, 'styling' — big rear fins on automobiles — so that 'styling' has become the opposite to 'designing' which is what students are persuaded they should be trained to do. By and large, the 'traditional' industries — furniture, ceramics — have been the ones that have preferred to train their own designers. 'New' industries — electrical goods, radio — have used art-school designers and ideas. Braun in Germany is the outstanding post-1945 example of this.

Naturally, even the idea of making the art school a major source of design ideas takes design even further away from consumer choice. A designer trained to do clever things with plastics is going to be wasted if what everyone wants is something closer to wooden furniture in the Hepplewhite tradition; which the furniture industry seems to have realised.

DESIGN TO SEE:
Art schools have annual exhibitions of the work of students graduating. In England these exhibitions (usually open for only three or four days) are held in June and July.

READING:
Nikolaus Pevsner, *Academies of art past and present.* He is concerned mostly with painting academies, but does discuss the Central School, and has an interesting early photograph of one of its workshops.
Quentin Bell, *Schools of design* Almost entirely about English schools in the mid-19th century.
See also BAUHAUS reading.

Arts and Crafts The Arts and Crafts Movement, at its most energetic from about 1880 to 1914, must be seen as a turning away from industrialised art, however much many of its practitioners may have had an influence on industry. It is a confusing and diverse movement, so much so that it is more like a federation of movements than one movement. The Arts and Crafts also had a tendency to create a mystery around the crafts — see GUILDS.

The Swedes began it all in 1845 with the foundation of the Svenska Slöjdföreningen (Craft Society) which still functions, together with the Hemslöjd (crafts for the home) movements. They feared that industrial production would overwhelm traditional crafts. (Sweden's own industrial revolution did not begin until nearly half a century after this.) The Swedes have cherished their folk traditions, not only in design but also, for example, in folk dancing. The Hemslöjd movements have not only preserved traditional techniques, but have encouraged creative work within those traditions, which continues today and has influenced Swedish industrial design, perhaps giving it that self-confidence that made it able to withstand the BAUHAUS crusade, and which thus made it (and Scandinavian design generally) so popular since 1945.

In the middle of the 19th century, Carlyle and Ruskin both wrote idealising the Middle Ages as a time when craftsmen were honest and free. They thought they saw a comradeship of the guilds, which Ruskin tried hard to recreate, and which were revived as far as they could be in the 1880's in England, and even by Gropius for a year or two at the Bauhaus. The Carlyle-Ruskin-Morris picture of medieval craftsmen is more interesting as a 19th century myth than as a true account of conditions in the Middle Ages. However, a kind of guild was set up by William Morris and his friends, all inspired by Ruskin, in 1861. They formed a company — some changes in business law since 1400 had to be accepted — 'Morris, Marshall, Faulkner and Co., Fine Art Workmen' ('Morris and Co.' after 1875). They were given work by sympathetic architects, some of whom, like Philip Webb, also designed for them. The work was, to begin with, mostly ecclesiastical — stained glass, painted reredos, etc. Later they designed furniture, textiles for the market and eventually had a shop in Oxford Street.

A few years later Ruskin founded the St. George's Guild (1871) and then groups of craftsmen came together and formed guilds, often gathering round a leading designer:

1882	The Century Guild, founded by Mackmurdo; it made, amongst other things some of his (proto-Art Nouveau) designs.
1884	The Art Workers' Guild.
1888	The Guild and School of Handicraft, founded by C. R. Ashbee in Toynbee hall in East London; moved a short distance to Mile End in 1891; then to Chipping Camden in 1902. Some pieces of silverware designed by Ashbee and made by his guild are on view in the V. and A.
1888	The Arts and Crafts Exhibition Society. This was the 'platform' for the various sections of the movement. They were otherwise reluctant to publish anything. Perhaps they felt that Morris had said it all.

In 1893 the first edition of the *Studio* was published; it continued to give space to arts and crafts. The Central School was started by Lethaby in 1896. The example of William Morris led a number of men to turn from other careers to take up crafts of one kind or another:
— Henry van der Velde did so in 1893 after a nervous breakdown.
— T.J. Cobden-Sanderson was a barrister, but fell under the Morris spell and started a book-binding business in 1884.
— Wilhelm von Debschitz was an officer in the Prussian army; resigned and taught himself painting. Then, under the influence of Morris, turned to the crafts and founded a school in Munich with Olbrist in 1902.
— Elbert Hubbard founded a community of craftsmen, the Roycrafters, at East Aurora, N.Y., also under the influence of Morris. They met in 1894.

As well as reviving declining crafts, the Arts and Crafts Movements had other ideas, notably the belief that designs should be 'honest' (see HONESTY); therefore much of their emphasis was on the way in which the work was done.

Lethaby's definition of 'architecture' as 'fine building' shows that this principle could be extended very far. It was probably on the grounds of honesty in workmanship that the Arts and Crafts guildmen could not bring themselves to appreciate Art Nouveau, a movement whose decorative motifs were often similar to those used in the Arts and Crafts workshops. With ART NOUVEAU, the method of construction is usually secondary to the effect desired. This 'healthy', 'honest workmanship' aspect of Arts and Crafts has been claimed as a 'pointer' by the Modern Movement. The Arts and Crafts, of all movements, thought of themselves as *being,* rather than *preparing.* It is doubtful, too, whether Philip Webb, for example, would have thought Corbusier's Villa Savoye 'honest'. Lethaby himself referred to the C.I.A.M.-Bauhaus products as 'Ye olde Moderne style' — see R. Macleod's *Style and society,* chapter eight.

After 1915, when Ashbee went to Cairo as a lecturer in English, and with the blight of the 1914-18 war, the Arts and Crafts Movements faded from their place at the centre of fashionable design, except perhaps in Scandinavia. Their influence abroad, especially in Germany, was also on the wane in the years before 1914 — nothing to do with the hostilities; see DEUTSCHE WERKBUND. It is easy to see the 'craft-expressionist' early years of BAUHAUS as an aberration caused by the disruption in Germany after the war, though one should be cautious about any too close explanation of art movements as a direct product of social upheavals. However, craft movements continued to flourish in Scandinavia, and have been revived — though now with a large amount of amateur, rather than guild, enthusiasm — in Britain and America.

The main heirs in England — and elsewhere — to the Arts and Crafts Movements are the many 'small' independent studio craft workers, particularly potters, who keep themselves going today on the wide popularity of hand-made goods where repetitive machine-finish is not the quality most desired. Some traditional craft workers have been organised into co-operatives, like the Scottish Harris Tweed weavers, where there is now an interesting clash between the method of weaving and the market for the cloth (or some of it). Hand looms can make only up to a certain width of cloth, and some of the potential buyers would like it wider, but to make wider cloth would need more industrialised machinery, thus destroying the independence of the weavers.

In 'polite' design, the Arts and Crafts influence was very wide. Many of the characteristic objects — beaten copper hoods for fireplaces, brass fire-tongs, for example — were taken over by manufacturers and mass-produced. In fact, the whole 'Ye Olde Worlde', a kind of Englysshe National version of the Art Deco of the Twenties and Thirties, is a child of the Arts and Crafts, even if on the wrong side of the hand-woven blanket. The almost unreadable 'Tudor' lettering on and in tearooms is like an unconscious parody of Morris's 'Chaucer' type. Some critics are worried by this and by the fake half-timbering and the electric log-fires, but do not write much about the one legacy from the Arts and Crafts which is indeed dangerous — the rough cast, or 'pebble-dash' finish to walls (they are not pebbles, but small sharp bits of gravel which are thrown up at the still wet plaster). This was popularised by C.F.A. Voysey, and was praised for its honesty.

DESIGN TO SEE:

Most museums with crafts have examples of the Arts and Crafts, or movements influenced by them; this is particularly true of Scandinavia, but the V. and A. also has good examples of their work. Leicester Museum and Art Gallery has a special section devoted to work of Ernest Gimson — some fine pieces of his furniture are there.

READING:

Gillian Naylor, *The arts and crafts movement.* This is, in addition, a good short introduction to English 19th century design generally.

Bauhaus German art and design school open from 1919 to 1933. Walter Gropius was appointed head of the Weimar School of Arts and Crafts in succession to Van derVelde in 1914. At the time this might have seemed a definite step away from 'arts and crafts' towards 'industrial design', because Gropius's work to date in architecture — the Fagus (shoe trees) factory at Ahlfeld in 1911, and the 'exhibition factory' at the Deutsche Werkbund exhibition at Cologne in 1914 — are both machine-style buildings. However, after the war in 1919, and after some confusion over his appointment, Gropius took over and renamed the school *Das Staatliche Bauhaus Weimar.* 'Bauhaus' had a medieval ring to it — the concept of the *building (Bau)* as the whole unifier of the arts. For the first three or four years the school was run on Morris — arts and craft — lines, with a considerable mystic influence from Johannes Itten, He was called in to run the famous *'Vorkurs',* a preliminary course which lasted six months and was aimed, as Gillian Naylor writes in *The Bauhaus,* 'at purging the student of all conventionally acquired knowledge in order to introduce him to workshop theory and practice' — a guild apprenticeship, in other words. As Gropius wrote in his 1919 manifesto — 'Architects, sculptors, painters, we must all turn to the crafts'. At this time, too, Gropius himself was an EXPRESSIONIST architect.

Then, some time in 1922-3, there was a kind of 'revolution' in the Bauhaus, staged by staff and pupils, who were probably under the influence of the DE STIJL movement. Its leader, Theo van Doesburg, was in Weimar in 1921-2. Gropius gave way to them; Itten was sacked; and the Bauhaus was reorganized as a school for industrial design, graphic design and industrialized architecture. Thus any claim that Gropius might have made after 1923, that his or the Bauhaus's work was in the tradition started by William Morris, must be false. The Bauhaus moved from Weimar to Dessau in 1925 where Gropius designed its new buildings. (These are still there; altered by the Nazis, they survived the war and have been partly restored, though not quite to Gropius's design.) In 1928 Gropius left; Meyer, Gropius's architect partner, was Principal from 1928 to 1930, Mies van der Rohe from 1930 to 1933. All three Principals, then, were architects. The Bauhaus moved again to Berlin in 1932, and Mies closed it in the face of Nazi threats after their coup in 1933. (Both moves made by the Bauhaus had been forced by opposition — Conservative in Weimar and Nazi in Dessau.)

Many of the Bauhaus teachers ended up in America; Gropius himself via

England at Harvard; Mies at the Illinois Institute of Technology in Chicago; Moholy-Nagy also in Chicago, where he founded a 'New Bauhaus', now the Chicago Institute of Design. In Europe, after the war, Max Bill, a Bauhaus-trained Swiss architect and designer, started the *Ulm Hochschule für Gastaltung* — the Design Polytechnic at Ulm — which was in the end closed by the Bavarian Land Government, an echo of Weimar.

The legacy of the post-1923 Bauhaus can be summarized:

1 Design becomes 'problem solving' rather than 'object shaping' — thus *seating function* rather than *chair*, or perhaps no *object* at all.

2 All 'problems' have to be thought out afresh. All earlier designs are thus reclassified as 'design-solutions' and no existing 'design-solution' should be allowed to influence the new solution, a contrast to Scandinavian design, particularly Danish furniture design of the same years as the Bauhaus.

3 An obsessive concern with manufacturing and use-function (rather than, say, aesthetic or cultural functions) led to a ban on all ornament. Even in textiles there seems to be a marked preference for those patterns which can be made by the weaving process. Sans-serif lettering, naturally. Some of the graphic work was uncharacteristic in not putting legibility first.

Much of this became the orthodoxy of the establishment, as much in Britain as in Germany after 1945. Like most orthodoxies which think themselves to be revolutionary, this one is difficult to serve, and design tends to fall back on 'production-functionalism' backed up by ergonomics. The 'new-solution-to-the-design-problem' method also throws away a thousand years of experience in the design of chairs, knives, cups and saucers. It is not surprising that the Bauhaus and its heirs have had more success in selling design for completely 'new' objects like telephones and refrigerators. Because of the needs of industry — and vanity of designers — 'solving a problem' by not having a design at all, has never been popular. The ban on ornament, however, is still with us, but perhaps weakening.

In spite of so much about 'design problems' which suggests that the question of 'style' has been by-passed, Bauhaus is a recongizable style in design: a certain stark heaviness. In architecture it is one of the main components of the INTERNATIONAL MODERN style. What are the origins of the Bauhaus style? Adolf Loos's work in Vienna at the turn of the century is one obvious source. Loos had an obsessional hatred of ornament, and even went to the lengths of publishing an article entitled 'Ornament and crime'. His may have been an over-reaction (in the Vienna of the last years of the Hapsburg empire) to the voluptuousness of Viennese baroque and the early Art-Nouveau years of *Jugendstil.* Loos's famous Steiner House in Vienna (1910) is as extreme as anything of *c*1930. The photographs show its square staring windows in a completely blank facade, like a face singed by an explosion. In the Bauhaus, machines — or aspects of them, like a smooth finish (unfunctional and expensive)—were admired for a similar lack of graces, if not grace. Otherwise, the main influence seems to have been DE STIJL, with its fondness for separate planes at angles to each other.

The importance of the Bauhaus lies in the changes it brought about in design education. Direct copies of the Bauhaus seem to have met with predictable opposition, but modified versions and partial imitations abound. The *Vorkurs* survives with similar aims in many of the 'Foundation' courses run by art schools today. Above all, though, by preaching a wholesale rejection of traditional design, the Bauhaus aimed at a total control by the designer of man's constructed environment. This is an aim that no designer is likely to give up willingly, and it may finally only be halted by the resources and environmental crises, which have been brought on by those industrial processes the Bauhaus so loudly celebrated.

Design can be seen in many museums, e.g. M.O.M.A.

READING:
Gillian Naylor, *The Bauhaus.* The best short guide, with good illustrations. She is not troubled by Gropius's about-turns, suggesting that the muddles of the first few years happened because neither staff nor students understood his message.
H.M. Wingler, *The Bauhaus.*
Herbert Bayer and Walter Gropius, *Bauhaus 1918-28.* Bayer—best known as a photographer — also trained at the Bauhaus.

Beaux-Arts The term 'Beaux-Arts' was coined by Perrault in about 1690. It was translated literally into English as 'Fine Arts' in 1767, and is still used for painting and sculpture in both languages. (The corresponding French phrase for writing, *'belles lettres',* of *c*1710 was used but never translated into English. See also the German *'Kunstwerk'.*) Batteus, who used the phrase 'Beaux-Arts' in an essay in 1746, did not include architecture, because it was a useful art. However, after the Revolution, the Royal Academies of Drawing and of Architecture in Paris were brought together as the *Ecole des Beaux-Arts.* Throughout the 19th and into the 20th century, the *Ecole* taught a disciplined classical architectural style and method. Few English architects went there, but many Americans did, and the style of the Beaux-Arts began to influence American architecture in the late 19th century, especially with the work of McKim, Mead and White. The Beaux-Arts ousted rival styles, including that of the CHICAGO SCHOOL, for many large buildings until the 1940's, as it did in England through the organizational efforts of R. Phené Spiers (who had studied at the Beaux-Arts) and architects like Reginald Blomfield, who admired the thoroughness of Beaux-Arts training. Anglo-French architectural firms secured commissions: Mewès and Davis were typical of such partnerships with their London Ritz Hotel in Piccadilly (1906) and, amongst many other buildings by them, Westminster Bank, Throgmorton Street, in the City of London (1923). They were joined by Anglo-American architects like Atkinson and D.H. Burnham for Selfridge's in Oxford Street, London, begun in 1908. (Even Burnham was working in a Beaux-Arts style by then.) Bush House, at the foot of Kingsway, the new avenue laid out through former slums by the London County Council, was designed by two American architects, Helmle and Corbett (1925-35). The special quality of the Beaux-Arts style was the method which enabled architects to organize very large buildings in a classical style. Its success made it the main target for C.I.A.M. whose architects wanted all large buildings to be designed in their styles.

H.R. Hitchcock points out (in *Architecture, 19th and 20th centuries*) that one of the ironies of modern architecture is that the grandest and most successful project in the classical style — the kind of thing the *Ecole* trained its students to do — was the layout and buildings of New Delhi, by Lutyens, who had been trained in the old, casual, English way.

Biedermeyer German art and design in the period 1815-1848 — from the end of the French wars to the outbreak of the 'Liberal' revolutions. In 1853 writers published some comic verse supposedly by 'Gottlieb Biedermeyer', but the name was not applied to the arts of the period until 1891, and then in mockery. However, it became a useful cover-name, not only for German design of that period, but also in the Netherlands and Scandinavia. It designated 'middle-class' or even 'bourgeois' taste, although the aristocracy also bought richer versions of the style. Biedermeyer furniture is a kind of heavy NEO-CLASSICAL, mostly plain and solid, but sometimes billowing out into extraordinary barometer-shaped secretaires, which look more like Art

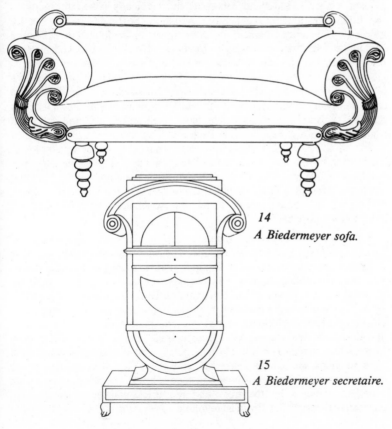

14
A Biedermeyer sofa.

15
A Biedermeyer secretaire.

Deco than Neo-classical. The paintings of Adolphe von Menzel show Biedermeyer interiors.

READING:
Georg Himmelheber, *Biedermeyer furniture.* He limits the 'essential' period to 1815-30, and has some superb photographs.

Brutalism Architecture since 1955. It seems hard to believe that architects should actually set out to make their buildings look *brutal,* but the term does not seem to be one of abuse, and has been accepted by many of the architects in the 'movement'. The term itself was probably derived from the French 'béton brut', or 'raw concrete' in English. Corbusier used concrete for both structure and as raw finish in his buildings after 1945. That it should be accepted by some architects and critics indicates an impatience with the smooth surfaces of the International Modern style. But when one examines the so-called Brutalist buildings, the idea of a *Brutalist Movement* evaporates. The Smithsons' Hunstanton school in Norfolk, built in 1949-54, is Mies without the many layers of paint, each one sanded down. The Smithsons' Hunstanton school looks and feels crude, but it is clearly in the same mould as the Illinois Institute of Technology buildings. Stirling's building for the Leicester University Engineering Department, or Rudolph's Architecture Building at Yale, may not look as the Bauhaus at Dessau once looked, but their brick bulges and concrete hiccups can be—and are—justified on functional grounds. Architects who express the different parts of their buildings in a forceful, disjointed way are understandably criticised by those who have a previous loyalty to 'the style of 1930' and are unmoved by the news that it is gone 1970. Architectural historians have taken up the idea and described some Victorian architects — S.S.Teulon in England, or Frank Furness in U.S.A. — as 'Brutalist', though Expressionist might be a better term for them. Teulon and Furness were able to use fine materials and take time over their buildings. When rough textures and a giant scale are employed in designing housing estates, on a much more limited budget than the Victorians had, so that there is not enough money for refinements, the result can be very drab indeed and a possible incitement to vandalism.

Reyner Banham, in *The new Brutalism, ethic or aesthetic?*, gives as one of his examples the London County Council's architects department, where he discerns a 'palace revolution' in the mid 1950's, when the 'Scandinavians' were ousted by 'Corbusierans'. The change-over can be seen in the different styles of the two halves of the Roehampton Estate in south-west London. Alton East was built in a humanist Swedish style — brick facings to the tower blocks, houses in small closes, four-storey maisonette blocks; and Alton West in a Corbusier style whose most spectacular element is the row of five mini-*Unités* which straddles one hillside in the estate. Unlike Marseilles, these slabs have no shops, etc. inside. Even the many point-blocks on this part of the estate are faced with concrete panels instead of brick. The place is saved from complete greyness by the tress and red brick maisonette blocks. An alternative theory to the 'Brutalist revolution' is that the L.C.C. decided to cut costs after looking over the bills for the first part of the estate. However, on a television programme about sixteen or seventeen years after they had designed Roehampton, the architects concerned agreed that their inspiration had been Corbusier, they had been down to Marseilles and seen the *Unité* and decided that this was the 'answer'.

Another contrast can be seen on the South Bank of the Thames, between the 'Swedish' Festival hall of 1951 and the 'Brutalist' Hayward Gallery and concert halls complex next door, of the 1960's.

Nikolaus Pevsner gave a talk on the radio in 1966 which he called 'The anti-pioneers', an explicit reference to his own book *Pioneers of modern design*. Much of his polemic was directed against architects who could be called 'Brutalist', and in particular Stirling for his engineering block. The architect Richard Sheppard (also criticized) replied to Pevsner in another radio talk about six months later. He suggested that Pevsner had confused 'functional' with 'machine-like' — a building does not have to *look like* a machine to be functional. There are, of course, other functions than those concerned with structure and opening windows. There is a 'cultural' function, and it is arguable whether a brutal appearance, of any shade of meaning the word 'brutal' can have, is ever culturally 'right' for anything except perhaps a prison, like George Dance's Newgate Prison of 1769 (demolished in 1900, to make way for the Old Bailey).

BUILDINGS TO SEE:
The origin of all Brutalist buildings is Corbusier's *Unité d'Habitation* outside Marseilles. Its pups at Roehampton are in south-west London, and there are many other L.C.C./G.L.C. blocks in London, especially in the boroughs along the south bank of the Thames.

READING:
N. Pevsner, 'The anti-pioneers' in the *Listener* of 29 December 1966 and 5 January 1967. The correspondence in the *Listener* of 12 January 1967 (including a letter from James Stirling), 19 January 1967 and 2 February 1967 (a reply from Pevsner).
R. Sheppard 'Monuments to the architect?' in the *Listener*, 8 June 1967.
Reyner Banham, *The new Brutalism, ethic or aesthetic?* This was published in 1966, before Pevsner's talk.

Chicago School The term has two meanings: 1 the group of architects who built the first skyscrapers (in Chicago) from c1880 to c1900, and 2 another group of architects and town planners who followed the first 'school' and among whom was Frank Lloyd Wright.

1 After the great fire of Chicago in 1871, rebuilding had to be on stricter lines: the structures themselves had to be fireproof (see IRON ARCHITECTURE). The architect who established the type was William Lebaron Jenney and his early buildings were mostly classical in style, so much so that some modern critics have tended to pass him by. However his buildings are interesting in two ways. The 'classical' buildings, like the Fair Store of 1890-1, should be seen as most people at street level would have seen them at the time: only the

lower storeys could have been seen clearly, and these three or four storeys were treated like a whole building, perhaps with rusticated ground floor, then pilasters and an entablature. Above that, six or seven storeys would have no architectural features worth mentioning, because they would not be 'seen' from the ground. At the top of the building would be a more elaborate entablature and cornice, which would be seen, perhaps repeating the design of the lower one, only more heavily, perhaps in a different style. This is not, from a designer's point of view today, a satisfactory solution, although Sullivan himself advocated something very like it, and most historians take care to point this out, if they discuss Jenney's buildings at all. But Sullivan used the same idea for his Carson Pirie Scott Store a decade later – an opulent couple of storeys at the street level, then ten storeys of offices, then a lid (since removed). Then, Jenney himself also designed an 'integrated' design for his second Leiter Store (now Sears Roebuck, at the south-east corner of State and Van Buren; 1891): two 'shop' storeys, six 'office' storeys in two groups of three, and a semi-classical entablature, but very plain. The building is twenty-seven bays long, also in groups of three, which are marked by thicker vertical dividers — and the ends have even thicker corners. This 'thickening' is quite unfunctional for a steel-framed building, but was quite common practice in the Chicago School.

Most of these 'Chicago School' buildings were designed as blocks to be seen as wholes, even if they were to stand in quite narrow streets. The Marquette building, perhaps the most satisfying design of them all (Holabird and Roche, 1895) has a podium of two-and-half storeys, a 'trunk' of eleven and a cornice of two (though this has now been altered); there are three distinct parts of the building and the facade was articulated by having the two end bays break forward slightly. The top and bottom storeys were decorated, the middle ones not, but the design was a whole. It makes an interesting contrast with, for example, the middle period of Corbusier, where the whole top of one of his blocks would be an undifferentiated slab, and the bottom a free-form 'sculpture' in a different material; the Swiss House for students in Paris of 1931 and the U.N. building in New York of 1951 are good examples.

At the end of the 19th century the taste of the Chicago rich turned quite decisively away from the 'Chicago School', preferring the work of architects who had been trained at the *Ecole des Beaux Arts* in Paris, France, or their associates. This change of taste was signalled at the Chicago World's Fair in 1893, when most of the buildings were in a fantasy Roman Imperial Style. Skyscrapers continued to be built — as much in New York as in Chicago, so that Manhattan became more famous for its tall buildings than the Loop in Chicago. The style of these later skyscrapers was not at all like the 'Chicago School', but the buildings were much more confidently designed than the early Jenney buildings had been. In Chicago itself the Wrigley building of 1921-24 (North Michigan at the River) looks uncannily like Soviet buildings of a decade later. In the famous Tribune Tower Gothic is very convincingly adapted to a thirty-storey skyscraper — whatever the critics may say; the winning design in the competition was by Hood and Howells (1925). In New York, Burnham designed the Flatiron building in 1902, still in a

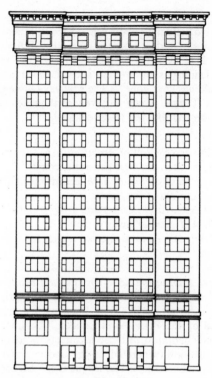

16 Holabird and Roche. The Marquette Building, Chicago.

'Chicago' style, but New York skyscrapers after that are a curious example of classical or Gothic turning into Art Deco before that fashion hit Paris: the Singer Building of 1906-8; Woolworth (Cass Bilbert, 1913); and of course Chrysler later on.

2 The work of the 'second' school is notable for private houses, including Wright's. His work is related to earlier movements in America, to the SHINGLE STYLE; to Richardson's ROMANESQUE; and to the decorative work of Sullivan, which may be Art Nouveau; Wright was a pupil of Sullivan's. After that, Wright's style took off on its own and has proved a considerable embarrassment to apologists for the Modern Movement, since Wright cannot be ignored, but does not fit into any of the clichés of C.I.A.M. or the BAUHAUS. Corbusier's buildings — and, according to the Smithsons, all characteristic buildings of the Heroic Period of the Modern Movement — stand 'poised' on the landscape; that is, they are held up by the thinnest possible steel columns so as to give the illusion of being 'poised'. Wright's buildings in contrast are settled into the landscape, partly because the Mid-Western climate favours not exposing buildings more than necessary in winter, and partly because Wright had 'irrational' feelings about being at one with the land.

BUILDINGS TO BE SEEN:
Many of the Chicago buildings of both schools are still standing, though often altered. The most useful guide is *Chicago's famous buildings,* which included (in 1965) four of F.L. Wright's buildings, among them the famous Robie House of 1909, a leading example of the 'second' Chicago School. Others of Wright's early buildings have gone — The Midway Gardens in Chicago; the Imperial Hotel in Tokyo, which survived earthquakes (as Wright often pointed out) and the war, but fell to developers.

READING:
C. Condit, *The Chicago School of Architecture* is a rewriting of his earlier *The rise of the skyscraper,* the best general account.
M. L. Peisch, *The Chicago School of Architecture,* about the 'second' school, where Condit's book is about the 'first'.
Vincent Scully, *American architecture and urbanism;* the Chicago school is discussed as part of a general history. Scully has some very interesting illustrations, including some of the rejected entries for the Chicago Tribune Tower competition.

C.I.A.M—*Congrès Internationaux d'Architecture Moderne* Active 1928-53. International congresses of architects had met regularly since the end of the 19th century, with topics like City Planning, the theme of the 1910 meeting organized by the R.I.B.A. in London. C.I.A.M. emphasised the *moderne* and it included most of those architects — then relatively few in number — who are now venerated as the apostles and teachers of the International Modern Movement. The second C.I.A.M. congress was held in Frankfurt to celebrate a mass-housing scheme carried out under the control of Ernst May, the city architect. Altogether ten congresses were held, the movement petering out in the 1950's (when the 'heroic' period had passed and doctrinal schisms had begun to appear).

BUILDINGS TO SEE:
See INTERNATIONAL MODERN, and individual architects in part 3.

READING:
Charles Jencks, *Modern movements in architecture.*
Anthony Jackson, *The politics of architecture*

Classic/Classical Although both words are often used to mean 'belonging to or derived from the civilizations of ancient Greece and Rome', the word 'classic' is more useful meaning 'perfect of its kind' (of any period). There is a large literature on classical design and architecture.

ON DESIGN:
Arthur Negus and Max Robertson, *Going for a song*
R. Edwards and L. G. G. Ramsey, *The connoisseur's complete period guides.*

ON ARCHITECTURE
John Summerson, *The classical language of architecture:* perhaps the best introduction to classical architecture, though he does not give much space to

the influence of the classical 'grammar' on 'polite' buildings.
For 'polite' building, there is some help from:
S.C. Ramsey and J.D.M. Harvey, *Small Georgian houses and their details.*
D. Cruikshank and P. Wyld, *London: The art of Georgian building.*
S.E. Rasmussen. *London, the unique city* has much useful information on
houses and street architecture.
John Summerson, *Georgian London* describes the major developments.

Comprehensive Development A British planning term for a practice in
vogue in the 1940's and 1950's, particularly appropriate to large areas which
had been destroyed by bombing in the war. These devastations gave architects
and planners the opportunities they had been looking for. The best example of
this kind of development is the city of Coventry in Warwickshire which lost
the whole centre of the city (including the cathedral) in one blitz. The
redevelopment centred round a long 'precinct' which slopes down a hill away
from the old cathedral tower, which survived the blitz. Access roads at the
backs of shops allow for deliveries and loading, and there are parking spaces
on the roofs of many of the buildings.
   The London County Council made plans in the late 1940's for eight
'comprehensive development areas', one of which, in Poplar, was begun in
time for the Festival of Britain — the Lansbury Estate, with a new market
place and shops and pubs as well as housing. Some of these C.D.A.s were
abandoned by 1960 (Lewisham, for example), but some were carried out: the
Elephant and Castle area was one. They are not much liked now, so the idea
has gone out of fashion: it tends to impose a monotony on an area, as well as
giving its inhabitants 'future shock'. Only the City of London's Barbican
scheme is steadily going ahead, and here one can see a version of what
architects' dream cities of the 21st century would be like — plenty of
pedestrian decks, above which rise an assortment of high buildings, which hold
a mixture of apartments and offices.

Concrete A mixture of mortar and small stones which sets like stone. Used
by the Romans, but then by nobody for 1,500 years. Some builders used it in
the 18th century but the chief experiments were carried out in the 19th century,
when the practicality of reinforced concrete was tested. Concrete is good for
compressive weight—it will stand a lot of pressure, but it cracks under tension.
Iron/steel, on the other hand, is good under tension—suspension bridges
— but buckles under pressure (and under heat). The two were combined as
reinforced concrete in 1871-2 by William E. Ward in his own house at Port
Chester, N.Y. Reinforced concrete was further developed by the French
engineer Francois Hennebique in the 1880's and '90's, and began to be used in
the early 20th century for some large buildings (the alternatives being
traditional load-bearing walls of stone, brick or rubble infill, which was
relatively expensive and not suitable for really large buildings because of its
weight; and iron frame — see IRON ARCHITECTURE — the Chicago
skyscrapers were iron frame. One of the most spectacular of the early
reinforced concrete buildings was the Centennial Hall in Breslau (now

Wroclaw) in Silesia, by M. Berg in 1913. Reinforced concrete became one of the most used of modern methods of construction, e.g. by Corbusier for the *Unités*, and even earlier by Auguste Perret, notably in the Théâtre des Champs Elysées of 1910 and at Nôtre-Dame at Le Raincy in 1922-3.

One problem about reinforced concrete — or ferro-concrete — is the difficulty in knocking down buildings which are no longer needed. The iron is under tension which may 'give' violently when released. As Geoff Scott says in his *Building disasters and failures* (London, 1976): 'about 90 percent of the stored energy of a pre-stressed member is contained in the tendons . . . (if released) the possibility of the tendon and its anchorage becoming a missile cannot be ignored in all anchored forms of pre-stressed construction'.

READING:
P. Collins, *Concrete, the search for a new architecture.*

Conservation The Society for the Protection of Ancient Buildings was founded in 1877 following a letter to *The Times* from William Morris. Since then, there have been many societies for preserving buildings and landscape in countries which have any worth preserving. In England there has always been a reluctance to *restore* when only ruins are left: most English work has languished under the heavy hand of historicism. The British are unwilling to restore in the old style, but fortunately loath to rebuild in the new. This tradition for not restoring goes back to Ruskin. Care in preserving 'documents of the past' has led to the interesting idea that buildings should not be cleaned, because the dirt is part of their history — many objections (not on the grounds of cost) were made to the cleaning recently of St. Paul's Cathedral in London. No such inhibitions have held back the Americans with remarkable achievements like Colonial Williamsburg where, for example, the Governor's Palace was rebuilt from the foundations which were all that was left on the site. In England, an American effort restored the ruined great hall and buildings at Dartington in Devonshire, and at the same time commissioned buildings in a variety of styles. In spite of such successes, historians will point out that the enthusiasm of some late-19th century architects, such as Philip Webb, and William Morris himself, for old buildings, indicates a sense of failure. Seldom, in the previous three centuries of English history, had architects and patrons felt it better to preserve even humble old buildings, than to rebuild.

Conurbation The word was first used by Patrick Geddes in 1910, and is now generally used to describe a built-up area created by the growth of several cities and towns towards each other, engulfing villages and small towns in between. It is a problem in local government as much as anything else: how far the advantages of regional planning are to be given priority over local loyalties. Most cities in the old world, and some in the new, absorbed villages as they expanded, but a 'conurbation' implies the absorption of large towns as well.

In 1882, the Spanish architect Soria Y Mata published the idea of a 'linear city', a long highway with development on each side. Three miles of such a city were actually built outside Madrid in 1894-96. This sounds much like 'ribbon development' — houses built in estates with occasional shopping parades along main roads or railway lines, which was the bogey of planning in the period 1920-60. But about 1960 the idea of development along 'fingers' once again became fashionable; supporters argued that it would leave the countryside in between 'untouched'. This is what ribbon development did, what Soria Y Mata meant, and what Boswash (Boston-New York-Philadelphia-Baltimore-Washington) does. There are still unspoilt bits of Connecticut. Two examples of such planning acceptance of ribbon development are the 'Hand' plan for Copenhagen — 'fingers' reaching along the Sound, etc. — and the *Randstad Holland* plan for *designing* the growing together of the towns between Amsterdam, the Hague and Rotterdam. 'Declaring' an area to be a conurbation may allow a cluster of towns to ask for central government funds to provide the kind of services which a city can have but which separately towns might not, and commerce and even banking might be attracted. The experience of the 'Five Towns' in Staffordshire shows that this does not always happen (they became one borough in 1910 and a city in 1925, but according to Pevsner's *Staffordshire* in his 'Buildings of England' series, there is still (1974) no proper centre). Conurbations ought to be distinguished from cities which have spread into open countryside, where there are no local government problems about where the centre should be.

READING:
P. Self, *World cities*. This has photographs and plans of London, Randstad Holland and others.

Dartington (see also CONSERVATION) The modern buildings at Dartington in Devonshire have not all been a success. Time does not deal kindly with the International Modern style. The Dartington Trust revived not only the old buildings, but old crafts and husbandry, somewhat as Ashbee's Guild and School of Handicraft had tried to do twenty years before the Elmhirsts started at Dartington. Money and better management, presumably, have helped Dartington to much greater success than Chipping Camden, so that it is one of the world's models for preserving and developing traditional crafts. Weaving, furniture and recently glass-making have been set up, and the products can be bought at shops on the estate, outside Totnes. The Trust has also interested itself in starting craft manufactures, etc. in areas outside Devon, where local industry has shut down.

TO SEE:
The Dartington Hall Estate is open most of the year (with its shops, restaurant at Shinner's Bridge, and garden shop) and the gardens are often open. Some of the school buildings can be seen from the road through the estate.

READING:
Dartington Hall and its work; a good introduction, with many photographs.
Anthony Emery, *Dartington Hall*.
Victor Bonham-Carter, *Dartington Hall, the formative years*.

John Seymour, *Bring me my bow*; a general book about Britain and its agriculture. He also has 'A plan for the redevelopment of Dartington Hall farms', prepared in response to an invitation from the Trustees.

De Stijl Dutch art movement of 1917-31. Its leaders were the painters Piet Mondrian, Theo van Doesburg and van der Leck, and the architects Oud and Rietveld. Rietveld's famous chair of *c*.1917 seems like an exaggeration of the style of the contemporary furniture of Frank Lloyd Wright who was much admired in the Netherlands at the time. Wright was also one of the main influences on the architecture of W. M. Dudok, architect to the city of Hilversum. His style was mature by 1921; his best known building is the Hilversum Town Hall of 1928-30. Dudok was also associated with De Stijl, and his buildings are distinguished from theirs mainly by his use of brick.

De Stijl, like the Futurist Movement in painting, was in love with the 'machine' and the members of the movement all seem to have believed that mankind could achieve a spiritual satisfaction only through art which is removed from the randomness of nature. De Stijl's propaganda for buildings and furniture which consisted only in planes at right angles to each other, and all of these planes visually separate, clearly played a part in the formation of the International Modern style. This influence was to a great extent unacknowledged, because International Modern (including the Bauhaus) claimed that 'rationality' and 'fitness for purpose' were the basis of their designs. (Who would confess to being irrational and unfit?) To admit a debt to De Stijl would have been to admit that purely fine art principles were also a component of their style, and the principles of fine art do not depend on either rationality or fitness for purpose. Rietveld's chair was not designed even with any ergonomic data in mind, let alone the experience of generations of sitters. As the Penguin *Dictionary of decorative arts* puts it — 'Some of his chairs can now be seen to have been among the most exciting three-dimensional works of art created at the time'. For the influence of Theo van Doesburg, see BAUHAUS.

TO BE SEEN:
Buildings in Hilversum and Utrecht, where Ritveld's Schroeder House is still standing. Dudok's architecture had an influence in England which can be seen in Charles Holden's Stations for the Piccadilly Line, mostly built in the early 1930's, and in Culpin and Bower's Greenwich Town Hall of 1939. Museums have examples of De Stijl work.

READING:
H. L. C. Jaffé, *De Stijl, 1917-31*; he also published *Piet Mondrian*.

Deutsche Werkstätten and **Deutsche Werkbund** Several *Werkstätten* (Munich 1897, Dresden 1898, among them) were set up on the lines of the English craft guilds. They brought together craftsmen in various fields and also undertook research into the development of traditional production, as, for example, the co-operation with cabinet-makers to design unit furniture *(typenmöbel)* — standardised parts as well as standardised units (cupboards, etc.). This in some ways foreshadows a similar co-operation between Danish furniture designers (particularly Kaare Klint) and the Copenhagen Cabinet Makers' Guild in the 1920's.

The *Deutsche Werkbund*, though in some ways an organisation sympathetic to the *Werkstätten*, was more concerned to encourage designers towards industrial mass-production. The guiding figure here was the writer and bureaucrat Hermann Muthesius, who had been sent over to England by the Prussian government to study English architecture and design in the late 1890's. The result of his stay was a book, *Das Englische Haus*, introducing the English developments in domestic architecture (Queen Anne, Arts and Crafts, etc.) to a European public. The *Deutsche Werkbund* was like a more organised version of the Arts and Crafts Exhibition Society, plus the fact that it was set up to bring manufacturers and designers together. Like the Arts and Crafts, it arranged exhibitions, and later on published a year-book. The best known exhibitions, and perhaps architecturally the most influential, were those at Cologne in 1914 and at Stuttgart in 1927.

Richard Riemerschmidt was the best known of the designers associated with the *Werkstätten* — examples of his cutlery are in museums. The most famous names associated with the *Werkbund* are Peter Behrens who, in the same year that the *Werkbund* was founded, 1907, was appointed art director for A.E.G. (the German General Electric Company), and Henry van der Velde, a craftsman inspired by Morris, who led an argument against standardisation during discussions at the 1914 Cologne exhibition. Muthesius was his chief opponent. Van der Velde was largely instrumental in having Gropius appointed to succeed him at the Weimar School of Arts and Crafts, and van der Velde's own ambivalence about industrial design can be seen reflected in the early years of the Bauhaus, which after 1923 settled down into a Muthesius version of a *Deutsche Werkbund* school.

Eclectic 'Choosing'. In architecture and design this means designing in many styles, sometimes in the same building or even in the same piece of furniture. In the first half of the 19th century in England particularly, when 'style' was being made a matter of faith by some designers, to design a series of buildings in different styles was a sign of the sin of eclecticism. Charles Barry is a good example of the 19th century 'eclectic' architect: he introduced the ITALIAN RENASCENCE style in London with his Travellers' Club in 1829; before then he had designed in NEO-CLASSICAL(Manchester Art Gallery) and in Perpendicular GOTHIC (St. Peter's Church in Brighton, and King Edward VI School, Birmingham, now demolished). Later he was to design in High Renascence (Reform Club, 1838), Elizabethan (Highclere, Hampshire) and again in Perpendicular (Houses of Parliament—1836 onwards). This kind of eclecticism became a standard practice in much 19th century building — especially 'polite' building: churches settled for GOTHIC, including eventually Non-Conformist chapels, but not the Roman Catholics, who favoured classical or ROMANESQUE; town halls were either classical or 'Flemish Gothic', or even 'Italian Gothic', because these had been the styles of the town halls of city states in Flanders and Italy in the early Renaissance, when they were at their most vigorous; Perpendicular Gothic was used for private schools, because the famous grammar schools had been founded in England in the 15th and 16th centuries.

The world 'eclectic' is almost certainly meant as a term of abuse and figures largely in the HISTORICISTS' vocabulary — it is part of their case that what was wrong with 19th century architecture was that its designers were eclectic. Since variety is the spice of life, eclecticism could be thought of as an enrichment; one has only to look around London today to sigh for it, and perhaps even Georgian Bath might seem a little unvaried if it were not built up and down steep hills. What is more, one of the most admired 'forerunners' of modern architecture, Philip Webb, was an eclectic *par excellence*, since snatches of various styles can be seen in single buildings by him; for example in Standen, in Sussex. The Butterfield-Webb-Lethaby tradition of 'negative' style, taking only what was suitable to the job in hand from any style (so Butterfield used sash windows — a 17th century invention — in his Gothic buildings), is clearly eclecticism, so perhaps the whole issue, though so often brought up, is only playing with words.

Elizabethan Originally architecture and design of 1558-1603, which carried on with few changes into the next reign, so that the similar styles are called Jacobean (1603-25). Both have close affinities with contemporary design in the Netherlands and Denmark (for example, the Rosenborg Palace in Copenhagen, 1606-17, for James I's brother-in-law, Christian IV). It was revived in England in the 1830's and 1840's, both for architecture and — in theory — for furniture. Country houses like Harlaxton (Anthony Salvin, 1831, inspired by the west front of Burghley House, 1577), and colleges like Lincoln's Inn in London (Hardwick, 1843) began a vogue which lasted until mid-century (Mentmore Towers, Buckinghamshire, 1852-54, by Paxton and Stokes) and was paralleled by a similar revival of Scottish Renascence architecture (for example, Balmoral, by Smith — with Prince Albert — 1853-55). See NATIONALIST REVIVALS. The furniture which the early Victorians called 'Elizabethan' was more like the furniture of the Restoration of c1670 — turned legs and upright backs to the chairs, etc. Turned legs were unfashionable in English furniture from the late 17th century until their revival for 'Elizabethan' in the 1830's; they are a carpenter's rather than a designer's motif. A modified variety of this kind of furniture lasted until at least the 1930's — gate-leg tables, a standard mid-17th century type, became especially popular.

Environment(-alism) 'Environmental architects' can be egomaniacs not content with designing buildings but aiming to design whole districts, the kind of design foretold by Colin Buchanan in *Traffic in towns* (1963) and to be seen in Philadelphia (Penn Center, which Buchanan cites) and the new centre of Stockholm. Everything — railways, roads, areas for walking, parking, shopping and even living — are all designed together as a whole concept. On the other hand 'environmental' can refer to the various movements concerned about the damage to the environment caused by modern industry, transport, etc. It can therefore signal a revived interest in traditional methods of coping with the weather, and a vernacular architecture and design which relies more

17 A chair in the style which would have been called 'Elizabethan' in the 1830's in England.

on natural materials than modern design usually does, but which also takes note of modern technical research (like solar heating). This kind of environmentalism has been attacked (e.g. in *The Aspen Papers*, ed. R. Banham, a statement by the French group: 'The environmental witch-hunt') as another move by the ruling classes to confuse the real issues. Meanwhile the conservation movements have been also attacked (e.g. over their energy policies) as helping Soviet Communism.

Exhibitions In the Middle Ages trade fairs were one of the main ways of trading. They became less important in the 16th and 17th centuries for a number of reasons, including the development of shops and a safer import-export business. When the practice of trade fairs was revived in the 18th century in the form of industrial exhibitions, the aim was not directly trading, but the encouragement of trade, together with other purposes such as national pride and the improvement of taste. This means that the objects (and later, buildings) on view are a bad guide to general taste. They were always exceptional 'turns', bravura technical feats in the 19th century, architects' pipe-dreams in the 20th. The trade fair does still exist, and business is done, but these fairs are more like super-advertising than a once-a-year chance to buy.

The Society of Arts in England (later R.S.A.) organised the first of the modern exhibitions in the year of its foundation, 1754. Later in the century the French began a long series of purely national exhibitions, designed to French trade. International exhibitions had to wait until international transport was good enough and quick enough for goods and people. Between about 1820 and 1850 there were perhaps thirty or forty large national exhibitions which attracted foreign observers, mostly in Europe and the U.S.A., including triennial exhibitions held in the rooms of the Royal Dublin Society from 1829 onwards. There were also, of course, exhibitions of painting and sculpture, once a year at the Royal Academy in London, once every two years at the Salon in Paris, and so on in other cities.

Between 1846 and 1849 the R.S.A. and Prince Albert, President of the Society since 1843, put forward proposals for an international exhibition which became, in the end, the Great Exhibition of 1851. This was the first international exhibition and like its many successors was partly national boasting on an international stage, and partly high-minded propaganda for peace, co-operation and the rest.

The building (by Joseph Paxton, developed from his greenhouses) became famous as the largest to date free-standing iron-frame building, ideally suited for its purpose, but, however admirable, not much use for anything else as they found when it was set up again at Sydenham in south London. The company which owned it went bankrupt, and the building burnt down in 1936. I.K. Brunel's own design for the Exhibition was a more conventional building of brick, with only top lighting — including a dome — in glass and iron. There were imitations of the Crystal Palace at Dublin and New York two years later, but soon there was a return to the Brunel idea of conventional building for exhibitions, even though few of them were kept after the exhibitions closed (the Palais des Beaux Arts in Paris is a rare relic).

International exhibitions became a regular feature of 19th century life. In the 50 years after the Great Exhibition there were more than a hundred major international exhibitions, besides minor ones and purely national events. The most important of them are set out here:

1851   London; 21 acres, 6,139,195 visitors.
1855   Paris; 24½ acres, 5,162,330 visitors.
1862   London; 23½ acres, 6,211,103 visitors.
1865   Dublin; 9 million visitors; in this year there were 11 international exhibitions.
1867   Paris; 37 acres, 10.2 million visitors.
1873   Vienna; 40 acres, 7,254,687 visitors — not as many as had been hoped for; there was a cholera epidemic.
1876   Philadelphia, the Centenary Exhibition; 60 acres, 9,910, 966 visitors.
1878   Paris; 60 acres, 13 million visitors (only 7 years after the defeat in the Franco-Prussian war); and also Amsterdam.
1888-9 Melbourne, the Centenary of Australia.
1889   Paris; 72 acres; the Eiffel Tower was built for this exhibition. It

was for the Centenary of the French Revolution, therefore many countries did not take part officially (including Austria, Netherlands, U.K., Russia); some (Germany, Sweden) not at all; others officially (including U.S.A. and most of Latin America, Norway, the South African Republic).

1893   Chicago; the 400th anniversary of Columbus's discovery of America.

1900   Paris; 39 million visitors, though 65 million had been expected; this was the first French exhibition that Germany took part in after the war of 1870.

Although the Great Exhibition of 1851 was an 'English' idea, it rapidly became a French speciality, the French government spending large sums on lavish displays, reaching a climax in the 1930's. The French were also the first to introduce architecture into these exhibitions. Examples of architectural work had been shown in 1851 — for example Pugin's 'Gothic Court' — but actual buildings were seen first in the Paris exhibition of 1867 (the one in Manet's painting); then there was a street of buildings in the 1878 exhibition, over half a mile long, the *Avenue des Nations*.

Most of these exhibitions were in Europe or in the United States, but many were in less likely places, some of them only recently settled or taken over by Europeans, and even more recently brought into the European industrial and commercial net — Madras (1853), Melbourne (1854), Sierra Leone and Dunedin (both 1865), Santiago, Chile (1869), Bogota (1872). Although trading itself was not a main concern, these exhibitions did lead to trade. The 1879-80 Melbourne-Sydney exhibition led to the starting of steamer services from Bremen and Marseilles to Australia and the opening of French banks there.

Exhibitions have of course continued to be held in the 20th century, especially in the 1930's, with peace and goodwill joining hands with trade and industry, as war became ever more certain. Among them were:

1925   Paris, the *Exposition des arts décoratifs* which gave its name to Art Deco.

1929   Barcelona; Mies designed the German pavilion, which was their exhibit.

1930   Stockholm; the first international exhibition in the International Modern style (designed chiefly by Asplund).

1936, 1937, 1938   Paris; 1936 was 'world', 1937 'international'.

1939   New York World's Fair.

The most notable post-war exhibitions have been:

1958   Brussels.

1960   Osaka, which showed off 'brutalist' Japanese architecture to the world (notably by Tange).

1967   Montreal; notable for Frei Otto's German pavilion with
                                 its tent-like steel-mesh roofs, and for Safdi's *Habitat*, an
                                 attempt — it was not built as large as planned — to
                                 design blocks of flats in stepped profile to create a more
                                 varied and humane arrangement; and Buckminster
                                 Fuller's Geodesic Dome for the U.S.A. pavilion.

Apart from the state-sponsored exhibitions, there were also many organised
by private groups and some of these had as big an influence on design — if not
on the setting up of shipping routes — as the state shows. The English Arts and
Crafts Exhibition Society held its first exhibition in October 1888 and then
annually, later triennially. The *Deutsche Werkbund* exhibitions in 1914
at Cologne, and in 1927 at Stuttgart, had a great influence on architecture.

Many manufacturing firms, including Morris and Co., sent work to the later
exhibitions of the 19th century, and there is no doubt that furniture design, for
example, was influenced by exhibitions as the modern production system
came into being. For instance, those features which might be good selling
lines, were picked, vulgarized, perhaps, and put into production for a year or
two. To a certain extent, this function has been taken over (from the middle of
the 20th century) by design magazines, and exhibitions are more interesting
for their architecture, which cannot so easily be understood from magazine
photographs and plans.

BUILDINGS TO SEE:
Few of them, of course, remain, and those that do have acquired a different
role — like the Eiffel Tower. The Bethnal Green Museum in London is the
South Kensington Museum of the 1850's, dismantled when the V. and A. was
begun, and rebuilt in East London. The exterior is a Romanesque brick
design, but inside, the appearance of a cast-iron 1850's exhibition hall is still
preserved: on a small scale, this is what the Crystal Palace must have looked
like in 1851.

READING:
Kenneth W. Luckhurst, *The story of exhibitions,* published in 1951.
John Allwood, *The great exhibitions* (1977).

Expressionism A style of architecture in the years around the 1914-18 war.
Like 'Baroque' it is a term which has a general use — a building in any style
can have 'expressionist' tendencies — and a particular architectural fashion
meaning; it is very much 'fashionable' architecture, and almost by definition
not 'polite' building.

If architecture has a 'language', then as Summerson has shown (in *The
classical language of architecture*) classical architecture had a Latin
vocabulary even if, compared with real language, a limited one. But what
about an abstract vocabulary? This is for most people incomprehensible, and
it is unlikely that more than a very few experts can ever 'read' the meanings of
an 'abstract' building. Julius Posener, in *The anti-rationalists,* uses the phrase
'sculptural architecture' in his article on the early 20th century German

architect Poelzig. All architecture is willy-nilly sculptural, nevertheless Posener's phrase is helpful in emphasising that particular quality in architecture, even if this gives offence to some architects who feel that their work is sculptural without being 'expressionist'.

Here are some examples:

A — 'Pre-expressionist' architecture not usually labelled as such:

Roumieu and *Gough*: architects of Milner Square in Islington, London, 1841 — and of much else. Milner Square seems to have a marked effect on some writers.

William Burges: the interiors of Cardiff Castle, designed for Lord Bute in the 1860's, are wilder than those of any other Gothic Revivalist. Many of the later 'Goths' show 'expressionist' leanings — S.S. Teulon, for example.

Gaudí: often included in ART NOUVEAU, though not by his admirers. Many of his buildings, especially the apartment blocks of 1905-7, Casa Milá and Casa Battló, in Barcelona, with their extraordinary roofscapes and moulded facades, do seem to be sculptural architecture. The occupants have to live with odd-shaped rooms. Gaudí could be said to be expressing religious fervour in his churches, but it is hard to understand what he may be expressing in his apartment blocks.

B — 'Expressionist' architecture:
The best examples are, or were, in the Netherlands and in Germany:

The Amsterdam School: The group of architects (labelled 'expressionist' by historians, not by themselves) is at the heart of Expressionism, in so far as it was more than a fashion. These Dutch architects are in many ways more interesting than the Germans because many of the Amsterdam buildings are domestic, whereas most of the accredited and even suspect Expressionist buildings in Germany are monumental types — concert halls, chapels, etc.

The doyen of the Amsterdam School was H.P. Berlage, who designed the Stock Exchange (1898-1903; 'a rather solemn building... standing on 5,000 piles' as the *Blue Guide* describes it). Other early examples of this 'Amsterdam' expressionism are the Hôtel Américain on the Singelgracht at Leidserplein (William Kromhout, 1898-1900) and the Scheepvaartshuis on the Prins Hendrik Kade (J.M. van der Meij, 1912). The Hôtel Américain's interiors — see the coffee room on the ground floor — are as remarkable as its exterior.

The housing estates, however, are perhaps the most interesting experiments. There are two particularly outstanding estates: Eigen Haard (Michael de Klerk, 1917) in north west Amsterdam, outside the Haarlemmerpoort, along the Zaanstraat beyond Cuijpers' Maria-Magdalenakerk (also a source for the 'Amsterdam school'); and Piet Kramer's De Dageraad estate in south-east Amsterdam on the city side of the Amstel Kanal. In layout the buildings are three and four storey apartment blocks, with some two storey houses. However, the detailing is quite sculpted: brick shapes and large pantiles which seem half way between Hansel & Gretel and Papuan village houses. The idea is clearly to bring art to the people by striking a compromise between the design (original) and the components (mass-produced). The result seems now quaint rather than moving, but both estates are a great deal cosier than for example Gropius's—the reformed Gropius—Siemensstadt housing of only six years later, to say nothing of post-war blocks (though there is an affinity with Darbourne and Darke's Vauxhall Bridge Road flats in London). The use of brick — red in Eigen Haard, buff-yellow in De Dageraad — is always a surprise. At De Dageraad, the houses around the Henrietta Ronnerplein are particularly delightful, and seem the ideal home for that lady's painting.

Gropius and *Mies van der Rohe*: in their expressionist phases. Above all, two monuments should be noted, Gropius's to the dead of the March rising, and Mies's to Rosa Luxemburg and Karl Liebknicht.

Mendelsohn: Many of his sketches have an obsession with streamlining, which is where 'expressionism' turns into Art Deco. His Einstein Tower (1921), an observatory near Potsdam, was the only one of these sketches that was turned into bricks and mortar — not the reinforced concrete it looks like. His Schocken store in Chemnitz was almost pure Bauhaus with its long strakes of windows, but the Schocken store in Stuttgart had a panache beyond the usual false-modest Bauhaus type: a dramatic semi-circular staircase at one end, and the work 'Schocken' in huge letters along the facade. After surviving the '39-45 war, it was knocked down for road-widening.

Poelzig: Grosse Schauspielhaus (1919) and Capitol Cinema (1925); both in Berlin and bombed in the war. The concert hall had a ceiling of stalactite-shapes which were said to help the acoustics.

C — 'Post-expressionist' architecture not usually labelled as such:

Le Corbusier: much of his post-war work, including the pilgrimage chapel at Ronchamp (1950-55), and the monastery of La Tourette (1957-61), especially the random lighting in the chapel.
L.C.C/G.L.C.: the Hayward Gallery/Queen Elizabeth Hall/Purcell Room group on the South Bank of the Thames. The shapes have been justified on functional grounds — 'service' wrapped round'functions' and marked out from each other in external finish which can be read (if you know the code): what looks like dirty planks are the air ducts, etc., and the pebbly bits are the halls themselves, etc. However, the Festival Hall next door has a completely different design, smooth where its neighbours are rough, and it too can be justified on functional grounds. The Festival Hall conceals its services behind a uniform exterior. Are the 'Hayward' group merely 'expressing' their plumbing? It does look as though they are also 'saying' something — or that their designers are — and that exposing the ducts was an excuse rather than a need. And most designers seem to respond to the buildings first of all as an exercise in sculpture; most of the rest of us react in this way too, even if in the opposite direction from the designers.

BUILDINGS TO SEE:
as listed above.

READING:
Dennis Sharp, *Modern architecture and expressionism.*
Reyner Banham, Nikolaus Pevsner, and others — articles, etc. in *The listener* — see BRUTALISM.
Jencks and Baird (editors), *Meaning in architecture.*

Festival The Festival of Britain commemorated the centenary of the Great Exhibition of 1851. As well as general festivities throughout the country, there was an exhibition on the South Bank of the Thames, opposite Westminster. It was not an international exhibition, though the style of the buildings and of much of the industrial design on show was close to Swedish International Modern, largely unfamiliar to British people in 1951. A certain spiky, splay-legged jokiness became a hallmark, especially of the furniture, and was soon despised by designers. Perhaps the exhibition did something to popularise modern architecture and design, but this is hard to be sure about — and the modern style popularised was a humane, light, Scandinavian style, soon to be out of fashion among designers — see BRUTALISM. Michael Frayn argues in his essay in *The age of austerity* that the Festival in general and the South Bank Exhibition in particular were characteristically middle-class ideas of what 'the people' ought to like.

   In 1976, to commemorate the Festival's 'silver jubilee', there was an exhibition at the V. and A. called 'A tonic for the nation' (i.e. after six years of austerity following six years of war), and that is perhaps what it was. In the book *A tonic to the nation*, published for that jubilee exhibition, Reyner Banham writes that the Festival had only a slight influence on architecture and design in Britain. Much of what it advocated was already in practice, or even becoming dated; only the landscaping of the South Bank was new. This

18 A 'Festival' chair. (Festival of Britain, 1951).

may be an art-historian establishing 'first appearances'; there had been nothing revolutionary about the 1930 Stockholm Exhibition as far as design was concerned; it was presenting it as something to be enjoyed by everyone that was so outstanding. Much the same was probably true of the South Bank and the Festival.

One of the most successful ornaments on the South Bank was a fountain in the Ships and Sea pavilion. It had columns of buckets filling and emptying into each other, that were interesting to look at, and that sounded remarkably like the sea washing on the beach. This fountain vanished from public view as soon as the exhibition closed.

BUILDINGS AND DESIGN:
The Lansbury Estate in Poplar, in the East End of London, was designed and built to be an 'exhibit' at the same time as the South Bank Exhibition. The area of the market, with its tower, and shops and pubs around it, remain more or less unaltered, and are the best example of 'Festival' architecture. The site of the exhibition itself remained a desolate waste for many years, and has been developed piecemeal. Only the Festival Hall of the original buildings remains. Both its exterior appearance and its setting (terraces, etc.) have been considerably altered since 1951, but the interior is largely unchanged, especially in its fittings. The remaining undeveloped part of the exhibition site was landscaped in 1977 as 'Jubilee Gardens', using many of the original 1951 ideas.

READING:
Mary Banham and Bevis Hillier (editors), *A tonic to the nation.*
Michael Sissons and Philip French (editors), *The age of austerity.*

Folk Art The visual folk arts of Europe and America are, by and large, a provincial variety of the fashionable styles of the 18th century. Swedish folk design, for example, shows the influence of court baroque and rococo. To have a folk art, one must have a folk, which in this context means a peasantry. A *peasantry* infers a social order in which the bulk of the population is engaged in farming. It may be poor and downtrodden, but its right to exist on the land is not challenged and the people's ability to survive changes in rulers also implies that collectively they have spirit enough to be able to adapt ideas from outside their communities to their own needs and traditions. Major social upheavals like the introduction of the feudal system, or of Christianity, may make profound changes, but even these can be absorbed — witness the number of ceremonies in England which are associated with Christianity, but have a pagan origin, and which survive almost unaltered. Christmas is not much to do with Christianity — and keeps its Norse name Yule — and 'Easter' itself is the name of a pagan goddess.

However, in England, the gentry oversaw their peasants' lives more closely than in most other countries, and from the 16th century up to the late 18th century began to change their estates from subsistence farming to business farming. The most spectacular episode in this process comes from Scotland, where the lairds, influenced by their fellow gentry in England, were able to establish that what had been thought of as clan lands were the laird's own property. The suddenness of this change in Scotland may have precipitated a love for some of the artistic aspects of Scottish folk art, lost in the slower English process. In both countries, the peasantry were changed into farm workers with few legal rights and no generally accepted right to be on the land at all. Such changes began to happen in England more than 300 years before the rest of Europe, and in Scotland at least a century earlier. They led, among other things, to the huge emigrations to America which began in the early 17th century. Peasants were still living in more or less traditional ways in Europe until the outbreak of the First World War in 1914. The collectivisation of the farms in Soviet Russia in the 1920's and 1930's was an attempt to concertina those 300 years of social change.

Thus, while folk art has survived in Europe long enough to be recorded and often to be preserved, in England — and to a certain extent in the Celtic lands in Britain too — there is very little left. Cecil Sharpe recorded old ballads in the late 19th century before the survivors died out, but he had to go over to Appalachia for many of them. In place of a peasant folk art, an industrial folk art did begin to appear in England. England had millions of industrial poor from the early 19th century onwards, and the time between the herding of the people into the industrial towns, and the blanketing of culture with the mass media in the 20th century, was longer than in most other countries — long enough for some kinds of folk ark to develop: music hall, work ballads, soccer, and visual arts like the Trade Union banners which are still carried in processions. These banners are in a NEO-BAROQUE style, an example of the way folk arts adapt the baroque styles more easily than others.

The Scandinavians, especially the Swedes, have done more than most peoples not only to keep their folk arts going but also to encourage their development. In no other country has an attempt to build a modern design aesthetic on folk traditions been so successful.

Without much in their own folk traditions to discover, cherish or use, many westerners will nowadays turn to the underdeveloped countries where a peasantry is still the majority of the population, and where its poverty makes the production of folk art for export good sense even to economists. Organizations like OXFAM have helped and also influenced many societies to market their designs. They may also be influencing the development of these arts in directions which will sell in western markets, and perhaps respond to changes in western fashions. While none of this may be too healthy for the folk traditions of these countries, there is no doubt that the popularity of folk art in middle-class western homes is a welcome sign that taste in the West is turning away from the wholesale ban on ornament that has been with us since the success of Bauhaus teaching.

READING:
Iona Plath, *The decorative arts of Sweden.*

French Renascence An historian's term for the style of the court of Francois I, King of France from 1515 to 1547, and that of his son Henri II

(died 1559). The style was imported from Italy and to some extent adapted to French needs and tastes. It was a richer version of the contemporary Tudor style, and can be compared to the later Elizabethan and Dutch Renascence styles. French Renascence was revived in the 1830's (see NATIONAL REVIVALS). Godde and Leseur's extension to the Hôtel de Ville in Paris (1837-1849), in a style close to that of the 16th century parts of the Louvre, was being built at the same time as the similarly Nationalist Palace of Westminster in London. With its high-pitched roofs on end pavilions, the French Renascence style merged easily into SECOND EMPIRE, which became the most influential French revival style in the 19th century, in France itself, too. The more characteristic Francois I mannerisms, such as the fantastic display of classical ornament on the otherwise predominantly Gothic building of the palace of Chambord in the Loire valley, found favour as the style of many large country houses outside France in the later 19th century: Waddesdon Manor in Buckinghamshire (Destailleur, begun 1874); Biltmore at Asheville, N.C. (R.M. Hunt, c1890; the grounds by F.L. Olmstead). Blocks of apartments too were sometimes in a French Renascence style (Archer and Green's Whitehall Court in Westminster of 1884, for example).

Functionalism draws its beliefs from a statement by Louis Sullivan that 'form follows function'. As the Penguin *Dictionary of architecture* disingenuously says, 'whatever the architect wishes to convey aesthetically and emotionally must not interfere with the fitness of the building or the object to fulfil its purpose'. Reading further in Sullivan, it becomes clear (as it does

19 Biltmore, North Carolina. A late example of the use of a French Renascence style for a large country house.

when one looks at his buildings) that he did not mean that 'function' should be the sole determinant of form, and he certainly did not mean his aphorism to be used, as it has been, as a ban on ornament. The Penguin *Dictionary*, too, begs some questions. How eccentric does an architect have to be, for his designs to interfere with the function of a building? Vanbrugh's King William block at Greenwich is certainly not unusable, even though the design means that many rooms have windows too high or too low for convenience. Street's Law Courts in the Strand in London, though lawyers have complained about the building ever since it was opened, have served their purpose for nearly a century.

The principles of architecture formulated by Vitruvius in the Roman Empire were translated by Henry Wotton in 1624 as *Elements of architecture*, and his version of Vitruvius's principles has become famous — 'well building hath three Conditions: Commoditie, Firmness and Delight'. Of these, Functionalism claims to stress Commoditie, though in fact it makes a fetish of Firmness; what it ignores is Delight — or it claims that Delight will automatically follow from the other two, which Vitruvius and Wotton knew to be false.

'Functionalism', if taken as a serious critical word, might also take into account factors like cheapness and simplicity of building or furniture-making (especially if plastics become too costly to use freely), and cheapness of maintenance, which would tell against plate-glass windows, with their expensive insulation problems, and throw-away cups and saucers, a waste of material and a rubbish problem.

Garden Cities Ebenezer Howard published *Tomorrow* in 1889 (republished in 1902 as *Garden Cities of Tomorrow*). The Garden City Movement was founded in England in 1899. Letchworth in Hertfordshire was begun to the designs of Parker and Unwin in 1903, and Welwyn Garden City in 1920 to the designs of de Soissons and Kenyon. These were not merely plans for pleasant or even ideal towns. The movement was inspired by a deeply held belief that cities, as they existed then, were not only decayed, but inherently bad environments — their decay due to their nature, perhaps. In this respect the Garden City Movement is part of a Romantic tradition going back to J.J. Rousseau, and even perhaps looking forward to the 'communes' of today. The movement had something in common with Ashbee's Guild of Handicrafts which moved out from London to Chipping Camden in 1902. Until the 1940's, *moving out* was an underlying assumption behind planning proposals, strengthened by the fear of bombing as war drew near in the '30's, and children were evacuated to the countryside. This *moving out* principle partly explains the effort the Local Councils like the LCC put into estates of cottages on the outskirts of London around the year 1900, long before they started large-scale replacement of houses with flats in the centre of London.

The idea of making an estate of middle-class houses look as though they are all buildings in a large garden is part of the English Picturesque Movement of the late 18th century and can be seen in Nash's various schemes for Regent's Park (1806), including the two Park Villages (his thatched village at Blaise, near Bristol, built in 1811, was more a garden ornament than an estate itself). Later examples like the Calverley Estate at Tunbridge Wells, begun by Decimus Burton in 1828, are suburban in feeling rather than, like Regent's Park, a picturesque addition to the city. The style of these suburban houses remained classical until mid-century. Many estates became 'leafy' as the years passed, to use Pevsner's poetic adjective, but the layout was often rigid — see Blackheath Park (begun 1825), or the later Cator Estate in Beckenham (begun 1864). Both these estates are in south east London.

In the middle of the century, more picturesque layouts were designed with houses in various styles — Swiss cottages, for example — to give the illusion of urban villages. A good example is The Vale in Southsea, Hampshire, built during 1850-60 with narrow lanes curving through high walled gardens. In America, some suburbs were laid out on picturesque principles, under the influence of A.J. Downing, who was himself influenced by the English writer J.C. Loudon. Riverside, Illinois, designed by Frederick Law Olmstead in 1869, is a good example.

In the different 'enlightened' tradition of 18th century grid plans, some manufacturers paid for model estates for their workers, the earliest being Robert Owen's in New Lanark south of Glasgow, begun c1800, and New Harmony, Indiana (1825). Similar utopian schemes for setting up friendly prisons for ideal living were put forward in France, one actually began in 1837 inspired by Fourier. Less utopian were the back-to-back rows of cottages built in 1847 by Colonel Ackroyd, a mill-owner, for his workers at Copley outside Halifax, Yorkshire. In 1849 Titus Salt began his more ambitious scheme on the

Aire above Bradford, about 10 miles from Halifax: Saltaire, which realized many of the idealist schemes of the past 100 years. The neat houses are in orderly rows, there is a church and an evening institute and a fine big mill; by the standards of most mid 19th century workers' housing, it was excellent. Ackroyd also built Ackroyden, larger than Copley, in 1859 — also on a grid plan.

The difference of a generation later is striking: Bournville, begun by the Cadbury chocolate firm for its workers south of Birmingham, Warwickshire, in 1879, was the first such town to be designed in a picturesque layout — it has claims to be the first Garden Town if not Garden City. It was soon followed by Port Sunlight, begun in 1880 for Lever, to house the workers of his soap factory.

Meanwhile the middle class suburb was given a new identity by the development of Bedford Park (begun 1875) about eight miles west of the centre of London; the style of the houses was in the newly fashionable QUEEN ANNE, many designed by R. Norman Shaw. They set the style of many suburbs for the next half-century. Bedford Park was eclipsed in fashion by Hampstead Garden Suburb, begun in 1906 with Parker and Unwin as designers, as at Letchworth which they had begun three years before. Lutyens, the 'heir' to the Queen Anne tradition in the 20th century, designed many of the buildings. Both Bedford Park and Hampstead Garden Suburb are said to have had a great influence in Holland, Germany and especially America, but their influence on the developments around them seems to have been random.

Thus we reach the Garden City. After 1920 few British middle class suburbs do not show at least that minimal influence — grass verges in the streets, which are often winding. The influence of 'Arts and Crafts Tudor', and of C.F.A. Voysey (pebble-dash Cotswoldy type villas), set the style of the English suburb. In America the idea of 'houses in the garden' is carried even further with the general practice of open lawns and shrubs instead of front gardens (Bedford Park has white picket-fences), and this idea too has come back to Europe in countless estates (e.g. an estate of middle class houses at Clondalkin, near Dublin, Ireland, of c1965).

The main 'legacy' of the Garden City is the early layouts of the New Towns built after the '39-45 war in England — Harlow, Stevenage, Basildon, Crawley, etc. are all reasonably close to London and laid out in Garden-City principles. The style of housing is an attempt to reconcile International Modern with the brick traditions of the Garden Cities, and it is not always successful. In the later New Towns, starting with the abortive plan for Hook, which was to have been a London County Council New Town in Hampshire, and most notably in Cumbernauld, the 'garden' layout is put aside in favour of a packed city centre and closer houses, all in a Brutalist style. These towns, are perhaps a wretched version of the Swedish SATELLITE TOWNS, where the architecture has been untraditional from the start.

Colateral relatives, as it were, of the Garden City, are various other plans for middle-cost housing, not necessarily houses, sometimes apartment blocks. The best known of the house-layouts is that of RADBURN, in New Jersey. The

New Town concept has also been experimented with in America at Columbia, mid-way between Baltimore and Washington.

PLACES TO SEE:
All those in England mentioned here are still to be seen (Saltaire has recently been cleaned), and Radburn has matured over the last 40 years.

READING:
Ebenezer Howard, *Garden cities of tomorrow.*
Frank Schaffer, *The new town story.*
F. J. Osborn and A. Whittick, *New towns, the answer to Megalopolis.*

Glasgow School A group of graphic designers and architects, all trained at the Glasgow School of Art when Fra. Newbury was Principal. The best known of this group are Charles Rennie Mackintosh and the two Macdonald sisters, one of whom, Margaret, worked with and married Mackintosh. Their graphic work is very like contemporary ART NOUVEAU work abroad, whereas Mackintosh's buildings are more like traditional Scottish architecture. His work also forms part of a vigorous late-Gothic Revival in Glasgow, which also has a number of office buildings in a style close to Art Nouveau. Mackintosh's interiors are also more like Art Nouveau, particularly his furniture, and the decorations he designed for walls — notably the walls for Miss Cranston's tea rooms, now mostly destroyed.

DESIGN AND BUILDINGS TO SEE:
Glasgow Art Gallery has a small Mackintosh section, and there is an even richer collection in the School of Art, which he designed in 1896 and 1907. Other buildings of Mackintosh's time in Glasgow are well catalogued in *Glasgow at a glance,* edited by Young and Doaks.

READING:
R. Macleod, *Charles Rennie Mackintosh.*

Gothic Like many art terms, it was abusive to start with (like Baroque and Biedermeyer). The Goths were one of the peoples who were thought in the 18th century to have caused the downfall of the Roman Empire. In the mid-18th century, the Roman Empire was uncritically admired as the acme of polite living. Roman architecture had been revived, and by 1750 connoisseurs could think themselves the equal of the Romans. Thus the architecture of the 1,000 years between the fall of Rome and the revival of Roman civilization in Italy was given the name of the 'barbarians' who had overthrown Rome — 'Gothic'. A century later, Ruskin (in 'The nature of Gothic' chapter in *The stones of Venice* that was to affect Morris and others so deeply) accepted 'barbarian' as an essential part of 'Gothic'—rough nobility, etc. 'The demand for perfection is always a sign of the misunderstanding of the ends of art' (section xxiii of 'The nature of Gothic').

Although many Gothic buildings (especially the monastic ones) had gone by 1800 — they became 'quarries', usually — the great cathedrals had been patched up over the years, and in the later 18th century were undergoing some particularly insensitive restorations. An interest in Gothic architecture that was, by then, more than antiquarian produced some guides, of which one of the most influential was by Thomas Rickman: *An attempt to discriminate the styles of English architecture* (1817, and many editions through the 19th century).

His categories have lasted, and are:

Norman: from 1066, of course, until $c1200$, depending on how up-to-date the part of the country was. This alone of his categories has been given up recently in favour of 'English Romanesque' which is what it is.

Early English: despite its name the most foreign of the Gothic styles, being a direct import from France. It is the style of the High Gothic cathedrals of the Ile de France, beginning with the abbey of St. Denis in the mid-12th century, and including the cathedrals of Paris, Chartres, Amiens and Rheims. In England, the style can be seen neat in the choir of Canterbury Cathedral, and in Westminster Abbey. Adapted by local masons, it is perhaps more 'English' in the cathedrals of Lincoln, Salisbury and Wells.

Decorated: in the style fashionable between about 1300 and 1350, e.g. Beverley Minister in Yorkshire, a much richer version of E.E., with more elaborate carving and flowing ornate window tracery.

Perpendicular: the plainer style of the late 14th century masons, which lasted until gradually replaced by classical styles in the 16th century. Above all it is the style of the parish churches of Somerset, Gloucester and East Anglia, rebuilt by merchants rich from the wool trade in the late Middle Ages. Ruskin hated Perpendicular.

These terms have been given generally accepted abbreviations by Nikolaus Pevsner in *The buildings of England* as E.E., Dec. and Perp.

Rickman was a Quaker, and the Ecclesiologists of the Gothic Revival were High Anglican. They could not stomach a Non-Conformist's terms, preferring a Catholic's — Pugin's — 'pointed architecture': early, middle and late pointed. This later produced some fine tuning, such as 'early middle late pointed', and so on, which is perhaps one reason why Rickman's terms, especially after the Gothic fervour waned after 1870, were preferred. The Ecclesiologists, following a false physiological analogy of youth, maturity and senility, favoured 'middle pointed', roughly 'early middle Dec.': see GOTHIC REVIVAL.

After their own High Gothic style, the French developed in the 15th century a style as wild as the English Dec. had been, called 'flamboyant' because of the flame-shapes in the window tracery. Other western European nations also developed their own versions of Gothic, the Iberian late Gothic being particularly rich. The 15th century Gothic of the Netherlands, north Germany and Scandinavia had much in common with the English Perp. style. The Gothic Revival of the 19th century was largely an English invention, and it was an English critic, Ruskin who popularised Venetian Gothic. Insofar as the Gothic Revival was taken up outside the English-speaking countries, it was adapted to the native traditional Gothic style, if one existed, as in Cuijpers's churches in the Netherlands in the latter half of the 19th century. However, there was, as with all these revivals, an open market, and the Votivkirche in Vienna (by Ferstel, begun 1856) looks like a small French High Gothic cathedral.

Gothic Revival High fashion architecture *par excellence*. As a movement it hardly affected the great bulk of 19th century building — polite architecture — let alone the population as a whole. They would have been aware of it (if at all) only when they went to church (which no more than a minority did) and only in those cities which happened to choose a Gothic style for their new town hall in the middle of the century. It is high fashion in that it had a well-organised, extremely bigoted group of lay propagandists, and in that its finer points were very much the small-talk of architects, designers and connoisseurs. So it is no surprise that the Gothic Revival figures so largely in histories of 19th century architecture. It is a British, even English, movement, and had little effect outside the English-speaking countries, even in those like France which had Gothic traditions of their own. Even in England, it is almost exclusively a religious architecture — churches, universities (in the 19th century largely staffed by the clergy) and muscular Christian schools. Only between approximately 1840 and 1870 was it a serious contender for public buildings, and even in these years 'Gothic' architects never attained the easy universality that the classical architects had from the middle of the 17th century onwards, and had until about 1930. The 'Goths' certainly tried to reach that universality, and there was much talk of 'developing' Gothic in the same way as Roman architecture had 'developed' after the Renascence, but it is significant that the two best known 'developers' in this sense, Philip Webb and W.R. Lethaby, designed 'developed' houses in a vaguely 17th century style. Webb's were more classical than Lethaby's, which were Elizabethan. Gothic's 'failure' to produce anything which could be seriously taken up by 'polite' architecture (trimmings on gables not being 'serious') kept it in fashionable circles. Also, Gothic Revival was *artists'* architecture.

Then there was the damage done to churches already standing: the 'Gothic' that was revived was the cathedral style that had been fashionable in about the year 1300, which was held by members of the Cambridge Camden Society (later the Ecclesiological Society: an oddly 'scientific' name) to be the 'mature' Gothic style. Earlier (e.g. Durham Cathedral) or later (e.g. King's College Chapel) Gothic styles were held to be either 'immature' or 'decadent'. So not only were classical churches savaged — that one would expect — but medieval buildings were not safe either. If the Camden tasters decided that the vintage was not quite the right one, these buildings were 'improved' — especially the Perp. style of the 15th century. Earlier architects could be excused on the grounds of immature ignorance, but there was no mercy for the designers of, for example, the Perp. windows of St. Alban's Cathedral. Only time and a shortage of money stopped these men from ruining some of the jewels of English architecture.

Why bother with the Gothic Revival at all? Why not pass it over like the neo-Egyptian style for example, which has one or two interesting buildings, including a fine one, Bindesbøll's Thorvaldsen Museum of 1839 in Copenhagen? Many of the thousands of Victorian Gothic churches built against the rising tide of scepticism are now predictably empty, and the Church has a more profitable use for their sites. Gothic has a minor importance, because it became a kind of genre architecture; just as Dutch painters in the 17th century might specialise in, say, tavern scenes, many Victorian architects found themselves specialising in churches, and some of them were very good. All of them tried to be very sincere: e.g. Pearson, architect of Truro Cathedral (begun 1879), Brisbane Cathedral (designed 1897) and St. Augustine, Kilburn (begun 1870); Street, who had both William Morris and Philip Webb in his office as pupils, and was architect of the Law Courts in the Strand, London, (1866), although most of the rest of his work was churches; the northern England firm Paley and Austin — for their churches, see eloquent descriptions in Pevsner's *Lancashire* volumes in *The buildings of England*. After 1870, for a purely 'Gothic' architect, the genre was churches.

Beyond this, the hidden importance of the Gothic Revival is in the effect it had on architects, their critic-supporters, and eventually on their patrons. 'Gothic' was one of the most important weapons in the assertion that all building must be designed by artists. It is easy to see why some of the most imaginative and the most ambitious artist-architects were drawn to the Gothic *idea* even if, after 1870, few of them stayed with Gothic *forms*. The classical styles were — and are — part of the general culture of educated people in the western world, with a quite easily understood 'vocabulary'. The patrons of a classical architect often know enough about it to make constructive comments. At first, the Gothic Revivalists tried to develop a 'Gothic' vocabulary to replace the 'Roman', but this failed, because there was no agreed set of rules from which developments could start. When 'development' did happen, it was away from strict adherence to Gothic forms. It is curious that there are remarkably few houses by Gothic Revival architects based on the plan of a medieval houses — hall, screens passage to one side, private rooms to the other. Instead, they built askew classical houses with cathedral details in the middle of the century — as can be seen in North Oxford. Later on, they designed askew classical houses with mainly classical details; only the 'informal' arrangement, and the artist's role as designer, were left.

What happened has been well chronicled by Mark Girouard. The best of the younger Goths turned to a free classical style which they called QUEEN ANNE. Their patrons also turned to classical furniture, giving up the heavy cupboards designed by Morris and his friends in the 1860's to be painted with medieval scenes.

There is a good account in Robert Macleod's *Style and society* of the 'Gothic' quality of the work of Webb and Lethaby at the end of the 19th century. Theirs was an architecture of omission rather than positive style; a kind of curious, sly joke they played on each other, whereby Gothic had come to mean something like avoidance of any style at all — a proclaimed 'fitness for purpose' though usually having 'features' which were beyond mere fitness. Lethaby designed in a plain Tudor style, without many of the classical trimmings which the Elizabethans used to enliven their buildings, and Webb in a 17th century country classical style. His buildings have a fussiness where every feature looks as though its architect had wondered whether it ought to be there at all. There is a very just assessment of Webb in Girouard's *Victorian country houses* (on Standen, near East Grinstead in Sussex).

Most of the Goths hated the regularity of classical architecture, and especially the repeated carvings for the capitals of columns, which must be alike. When machinery for carving was invented, they hated that too, because the 'freedom' of the artist was one of their chief arguments in favour of Gothic. Drawing from Ruskin's chapter 'The nature of Gothic' in *The stones of Venice*, William Morris proclaimed that Art was the product of a workman's joy in his work. They very much wanted to believe that this had been true of medieval workmen, but it does not seem to have been likely. For every one privileged carver who was allowed to cut capitals like those in Southwell Minster chapter house, there must have been a hundred condemned for all their working lives to do the monotonous rough work, and many who did only the rough carving on the capitals before the master came along and finished them.

Critics and art historians, by overrating the Gothic Revival, have made it appear the great rival of classical — the 'battle of the styles'. That battle between classical and Gothic was comparatively short, fought almost entirely in England, and was won outright by classical. ROMANESQUE was, for certain types of large public buildings — including many churches — the main rival of classical in the second half of the 19th century, but only for fashionable architecture, not at all for 'polite' building, where Gothic too had made few inroads. But critics persisted with Gothic. Lethaby allotted only a page or two to the architecture of 1500-1800 (less, as has been noted, than he gave to Crete and Babylon) in his Home University Library volume *Architecture,* 1912); a rearguard action against classical. However, the truth was that even at the height of Gothomania — 1840-70 — some of the most convincing of classical buildings were rising: St. George's Hall, Liverpool, 1841-56; Wellington College, 1856-59; Leeds Town Hall, 1853-8; Bolton Town Hall, 1866-73.

The main stages of the Gothic Revival are:

1. Gothick: amusing aristocratic toys, either complete houses like Walpole's Strawberry Hill, Twickenham (1749 onwards), or rooms, like the library of Milton House in Berkshire. Unlike the serious Gothic Revival, this did have an effect on 'polite' building: fretwork details, applied to classical houses — 'Bargeboard Gothic' in both Britain and America.

2 A more serious phase was inspired by the novels of Walter Scott, as writers on architecture at the time agreed (*Waverley*, the first of them, was published in 1814). A 'romantic' interest in Gothic followed; castles were built or rebuilt, notably Windsor Castle, remodelled by Wyatville in the 1820's. The

upper classes in England were alarmed at the growth of towns without churches to oversee them, and Parliament passed a Church Building Act in 1818 which appointed Commissioners to decide on sites and funds — hence 'Commissioners' Churches'. Many of them were in a thin Perp. style which perhaps helped to give it a bad name.

3   Gothic became acceptable for large public buildings when the conditions for the competition for the new Palace of Westminster (the old group of buildings, including the House of Commons and Soane's House of Lords, having been burnt down in 1834) specified an Elizabethan or a Perpendicular style (see NATIONALIST REVIVALS). Barry's winning design was in Perp.

4   Then the pedants moved in; first Pugin in *Contrasts* (1836), and *True principles of pointed or Christian architecture* (1841), which first identified Gothic with, in general, 'honesty' and, in particular, with Christianity. Hard on Pugin's heels came the Camdenians and their favoured architects, Butterfield and Carpenter, who designed St. Paul's, West St., Brighton, a classic Camdenian church (1846-8).

5   Then came Ruskin with *Seven lamps of architecture* (1849) and *The stones of Venice* (1851-53). He borrowed ideas from Pugin — 'honesty', the decoration of the structure. He advocated not the style of 1300 in England and France — until then the chosen style of the experts — but Venetian Gothic. Almost as intolerant of Renascence architecture as Lethaby (a follower) was to be, he at least admired the general shape of the Salute in Venice. Ruskin's direct 'Venetian' influence can be seen in the designs of Oxford University Museum (Woodward, 1855-9) and Northampton Town Hall (an early work of E.W. Godwin, 1861-4).

6   The 1850's and '60's saw the high point of Gothic in England and overseas:
Parliament House, Ottawa (Fuller and Jones, 1859-67).
Memorial Hall, Harvard (Ware and van Brant, 1866-78).
Manchester Town Hall (Waterhouse, begun 1868).
Law Courts, Strand, London (Street, begun 1868).
Farnham Hall, Yale (Sturgis, 1869).
St. Pancras Station Hotel (Scott, 1868-74).
Glasgow University (Scott, finished 1870).

7   Then Gothic went out of fashion, except for the steady stream of churches including some outside Britain:
Votivkirche, Vienna (von Ferstel, 1856-79)
St. Denys de l'Estrée (Viollet-le-Duc, 1864-7).
Maria Magdalenakerk, Amsterdam (Cuijpers, 1887 — and others in Amsterdam by him, in the last twenty years of the century).

8   The Art Nouveau period, or at least the late 19th century, brought back a kind of whimsy Gothic — Nyrop's Copenhagen Town Hall (Flemish Gothic) of 1892-1902; Middlesex Guildhall in Parliament Square, Westminster, by Gobson and Russell, 1905; Woolworth Building, New York, by Gilbert

1913; Tribune Tower, Chicago, by Hood and Howells, 1925. There was also a come-back for Perp. in the late 19th century, sometimes with an Art Nouveau twist, and, unexpectedly, in Methodist churches in England.

Gothic Revival design went with the architecture every now and then, with each spurt of enthusiasm. Thus Pugin designed everything for the interiors of Parliament — inkwells, floor-tiles and door-handles as well as furniture. This may not have been much like real medieval furniture, nevertheless the whole Palace of Westminster is clearly an attempt to realise a gorgeous 15th century palace. On the other hand, Butterfield's furniture for Milton Ernest Hall in Bedfordshire, which he built in 1856 in a 14th century style, was in a style very close to Biedermeyer. Morris and his friends made heavy, plain furniture in the 1860's and painted scenes on it. Later they tended to produce furniture which had more in common with late 17th century styles than with those of the 14th. William Burges had the interesting idea that medieval furniture does not survive because it went from gentleman's hall to spare room, to servants' hall and, in the end, for firewood. He inferred that it was plain furniture whose chief attraction was the painting on it, not the workmanship in wood which was the characteristic of furniture from the 17th century onwards — once the painting had worn off, the furniture would have no particular value.

BUILDINGS AND DESIGNS TO BE SEEN:
There are guided tours round the Palace of Westminster when Parliament is in recess (roughly, in school holidays). The church of All Saints', Margaret St., north of Oxford St. in London, designed by Butterfield, 1849-59, is the most complete and spectacular of the Ecclesiological churches. The V. and A. has examples of Gothic revival furniture and design.

READING:
K. Clark, *The Gothic revival.*
R. Macleod, *Style and society.*
Mark Girouard, *Victorian country houses.*
J.F. White, *The Cambridge movement.*

Guilds The medieval guilds were business clubs which regulated standards and controlled entry into most professions and trades. By the 16th century, English guilds had become family hierarchies which were more or less closed to outsiders, so that apprentices rarely became masters unless they had connections. They had to make do with being journeymen, with few privileges. Nevertheless, a myth lasted, as can be seen in Hogarth's series *The industrious 'prentice and the idle 'prentice,* so perhaps it was not impossible, even in the 18th century, for a bright lad to succeed (and marry the boss's daughter).

The breaking of the guilds' control is generally reckoned by economists as one of the essential steps in economic development, moving from a traditional society into an industrialized economy. Hatred of industrialization, common among thinking people in England in the early and mid-19th century, led some of them to idealize the guilds. Ruskin was among those who proposed a 'guild' type of organisation to work towards a thoroughgoing reform of English society. Guild Socialism in the later years of the 19th century was one of the developments from this. The Trade Unions which began to organize themselves slowly in the 1850's (after the débâcle of 1848) were a wholly different kind of organization from either the medieval or the 19th century guilds, although since they were engaged in trade and industry, they inevitably had to deal with some of the same problems as the guilds had done — but not until well into the 20th century.

Two 'Arts and Crafts' guilds survive in England:

1 Ruskin's own St. George's Guild, founded in 1871. It now has funds which are used for conservation and rehabilitation work.

2 The Art Workers' Guild, founded in 1884, which still keeps to its semi-secret rituals, and in this way is much more like a medieval guild: the 'craft', whatever it is, is something of a secret which has to be kept from outsiders. During the discussions on craft and design education in the last decade of the 19th century, the Art Workers' Guild always refused to make any collective comment. Nevertheless, when Lethaby, a member, became first Principal of the Central School of Arts and Crafts in London, he saw to it that his staff were drawn from the Guild.

Accounts of the life-style of Ashbee's Guild of Handicrafts in Chipping Camden, in the early years of the 20th century, make it sound much like similar attempts in modern 'communes' to revive a self-sufficient life. These might find it useful to study why the Guild of Handicrafts in the end failed.

The attitude of the English craft guilds (especially the Art Workers') is in marked contrast to the Swedish Slöjdföreningen, which, from the start, has publicised its activities with lectures, courses and literature.

Historicism The theory that everything in human society, including the arts, is historically determined; that there is a force, for convenience called 'history', which controls human affairs in ways in which only the enlightened can understand. Historicism holds that there are 'epochs' in human life, with characteristics which can be understood only in terms of the guiding 'Spirit of the Age', or 'Zeitgeist', as the German philosophers of the late 18th century, who are chiefly responsible for Historicism, called it. Through Hegel to Burckhardt (who wrote *The civilization of the Renascence in Italy* — a significant title, extending the idea of 'rebirth' from the arts and learning into the whole of Italian society at that time), and from Burckhardt to Wittkower, there is a strong tradition of Historicism in writing about the arts, which has found a home in these years, where there is so much talk (prompted by a variety of causes) of 'revolution', 'progress', 'change', 'novelty' and so on. It is easier to defend a revolution (in design or anything else) by claiming that it is in the 'spirit of the time', than by having to defend it on aesthetic or any social grounds.

Writers in this historicist tradition have tried to pre-empt the use of the word 'historicist' to brand their opponents rather than be branded themselves. However, when called upon to defend this eccentric usage of the word, the answer is usually unsatisfactory. There is a question-begging 'definition' of 'Historicism' in H-R. Hitchcock's *Architecture, 19th and 20th centuries:* 'quite simply, it means the re-use of forms borrowed from the architectural styles of the past, usually in more or less new combinations'. Apart from the fact that, simply or not, this is not what 'Historicism' means in the world at large, this 'definition' is puzzling, unless perhaps, one is an historicist thinker oneself. The rider, especially, is confusing — 'more or less new combinations' — would not the new combinations be 'of our time'? It is significant that Hitchcock has to apologise for putting off his 'definition' until so late in the book — page 469, a note to page 392 — because his book is not particularly historicist until the last chapter or two.

There are a number of books intended for the popular market which are badly flawed by Historicism — R. Furneaux Jordan's *Victorian architecture,* for example, does little more than use its nominal subject-matter — or an odd selection from it — to justify the 'revolution' of the International Modern Movement. In the list of books at the end of this book, there is some indication of those which are so biased by Historicism as to be of only marginal utility.

READING:

David Watkin, *Morality and architecture,* and
K.R. Popper, *The poverty of Historicism,* which he discussed.

Honesty   This can refer to 'honesty of construction' and to 'honesty to materials'. It is more metaphysical than simply not cheating, and no-one seems to have wanted to call Frank Lloyd Wright's houses 'dishonest', even though the rain came through some of the roofs. Both the Gothic Revival and the Internation Modern Movement claimed exclusive rights to 'honesty'. David Watkin has disposed of these pretensions in his *Morality and architecture.* In the real world, the words 'honest' and 'truthful' can apply only to persons and their statements. Except in a trivial way, the 'language' of architecture (see EXPRESSIONISM) does not extend to such subtleties as lying. A well-known example of this kind of 'dishonesty' is Louis Sullivan's Guaranty Building in Buffalo, N.Y. of 1894-5. The main visual effect of the building is achieved by the insistent vertical lines, twelve bays on one side, fourteen on the other. The building is clearly an iron-frame, and one would be led to suppose that these verticals *are* the iron frame. A glance at the ground and mezzanine floors, however, shows that the building is really only six by seven bays; half the pronounced verticals are, then 'false'. What is more, the corners of the building have thicker verticals than the facade; an 'effect' not reflecting the structure. A thoroughly 'dishonest' building, then. However, this has not stopped it from being thought of as one of the jewels of American architecture.

Although he was not the first to do so, Pugin often used the word 'honest', but seems to have meant by it little more than 'Catholic'. Morris, Lethaby and the Arts and Crafts seem to have used the word for, amongst other things, a certain kind of heavy furniture. A late example of this kind of furniture flourished in England in the 1939-45 war, under the name of UTILITY. Utility furniture is the good, solid woodwork that answers the Arts and Crafts demands. The pressures of wartime economy demanded a careful use of materials. The same amount of wood that went into a Utility chair could as well have gone into a simple 18th century English provincial design, or an even simpler 19th century Shaker design. What then makes the Utility chair, the Morris design, *honest*? There is a considerable grace and elegance about even the Shaker chair which is lacking in the Utility; so one must conclude that 'honest' means 'unsubtle'.

Industrial Design In spite of repeated attempts throughout the 19th century, aided by offical and private exhibitions, designing for industry did not become a recognized profession until the 20th century. Industrial design falls roughly into two categories:
1 Designing industry itself, and designing major engineering works: Jodrell Bank telescope, for example. Such objects were not considered Art in the 19th century, though they were admired. Aeroplane and ship design come partly into this category.
2 Designing products, which is the more familiar aspect of Industrial Design today. In the 19th century this was not easy to organize because of the diversity and small scale of firms. In 1907 Behrens (an architect) was appointed head designer for the German firm A.E.G., an early example of such an appointment and a significant one, in that it was in the electrical goods industry.

With the development of mass-production consumer industries in the U.S.A. after 1920, came the industrial designers. Sometimes they were employed by the production firms, sometimes in large consultancy firms of their own. Examples of these consultancies are the firm Raymond Loewy set up in 1929, designing for Westinghouse, Gestetner, Sears Roebuck and others, and the firm founded by Lippincote and Marguiles in 1946, whose clients also tend to be the electrical goods industries and large transport companies. Mass production implies constant replacements to keep the wheels turning (or 'built-in obsolescence'), and so a constant supply of slightly different designs.

The outstanding example of British Industrial Design in the period between the First and Second World Wars, was the London Transport Passenger Board which appointed Frank Pick to be in charge of design. He organised a compiete restyling of the Board's graphics, architecture and fittings, employing a number of freelance designers and architects.

International Modern The usual term for the style of architecture and design which has been orthodox since at least 1945. There was an exhibition at the Museum of Modern Art in New York in 1931 (and a book that went with it) by Henry-Russell Hitchcock and Philip Johnson, called *The international style: architecture since 1922.*

The characteristic of International Modern architecture is to reduce everything to a smooth white cube or cubic box, with the windows flush with the outside wall. (Modern architecture which has broken away from International Modern has returned to the Pugin idea that the design of a building should not be symmetrical but should express the differing functions of the different parts.) Corbusier's Villa Savoye of 1929, which is the classic example of this style, is a half-cube held above the ground by a smaller central pedestal and by thin columns; this white cube has a continuous band of window all the way round. Some of it is empty (giving on to a terrace at first floor level), the rest glass, but there is no differentiation in shape between the terrace 'windows' and the real ones, and none between, say, the lavatory windows and the living room windows — the kind of sacrifice to symmetrical effect for which the Georgians are often condemned. Above this white cube rose two sculptured shapes, painted pink and blue, housing services. In this, Corbusier was deviating from the Bauhaus/C.I.A.M. rule somewhat, almost to the extent of making the standard product no more than a podium for his sculpture, and thus emphasising a part of the whole. Nevertheless in all other respects it is a perfect International Modern product. In standing off the ground, and providing 'windows' as the only way to view the scenery from the terrace, Corbusier was deliberately reducing Nature to the role of a picture to be looked at, rather than an experience to be felt. In this he, and the International Modern Movement generally, differ markedly from the work of Frank Lloyd Wright, whose buildings were meant to harmonize with nature. During World War Two, the Savoye villa was nearly ruined through neglect. Poissy has become an industrial suburb, and the Savoye family could not afford to rescue the building, so the state had to step in. It is not a good advertisement for that *'Sachlichkeit'* — sensible practicality — which C.I.A.M. and the Bauhaus claimed; all their buildings were faced in stucco to look like smooth machines, and so need upkeep every year. It is significant that in his Illinois buildings after the war, Mies used brick instead of stucco as infill, as did Gropius in his Harvard graduate blocks.

In the 1950's and 1960's the chief representative of the International Modern Movement is the work of Mies van der Rohe and his imitators. Mies in 1922 had designed a 'glass skyscraper' but it was not until he was in America that one of these designs was built. The classic examples of the style both went up around 1952 — Mies's Lake Shore Drive Apartments in Chicago, and the Lever Building in New York, designed by Gordon Bunshaft of the firm Skidmore, Owings and Merrill. These buildings and their successors are usually tall, of grid construction and are finished in what is often described as a 'skin' of glass. The glass is arranged in a graph-paper pattern decided by the architect, and behind this glass is either space, when there is a window, or a screening material which both hides the services and does not interrupt the appearance from outside. In order to maintain this outside appearance, blinds are operated in unison, so that the facade will not look bitty — it is not up to individuals to decide whether they want the blinds down or not. A glass-walled building of course creates yet more problems in heat control (New York is said to use more energy keeping its buildings cool in summer than warm in winter). The glass skyscraper, an anonymous block which does not disclose whether it is offices (the most usual), apartments, hospital, etc., became the ubiquitous cliché of architecture in the years 1952-

*c*1970, and a return to more expressive concrete — e.g. Barbican flats in London — is perhaps indicative of a desire to solve problems again.

In the *Architectural Review* for December 1965, Alison and Peter Smithson (architects in the 'Brutalist' Movement; designers of the Miesian Hunstanton School, Norfolk, and the Economist Building in London) published a photographic record of what they called the 'Heroic Period' of modern architecture (the 1920's and early '30's). They wrote: 'The Heroic Period of Modern Architecture is the rock on which we stand. Through it we feel the continuity of history and the necessity of achieving our own idea of order.' For them essentially, architecture was:

a Cubic, or appeared to be carved out of cubes.

b Geometrically organized and highly abstract in the interpretation of human activities.

c A complete thing in itself.

d Was poised, not rooted on its site.

e Was usually white, or lightly coloured, or made of shining materials.

f Natural materials when used appear to be substitutes for artificial materials not yet invented.

It is significant that in their photographic survey, the Smithsons make no reference to the Stockholm Exhibition of 1930, or to any Swedish work. For the hard-line International Modern, the Swedes were too soft towards humanity, not nearly 'abstract' enough in their interpretation of human activities. The characteristic noted in (f) is presumably a throw-back to the De Stijl-Futurist belief in spiritual value through the 'machine'.

The International Modern Movement and its supporters have made much of the idea of 'service' — that the function of design, if not of art, is to 'serve' people. Although this statement sounds unexceptionable, one should always be suspicious of claims to be 'serving' other people, especially when these claims are made by, or on behalf of, 'artists'. The role of servant is not a dignified or a free one. When this role is assumed voluntarily, it usually masks a plan to control — as with the Civil Service, which, in theory at least, is in any case serving the Crown in Britain, not the people. Similarly, modern architecture and design serve the needs of the big corporations. Whatever hypothetical kind of service they are offering ordinary people, it does not include asking them what they want. It is unfortunate that the International Modern Movement became so closely linked in many people's minds with left wing and even liberal political and social movements.

BUILDINGS TO BE SEEN:
There is hardly a city now which has not some International Modern building with its characteristically obsessive horizontality; long lines of windows, and the structure 'honestly' expressed, so that the building looks as if there were no reason why it should be that size rather than more or less. For individual architects, see the guide to names.

READING:
Henry-Russell Hitchcock and Philip Johnson, *The international style.* The 1931 book has been reissued, with an essay by Hitchcock, 'The international style twenty years after'. The photographs give the best record available of

the style, and, unlike the Smithsons', include a few Swedish examples.

Reyner Banham, *The architecture of the well-tempered environment*; very useful descriptions of the ventilation and heating arrangements in high-rise glass buildings, and in Wright's prairie houses; and much else.

Theo Crosby, *How to play the environment game.* It has a good section on the way in which the large construction firms have profited from the International Modern style, and cites some useful books.

Iron Architecture Improved production methods in the 18th century made iron available for building: or perhaps the iron manufacturers needed outlets for the stuff? The first serious use of iron in buildings was for the mills that were being built in northern England in the late 18th century. Here the fire-risk was very great — wool and cotton waste floated about; lighting was by oil lamps, with continuous shift-work, and there were long hours of lamplight in the winter months. After a number of bad fires, insurance companies began to refuse to underwrite mills. A new method of construction had to be devised. Iron columns and beams were introduced, with the floors supported by brick arches resting on the beams. Charles Bage's flax mill at Shrewsbury for Benyon, Marshall and Bage in 1796-7 was the perfected type: an internal iron frame resting against brick (or stone) outer walls. The floors were of hard wood on rubble resting on the brick arches. A competely free-standing iron frame building (i.e with no outer load-bearing brick or stone walls) was not achieved until Fowler's Hungerford Market in London (near Charing Cross) of 1835. The need was for a bracing system to keep the joints rigid so that the whole structure did not fold down. With the Crystal Palace (1851) these braces were incorporated into the design of the girders.

Iron gradually replaced wood as the framework for glass walls and roofs, though some greenhouses have continued to be built in wood to this day. Wood was used in the train sheds of King's Cross Station in London (1851), but it rotted in the steam and had to be replaced by iron. Iron was used for large greenhouses in the early 19th century, and since iron can be cast into many shapes some of these greenhouses were given a 'camp' design, like the greenhouse for Carlton House, which was like a perpendicular chapel in iron and glass instead of stone and glass (used for parties as much as for plants). Some churches had iron frames, and of course there were the bridges starting with Ironbridge itself, over the Severn (1776), and attaining grandeur by 1819 with the start of Telford's Menai Strait suspension bridge.

Between about 1835 and 1860, iron architecture has its greatest vogue, but was confined to stations, greenhouses or anywhere a large clear space was needed with light coming from above: market halls and exhibition halls like Paxton's 1851 Crystal Palace and also exchanges (as in Bunning's Coal Exchange in London of 1846 — demolished now); libraries, especially when infilled into other buildings, as were Sidney Smirke's reading room in the British Museum in 1852-7, and Labrouste's reading room in the National Library in Paris in 1862-8. Labrouste had earlier designed another reading room — the St. Geneviéve Library near the Sorbonne in Paris, of 1843-50, where the long reading room is divided down the middle by a colonnade of thin, elegant, iron Corinthian columns holding up an iron roof.

Then, about 1860, the fashion for iron architecture waned. A number of buildings had been given iron facades (Oriel Chambers in Liverpool of 1864 is a survivor of the fashion), but it was found that in fires these gave way disastrously and so had to be cased with ceramic, cement, or anything that would insulate the iron framework of the building from heat. One of the most serious of these fires was in Chicago in 1871, and the subsequent fire regulations for iron-frame buildings were the starting-point for the architecture of the CHICAGO SCHOOL.

Although the Crystal Palace had been such an admirable and admired exhibition building, it was sitting out its time at Sydenham, a white elephant unusable except for exhibitions and for mammoth performances of *Hiawatha*. Later exhibition buildings reverted to the kind of structure Brunel had proposed for 1851 — massive bricks walls with iron used only for glass domes.

There are two areas where iron survived the change in fashion:

1 Decorative wrought iron had a long tradition going back to the 16th century, and even earlier, for gates and screens. Some 18th century examples are the finest of their kind. With the development of a fashion for first floor balconies, wrought iron railings were much in demand, and there are many examples still *in situ* on houses of the late 18th and first half of the 19th century, especially in England and America: New Orleans has some fine examples, and so has Sydney in Australia (the King's Cross district). In the later 19th century, this decorative ironwork was mostly to be found in England at the seaside, not only on hotel balconies (some fine examples in Brighton) but on piers — especially the many piers built for pleasure, as much as for landing passengers from boats. West Pier, Brighton, of 1863-6, and South Parade Pier, Southsea, Hampshire, of 1908 (now being repaired after a fire), are two good examples.

2 Shopping arcades, a sensible idea and surprisingly rare in countries like Britain where it does rain. One of the grandest of these arcades is the Galleria Vittorio Emmanuele in Milan (by Mengoni, 1865-77) which is wide enough for outdoor cafés as well as a pedestrian street. A similar 'street' in Moscow is now G.U.M.

BUILDINGS TO SEE:
Many of the piers are still standing, though most of them are by now in need of expensive upkeep. Many of the mills have been demolished, but one or two are being preserved by Industrial Archaeology societies. The Crystal Palace was destroyed by fire in 1936, but a much smaller version of it exists in the Bethnal Green Museum (see EXHIBTIONS).

READING:
H-R. Hitchcock, *Architecture, 19th and 20th centuries*; the chapter on 'Building in iron and glass' is one of the best in the book.
G.F. Chadwick, *The works of Sir Joseph Paxton.*
A.W. Skempton and H.R. Johnson, 'The first iron frames' in the *Architectural*

Review for March 1962 (CXXI, pp 175-86).
Kenneth Lindley, *Seaside architecture.*

Kitsch A vague (originally German) term, perhaps meaning very little more than 'we do not like it', because there is no sharp dividing line in a sequence of objects ranging from Cellini's Salt Cellar at one end, and downmarket lavatory-pan mustard pots at the other. Unlike 'no dividing line' between black-grey-white, what one calls Kitsch depends entirely on shifting snobberies. Thus many of the works of the admirable Royal Copenhagen Porcelain Factory — like its little mermaids — do seem sentimental, but so are Meissen shepherdesses.

READING:
Jacques Sternberg, *Kitsch.*
Gillo Dorfles, *Kitsch: an anthology of bad taste.*

M.A.R.S. Modern Architecture Research Group, formed in April 1933, mainly by architects who admired the work of the C.I.A.M. group. They held an exhibition at the new Burlington Galleries early in 1938 (catalogue published as a booklet). In the late 1930's the group produced a megalomaniac plan for the development of London, which was published in 1942 after the bombing, when there seemed a better chance of something like it getting done; no success, though. The group was disbanded in 1957; it died at about the same time as C.I.A.M., for much the same reason — a new generation of architects wanted their own show.

READING:
Anthony Jackson, *The politics of architecture.*

Nationalist Revivals Elizabethan; French Renascence; Dutch, and, for Austria, Baroque. Once the restraints of the classical tradition had become unfashionable, any style from the past became novel, and buildings which would have seemed merely ridiculous in 1800 could be the latest chic in 1820. Reactions to the Gothick style of Strawberry Hill, which started around 1750, teetered on the edge of scorn for some time. As suggested in GOTHIC REVIVAL, it may have been Scott's novels, beginning in 1814, coupled with the revival of national feeling brought on by French imperialism, and also by German romantic idealism,which made it accessible. History, and nationalism, and the glories of war for those who had not had to fight in it, were the fairy godmothers of a revived interest in a national style from the past. Most European countries fostered a revival of past national styles — even to fancy dress: there are photographs of English Royals dressed up as Elizabethans, and their Russian cousins dressed up as Muscovite warriors and maidens. Not surprisingly, the styles chosen were those fashionable at a successful, or at least heroic, period in the past. After all, one of the reasons why the Italians in 1400 had begun a revival of Roman architecture was to recall the greatness of what they considered was their own — as opposed to the German — Roman Empire.

Perp. Gothic (the church-style of the 15th century in England) was early on the scene, as a distinct movement in the Gothic revival: Pinch's St Mary, Bathwick, on the eastern edge of Bath, an archaeologically good example, was begun as early as 1814. Elizabethan followed with Salvin's design for Harlaxton, Lincolnshire, in 1831, and was one of the two styles allowed in the competition for the new Houses of Parliament announced in June 1835 — the other being Perpendicular. Both were chosen deliberately as English national styles. In Paris the Hôtel de Ville was extended from 1837 onwards in a similar style not unlike the 16th century parts of the Louvre. This French revival (like its original) developed into a kind of Baroque, called Second Empire, shown first in the new north wing of the Louvre itself (begun 1852). Eventually there were nationalist revivals in most countries:

Germany: the Krupp model villages of the 1880's are built in a 16th century German village style (almost Hansel & Gretel architecture, one might say); Gropius tried to convince Goebbels, unsuccessfully, that the BAUHAUS was a national German style, too; maybe he was right.

Holland: Cuijpers not only built churches in a style like that of the great town churches (e.g. Haarlem, 15th century; Amsterdam — Oude Kerk, 14th century, Nieuwe Kerk, late 15th) — see his Vondelkerk and Maria-magdalenakerk; but designed the Rijksmuseum (1876-85) and the Central Station (1885) in the style of the late 16th, early 17th century — of Lieven de Key.

Denmark: Nyrop's Copenhagen Town Hall (1892-1902) is in a Danish/Flemish late Gothic/Renascence style — quite unlike Hansen's neo-classical Town Hall which it superseded; and Jensen Klint's Grundtvig Church of 1921-6, which is a development from the traditional brick, step-gabled country church.

Sweden: Östberg's Stockholm City Hall (1909-23) has many features (inside as well as out) which recall the Swedish Renascence, as well as Italian and Baroque features.

Russia: The cathedral built on the spot where Alexander II was assassinated in 1881 in St. Petersburg (Leningrad) is in a traditional Russian-Byzantine style.

Austria & S. Germany: Apart from the neo-Baroque buildings round the Ringstrasse in Vienna laid out in 1858, there is the Schloss Linderhof, near Oberammergau, designed by Dollman for Ludwig II of Bavaria (built 1870-86) and while Herrenchiemsee (begun 1878) is a German-Baroque Versailles, Neuschwanstein is German medieval again.

Spain: Whatever subconscious affinities Gaudí may have had with ART NOUVEAU or EXPRESSIONISM, his architecture can be reasonably seen as a revival of, and development from, Catalan Gothic.

How much of this national revival could be used in 'polite' building and furnishings? It would seem to have been potentially popular. In England, one has to wait until the influence of the Arts and Crafts Movement, with its revival of country, and pre-18th century, crafts and styles. These became fashionable in the last decades of the 19th century, and then permeated general ideas. Thus one can picture a typical middle class house in the suburbs, detached or semi-detached, half-timbered at least on the upper floor, with leaded-light windows. (Oak panelling and oak furniture, particularly gate-legged tables, all derived from the 17th century, and much more faithfully than the style the Victorians called 'Elizabethan'). There was also a revival of interest in pewter (for mugs, trays and teapots) where electroplate would have been normal 50 years before, and, continuing up to the present day, a revival of interest in 'traditional' English earthenware patterns for both ornamental and everyday wear — replacing the formal patterns of the 19th century.

Neo-Baroque (Second Empire; Edwardian Baroque, 'Wrenascence'). The almost universal style for large buildings from about 1860 to 1930 in Europe, America, and their colonies. Buildings in other styles (e.g. Manchester Town Hall, 1868; the Chicago skyscrapers of 1890-5, or the International Modern of c1925-30) are numerically exceptional. 'Baroque' itself is of course a term covering quite a wide variety of sub-shapes, but generally the characteristic is as follows. Classical architecture relies on a 'vocabulary' of proportions motifs and details based on the Greek and Roman *orders* of columns and their beams. There can be storeys raised one above the other (as in the facade of the Colosseum in Rome) but no more than five; each storey can only be a certain height — the columns of the British Museum are about as high as one can go for comfort, and without somehow destroying the whole aesthetic. For the really large buildings, a solution was devised by Michelangelo for St. Peter's in Rome and for the Senators' Palace on the Capitol — to have a 'giant' order of columns, with two ordinary sized 'orders' behind and between them. Both palladian architecture in 18th century England, and neo-classicism had been styles which were a reaction to the swagger of Baroque. For the empires of the early 19th century, however something grand was needed. One solution was to keep the proportions of neo-classical architecture, but shed all or most of the 'vocabulary' of the orders, while increasing the scale of the building. The General Staff Arches in St. Petersburg (Leningrad) by Rossi (1819) are a good example of this.

The other solution was a return to Baroque; and most large cities in Europe and America have examples of it. The whole story can be seen in the development of the Capitol building in Washington D.C. Built first in a restrained neo-classical/palladian style by William Thornton and others between 1792 and 1828, it was enlarged, and the first part overwhelmed,by the dome and wings added by Thomas U. Walter in 1851-65 — right through the Civil War. Pictures of Lincoln's inauguration show it under construction. Other Washington buildings are in the 'second empire' variety of Baroque — for which see *Paris* below.

Vienna: The Ringstrasse was laid out around the old city of Vienna in the space where the fortifications and glacis had been. For Austria, Baroque was something of a return to a National Style. The Burgtheater of 1874 is a good example of the 19th century Baroque that was the style of many of the buildings put up along the Ring.

Paris: Some of the monuments (Arc de Triomphe, Stock Exchange, Madeleine) are in a Roman neo-classical style, but the great 19th century re-ordering of Paris began under Napoleon III. The period, 1852-1870, is known as the SECOND EMPIRE, following the first empire of Napoleon's uncle Bonaparte. The first monument of the style is the new north wing of the Louvre, begun by Visconti and Lefuel in 1852. The French always disclaim having any Baroque architecture: theirs was always pure classical. However, they certainly had a neo-Baroque. The rich over-ornament of the new Louvre with a much textured surface of sculpted figures, is topped by typical 'square domes' on the corners, either convex or concave (when they look like medieval Bohemia). They were used by Le Vau at Vaux-le-vicomte (1657), but topping a much more restrained facade than the new Louvre. European classical architecture was already going back to Baroque, as noted above (see Cuthbert Brodrick's Leeds City Hall, 1855-9), and the new French style was seized on very quickly as, in the Grosvenor Hotel, Victoria Station, London (Knowles, 1860). In the same year Knowles built two huge apartment blocks facing south over Clapham Common in south-west London, then an outer suburb, Cedars Terrace and Thornton Terrace, each with five high storeys and the characteristic pavilion roofs. In Washington D.C. there is Mullet & Gillman's State, War & Navy Department Building, 1871-5. Other examples — well on into the end of the century — are discussed by Hitchcock; most European cities have a quarter full of this kind of building.

In Paris itself, the last fling of the Second Empire was to commission a building more Baroque than anything else in Paris, and owing little to classical French architecture: the Opera House. This was begun to J.L.C. Garnier's designs in 1861, but not finished until 1874, so that the soldiers lining the grand staircase on gala nights guarded a president, not an emperor. The Opera House is a building in the lush style of 16th century baroque — Michelangelo and the Sansovino library in Venice.

Opera Houses: Not only in Paris, but throughout the Western world, a kind of Baroque became standard for large theatres, especially opera houses — as far away as Manaos, one of the most spectacular, half-way up the Amazon. Grand Opera was one of the most fashionable public art-forms in the middle and later 19th century and popular, too. It was the Italian variety, established by Rossini, and followed by Donizetti, Verdi and later Puccini. The natural setting for these florid — and highly artificial — operas was a Baroque opera house: gilt caryatids, curved boxes and red plush. It is no coincidence that the other great popular 19th century entertainment, the circus/carousel/fair was also decorated in a kind of 'people's Baroque'. It seems justifiable, then, to recognise that in the endless quest, then and now, for a 'style of the century' — however meaningless this quest may be — that style is undoubtedly a kind of secularised Baroque, and ought to be studied as such.

England: Brodrick's Leeds Town Hall of 1855-9; then 'Second Empire' as in Knowles's buildings of the 1860's. Gibson's National Provincial Bank in Bishopsgate (1865), however, is not at all French in style — nor are the Guildhalls of Bolton (1866) and its larger brother at Portsmouth (1886-90), both by Hill. Later examples of Baroque are usually called *Edwardian*

Baroque after Edward VII (1901-10), but the style was fashionable for a longer time — around 1885 to at least 1914. 'Edwardian' are R. Norman Shaw's Piccadilly Hotel of 1905-9; Admirality Arch over the entrance to the Mall (1911), the wide tree-lined avenue itself, and the refronting of Buckingham Palace (1913), together with a re-arrangement of the *rond-point* in front of the palace, all the work of Aston Webb. Next to Admirality Arch is the 19th century extension to the Admiralty. This (by the Leemings, 1894-5) is in a style called 'Wrenascence'; Wren especially in his later years presided over the only architecture in England which could be called Baroque (before the 19th century revival), and designed some of it himself, particularly the royal palaces of Hampton Court and Winchester, grand but sober designs, characteristically using red brick for the body of the building and white stone for the trimmings. Reviving Baroque, it was quite likely that architects would turn to this English style — Cockerell, the greatest English neo-classical architect of the mid 19th century, had always been one of Wren's admirers, and several buildings had been designed in a 'Wren' style — notably John Shaw's Wellington College in Berkshire (1856). The latest and grandest of these neo-Baroque architects was Lutyens, even though he came to Baroque late, after an Arts and Crafts beginning. His Liverpool Cathedral for the Roman Catholic diocese, designed in 1932, would have been one of the largest Baroque buildings anywhere. The model survives in the crypt, the only part built before the war and rising costs put an end to the scheme. His Governor's Palace in New Delhi was one of his finest buildings, an original development within Baroque.

Baroque, and neo-Baroque, are public styles of architecture. Scaled down to 'polite' building, their motifs became merely classical. In 'polite' furniture, however, the popularity of Second Empire, Rococo, and Baroque forms lasted well into the 20th century, contributing a lot to High Street Art Deco. There is a lot of bulgy furniture, much of it ugly, still coming into the second-hand shops. Baroque probably remains the only one of the high-fashion styles of architecture which has ever been really popular and loved, in music halls, public houses, fairgrounds and seaside piers.

READING:
H-R. Hitchcock, *Architecture, 19th and 20th centuries.*
Alistair Service, *Edwardian architecture.*

Neo-Classical (Greek Revival; Roman Revival; Classical Revival; Empire; Regency; Federal; Biedermeyer; *Restauration* [the French monarchy after 1815, not the English Restoration of 1660]; Karl Johan)

The roundest definition is: the style, or group of related styles of architecture, furnishings, clothes and ceramics of *c*1750 to *c*1850, partly (sometimes wholly) inspired by archaeological discoveries of the ancient Mediterranean. After some overlap in mid-century, neo-classical was succeeded by neo-Baroque.

The term 'neo-classical' is itself a confusing one and has been used for both shorter and longer periods than 1750-1850, and for a completely different

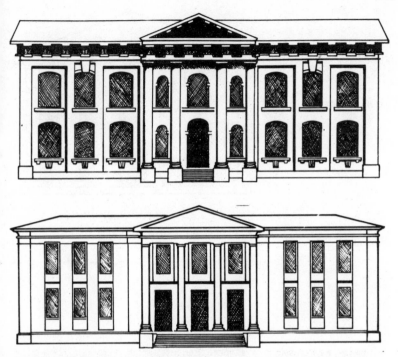

20 The difference between Baroque and Neo-classical: the buildings (like the Clarendon Building in Oxford, above, and Oslo University, below) have similar components, and are 3x3x3 bays wide, but the detailing and proportions are different.

one. Hugh Honour in *Neo-classicism* insists that the true period of the neo-classical idea was only 1750-1790 and that the Empire, Regency, etc. styles that followed it were a coarsening of exactly those things which 'neo-classicism' had been meant to purify. But a style is still a style even when it is coarsened and the coarsening was of contemporary forms and ornament, not of anything earlier.

Then, 'neo-classical' was used in the 19th and early 20th centuries for the whole of European and American architecture from 1420 onwards which owed anything to the arts of Greece and Rome. This unhelpful usage had dropped out of use and can be found only in older books. Finally, 'neo-classical' is used quite reasonably for the revived interest in neo-classicism itself which happened in some parts of America and Europe (notably in Scandinavia) around 1900, and could also be seen in a revival of interest in Adam, Chippendale and Sheraton furnishings in British upper-class society in the last decades of the 19th century (and which has lasted to this day). This last use of the term will be discussed at the end of this section separately.

front elevation

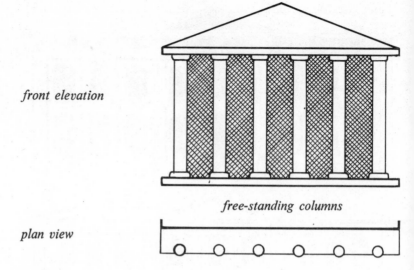

free-standing columns

plan view

However, neo-classicism was more than just the latest classical fashion, as its predecessor, Rococo had been. It was one of those periodic movements for a return to basic principles which happen every now and then in architecture and which in the classical period after *c*1450 usually meant going back to the ruins, measuring them up again, publishing the drawings and condemning all the 'incorrect' changes which had crept in since the last reformer. Alberti in the 15th century, Palladio in the 16th, Perrault in the 17th, Burlington in the early 18th, and finally the Abbé Laugier in 1753, who argued, amongst other things, that columns must be used only to support beams and not as mere decoration (as the Romans themselves had used them on the Colosseum).

Most of these reform movements leant on the abstract puritan side, and the targets for their abuse were invariably the jolly, scrolly buildings that can just as well be put together from the classical kit as the purist's own buildings. The graceful, arched style of the early Italian Renascence, the wilder jokes of Italian Mannerism, the confidently incorrect Jacobean, grand Baroque and frivolous Rococo, were all savaged by zealots. It is not surprising that all these varieties of classical styles were exuberantly revived in the 19th century when neo-classical purism fell out of fashion. Nor is it surprising that architects like Corbusier should claim that the International Modern style fulfils the proportions of Greek architecture, without any of the decorative elements at all.

Neo-classicism was the austere, puritan style to end all classical styles, which indeed it nearly did, falling an easier victim to exuberance than other

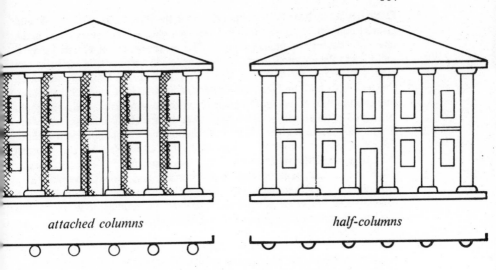

attached columns   half-columns

21 Neo-classical 'purity'. Writers from Laugier onwards argued that columns must be used only to support beams, and not merely for decoration. Only the free-standing columns do any serious 'work'. Half columns and pilasters, which are flattened half-columns, have a purely decorative function.

classical styles might have done. Classical survived in the 19th century as a fashionable architectural style by returning to Baroque. Perhaps a good architectural climate is one in which adaptation and variety can have full play. The 'incorrectness' which disgusted Laugier — apparent columns not really holding anything up, for example — is part of the pleasure we can get in architecture.

At the time that Laugier published his *Essay* in 1753, teams of European draughtsmen were beginning to explore Greek architecture, both in lands which had always been open to them, but whose Greek buildings had been ignored (Naples and Sicily) and in lands which had been under Turkish rule, and therefore largely closed to Europeans since the Renascence. As well as Greek buildings, the Eastern Mediterranean countries also had Roman ruins of different, sometimes richer, styles than those in the West. The results of these drawing expeditions were published in large volumes and had a great effect on both architecture and design. Partly in response to this Greek inflow, an Italian, Piranesi, published architectural engravings, many of them fantasies, but all investing Roman architecture with an awesome grandeur.

Thus from the 1760's onwards, several 'purer' (or at least earlier) models of classical architecture were available for architects and connoisseurs to ponder over, and they might commission and design buildings in any one of these styles — or, after a time, in combinations of them.

Greek Revival: Distinguishable from Roman (and thus from the proportion-system of architecture since the Renaissance) by slight variations in the proportions and ornaments of the columns, above all the Doric order — Greek

Doric having no base to its columns — as in the Parthenon. Almost the only Greek buildings surviving, however, were temples, and not every client in the late 18th century wanted a temple. The most successful Greek Revivial buildings in Britain and Europe are those which do not need side windows, like picture galleries, for example. W.H. Playfair's Royal Scottish Institution (begun 1822) and the National Gallery of Scotland (begun 1850) are both fine examples of an uncompromising Greekness. Academic buildings could be shaped into a plausibly Greek form, notably again in Edinburgh (one of the finest neo-classical cities). Thomas Hamilton's Edinburgh High School (begun 1825) is versatile enough to be the likely seat of the Scottish Assembly when the time comes. The Stock Exchange in Oslo (also begun 1826) has a fine heavy Greek Doric portico, and Oslo University (also Grosch, 1841-51) has the kind of Greek Corinthian detailing applied to a basically Baroque group of buildings. The wings in particular look remarkably like the Clarendon Building in Oxford, but with Greek rather than Roman proportions:

This became the standard adaptation of Greek Revival to the needs of modern buildings, not only in the British Museum (R. Smirke, finished in 1847), which hides its activity from the street behind a continuous Ionic colonnade, but also in the work of Wilkins — National Gallery (1832-8) and University College (1827-9), both in London, and even more his Downing College, Cambridge (begun 1807). Here the windows are set in a framework which echoes the columns of the entrance portico. St. Pancras Church in Euston Road, London (Inwood 1819-22) has many 'Greek' features including two copies of the caryatid portico of the Erectheum.

In America, 'Greek Revival' means not only a number of buildings with porticos, etc., which have Greek orders (Clarke's Insane Asylum at Utica, N.Y., 1837-43, for example), but also many country houses, especially in the southern states, which have porticos sometimes of Greek proportions, applied in an entirely Palladian way.

Roman Revival: In turn, architects who preferred Roman proportions could forget everything that had been learned since 1450 and go back to the genuine Roman article. The Town Hall of Birmingham, England, looks very much like a Roman temple, especially since it was cleaned. It was modelled on the temple of Castor and Pollux in the Roman Forum, and it was designed and built by Charles Edge in 1835-61.

Roman also became the more fashionable style for some time after 1800. The empires of Bonaparte and the Romanovs were more likely to look to the Roman Empire for a style than to the Greek city-states. Paris has its Arc de Triomphe, St. Petersburg (Leningrad) its General Staff Arches. In the face of such grandeur, Greek, if it were to survive at all, had to become grander too. It did so, in museums, like Schinkel's long, even, eighteen-column front to his Altes Museum in Berlin (1824-8), and perhaps in replay, Smirke's even longer forty-four column front to the British Museum (1823-47).

It was also open to an architect to start from the purest of all classical ideas, the forms alone, without any columns or entablatures at all. Some Roman buildings gave a lead in this — the aqueducts, for example, with their arches showing a brotherhood with classical proportions, but without the trimmings of the orders which mark the Colosseum. In France, in the late 18th century, two architects made drawings of such structures. Boullée did not become generally known until the 20th century, but Ledoux built several interesting buildings, most of which have been pulled down. The Barrières — toll gates on the roads into Paris — had some remarkable shapes, as we can see from photographs, including one of the most basic, a drum on top of a cube, the Barrière de la Vilette. This sculptural arrangement was used again with even greater simplicity by Gunnar Asplund in his city library in Stockholm of 1924-9, in the neo-classical revival.

Many of the most original architects of this period could be included amongst those who took classical shapes as their starting point. John Soane in England designed some of the most remarkable interiors in Europe. With few exceptions, they have been destroyed, not by war but by other architects — Baker in his remodelling of the Bank of England, and Street indirectly by designing new Law Courts in the Strand, London, thus making Soane's marvellous rooms around Westminster Hall redundant. The Bank survived until the 1920's, so we have many photographs of Soane's work. The Law Courts were built in the 1870's, and no-one seems to have bothered to photograph Soane's courts before they came down. 1883 was probably the nadir of Soane's reputation, and also of the taste for neo-classicism.

Mixed Roman and Greek: Some architects took elements from both Revivals. One of the most successful to do this was the great Danish architect C.F. Hansen; his Town Hall and Law Courts, in one building, and his cathedral (Vor Frue Kirk) of 1811-29, both in Copenhagen, are a brilliant neo-classical mixture of Greek and Roman styles.

With its massive archaeological learning, and its preoccupation with the designing of heroic or grand monuments, neo-classical is very much a 'fashionable' style. However, as a classical style, it was possible for many of the incidental features to be taken up by 'polite' building and design. The most common feature in England was the Greek Doric portico, often of only two columns, and quite small. The 'window solution' worked out at, for example, Downing college, became an accepted feature of many middle class houses in the first half of the century — windows set into a vertical recess reaching up through two or more floors, so that the intervening 'pilasters' could echo Greek proportions. Most of the national terms for neo-classical refer more to furnishings than to architecture: e.g. Regency, Federal.

Furniture design in the late 18th century was generally more severe in outline than in the earlier part of the century. 'Neo-classical' covers both the formal, rich, 'Louis XVI' (1774-89) designs and the pattern-books of Sheraton and Hepplewhite in England (and America), where the decoration was usually in inlay patterns in different woods rather than in gold and enamels. Before 1800 many specifically Greek and Roman motifs were used in decoration (as in the 'Etruscan' room Adam designed for Osterley Park in 1777), and after 1800 actual Greek designs were imitated. The two best known are the 'sabre' legged chairs with wide, curved back-rests, and the fashion for straight-skirted, high waisted clinging women's dresses. Both types were copied and adapted from drawings which could be seen on Attic vases of the 5th century B.C. Pattern-books for whole interiors as well as for items of furniture were also published, and used. The most distinguished of these were by Thomas Hope, who designed his own house and its furnishings at Deepden, outside Dorking in Surrey.

Neo-classical Revival: In the later 19th century in America and Europe there was a more or less complete acceptance of classical ideas in architecture and design. In some countries, the U.S.A., Scandinavia and Germany in particular, there was also a revival of neo-classical architecture (in contrast to the more general baroque). Good examples of this revival are the Faaborg Museum in Denmark (by Carl Petersen, 1912) and the Lincoln Memorial in Washington (by Henry Bacon, 1917). Neo-classical interior design was at first only partially revived in England, especially for wall and ceiling decorations, where the designs were usually adaptations of Robert Adam, and his chairs were made again. In the 1920's, especially in Paris, very expensive and fashionable interiors were designed in what is a more-or-less neo-classical mode; this is also the period of 'neo-classical' music — Stravinsky's ballets and early Prokofiev. Echoes of neo-classical women's fashions can be seen in the designs of the 1930's, although *any* straight skirt with sculptural folds, especially if worn with tightly-curled permanently waved hair, can look like *Mourning Athena.*

BUILDINGS AND DESIGNS TO SEE:

Many of the buildings mentioned in this note are still standing. The British Museum has just been cleaned, and looks more 'Greek' than when sooty. All major museums of design have examples of neo-classical furniture. In Stockholm there is also the *Rosendals slott,* more a country villa than a *slott,* built for King Karl-Johan, and now a museum which is a treasury of the style named after him. In Copenhagen there is the C.L. David collection, with neo-classical furniture (and a painting collection). The Sir John Soane Museum in Lincoln's Inn Fields, in London, is Soane's own house, with its series of remarkable rooms, and his collections.

READING:

Hugh Honour, *Neo-classicism.*

David Watkin, *Thomas Hope and the neo-classical idea.*

Neo-Liberty The 'Liberty Style' was the Italian term for ART NOUVEAU, after the London shop. So, Neo-Liberty is the revived art-nouveau fashion in Italy in the 1960's. Some Italian architecture, especially some of the new office towers in Milan, have been designed in a more Expressionist style than the usual post-Miesian International Modern; because they do not all look like the Lever Building in New York, they have aroused much harsh comment from orthodox critics, and the term 'Neo-Liberty' has been applied to them, as well as to more obviously art-nouveau inspired designs.

READING:

Charles Jencks, *Modern Movements in architecture.*

Neo-Wren or 'Wrenascence'. The swagger style Wren used in about 1690, especially at Hampton Court Palace. Much used for English town halls, from Brydon's Chelsea Town Hall of 1885-7 to Atkinson's Bromley Town Hall, of 1906. After that, it becomes more obviously Neo-Georgian. The American is perhaps 'Neo-Williamsburg', and there are similarities to the brick architecture of c1900-1920 in Scandinavia. They all come together in a late example, County Hall, in Winchester, England, by Cowles Voysey, Brandon -Jones, Broadbent and Ashton, a fine building of 1959-60, which looks much like the architecture of the Royal quarter in Copenhagen, and leaves Dr. Pevsner's pen quivering with 'entirely untouched by the last 30 years of architecture' *(Hampshire)*. Behind it is a grim horizontal-emphasis building in grey aggregate, very much touched by the last thirty years.

New Towns, see GARDEN CITIES.

Queen Anne The name given (at the time) to the free classical architecture, mostly houses, of the 1870's to about 1900. The early fashionable practitioners of the style were the pupils of famous Gothic Revival architects, the best known being Richard Norman Shaw, who had worked with G.E. Street. However, before springing into fashion, there were several buildings by quite well known architects which 'herald' the style: particularly John Shaw's Royal Navy College at New Cross in south London of 1844 (later Goldsmith's College), and his Wellington College at Sandhurst, of 1856-8. These are in a markedly 'Wren' style, not unlike Queen Anne, but even more like what Queen Anne itself developed into in the 1890's. There was, too, the house that Thackeray designed for himself in Palace Gate, Kensington, in 1861, in an early 18th century style; but the 'first' building in the new style is usually recognised as being the lodge at Kew Gardens designed by Eden Nesfield, R. Norman Shaw's partner, in 1867. Soon after this, Nesfield was designing Kinmel Park, a great country house in North Wales, finished in 1874.

Another architect who is important in the movement is Philip Webb, though he might not have been pleased to be classed with Queen Anne. One view of the Queen Anne is that it married 'Gothic' freedom of planning with 'classical' details — avoiding the symmetry which had been especially pronounced in late neo-classical architecture — (though not in 'Italian Renaissance'). Webb's idol, Butterfield, began the transition from faithful copying of archaic details into what some of his admirers at the time called a Gothic 'spirit' — using 'whatever style came to hand' in order to provide a serviceable form. Thus at his High-Anglican All Saints', Margaret Street, London (1849-59), Butterfield designed sash-windows for the clergy house, etc., alongside the church. In his vicarages of the 1840's, Butterfield had not held rigidly to to Gothic forms. Webb took this a stage further in his Red House at Bexley Heath (1859) for William Morris. The outline looks medieval (however unlike any actual medieval house), but the brickwork and sash-windows are very close to what would soon be called 'Queen Anne'. Webb became one of the most eclectic of late 19th century architects, his buildings looking like a country version of perhaps around 1680, with many local finishings — tile-hanging, for example — mixed with sophisticated late 17th century classical details. In R.N. Shaw's hands this kind of thing became much more fashionable. It soon moved from High Fashion architecture into a fashionable trend, with the development of Bedford Park, London, the first Garden Suburb, begun in about 1875; Shaw was appointed Estate architect in 1877. His designs for some of the buildings look, if anything, early rather than late 17th century. He perfected the type of large suburban house which spread all round London and other cities in those years: red brick, often several shades; white painted woodwork, sometimes sash windows, sometimes casement, but nearly always with the glazing bars and the rest of the window frame painted white — leaded lights in diamond panes came later, with a diffusion — a debasement — of arts and crafts. As Mark Girouard tells us in his book *Sweetness and light,* many Queen Anne developments were carried out at the seaside, so that some watering places look entirely in the style — for example, Cromer, Bexhill-on-sea.

Queen Anne was used for many public buildings, as a precursor, as it turned out, of neo-Wren. The best known are the London Board Schools of the last quarter of the 19th century. Following the Education Act of 1871, local school boards were set up throughout England, elected on separate votes. Not until some years later were these boards taken over by the Local Government Authority of their area. The architects of the London School Boards were Robson and Stevenson, and many of their buildings still stand. At the time they towered over the small houses, especially in the Thames valley south of the river.

The 20th century heir to the Queen Anne movement was Lutyens, and though his later buildings moved away from the style, his world of brass candlesticks, oak furniture, blue table cloths and white china seems to conjure up much of the spirit of the movement. The Queen Anne Movement was admired and sometimes imitated in America. It contributed to the SHINGLE STYLE.

READING:
Mark Girouard, *Sweetness and Light.*

Radburn Planning Radburn is a town in New Jersey near New York, where a layout of houses with access roads was designed by Clarence Stein in the 1930's. Based to a certain extent on the English Garden Cities, it is a definitive method of planning to ensure that many local activities can take place (e.g. young children walking to school) without anyone having to cross a road where they will meet fast traffic. The type of layout has become known as Radburn planning, though much of the rest of the town of Radburn is not laid out in this way. It is less profitable to the developer to arrange his new houses like this — a large area has to be set aside for communal use, outweighing the possible gains on space taken up by roads. It is interesting, though, that this development should take place in the U.S.A. in the '30s, where the private car already had to be taken into consideration in layouts. In Britain and Europe if such 'closes' were designed, they might well have had no direct access to a road. Even as late as the 1950's no provision was made at the L.C.C.'s famous estate at Roehampton for private cars. Tenants leave their cars scattered round the estate. Those living in the very charming little rows of houses cannot bring a car anywhere near their front doors, which are connected to roads by access paths only. In many suburbs since Radburn the idea of the cul-de-sac has been taken up, but seldom the idea of groups of cul-de-sacs backing on to each other and to school, library and shops.

Regency For Britain, 1811-20, when the future George IV (1820-30) was Regent for his father George III. Regency is not a particularly popular word with art historians, but in very general use. However, it is not as precise as 1811-20. 'Georgian' itself covers 1714-1830 and 'Victorian' from 1837-1901. What then about 1830-37? William IV should give us 'Wilhelmine', but this has never caught on. ('Adelaide style' has been suggested, after William's wife.) To fill the gap 'Regency' is often used loosely for the whole period 1811-37, not inappropriately, because there were no major stylistic changes in Britain between those dates. 'Late Georgian', also a frequently used term, presumably covers at most only 1800-30, though one suspects it too is loosely used for 1830-37. (see NEO-CLASSICAL). 'Regency' applies more closely to furnishings than to buildings.

Brighton is, of course, the Regency town *par excellence* though many of the crescents and terraces were put up even after 1837; and the Mecca for the Regency style is the Brighton Pavilion; upstairs there are some rooms furnished in an elegant late 18th century neo-classical style, too.

READING:
Donald Pilcher, *The Regency style.*

Renascence (alternative spelling, Renaissance). The 'rebirth' of classical culture in Italy in the 15th century (arguably a 'Nationalist' reaction against 'Gothic' which was seen as a German or French style and culture). However, this 'rebirth' produced a whole new set of attitudes and styles which slowly spread all over Europe and so to America in the next 200 years. At no time did any society suddenly change completely over from its own traditional styles to classical, with the possible exception of Russia under Peter the Great's reforms of c1700, when the whole culture was shifted into a European style (by then, Baroque), including a new, fashionable, capital city at St. Petersburg (Leningrad). Each society modified the new fashion, so that there is a French Renascence style, an English Renascence, Dutch, Swedish, etc. in the 16th and 17th centuries; but no Russian Renascence. All these styles, mentioned above were revived in one form or another in the course of the 19th century, and in fairly quick succession, from c1829 to c1850; then in America from c1880 to 1900.

1829   Charles Barry's Travellers' Club, London (finished 1832).
1837   Charles Barry's Reform Club, London (finished 1840).
1843   Henri Labrouste's St. Genevieve Library, Paris (finished 1850).

1883   McKim, Mead and White's Villard Houses, New York (finished 1885).

1888   the same group's Boston Public Library (finished 1892).

1899   and their New York University Club (finished 1900).

There is no real corresponding trend or fashion in interior design (as with the Greek Revival, for example), only a fashion for particular objects — vases — in a Renascence style. On the other hand there was a fashion in painting: the Nazarenes, a German group living and working in Rome, their English follower Dyce, and then the Pre-Raphaelites themselves (from about 1849) all revived the painting styles of the 15th century Italian masters.

As an influence on 'polite' architecture, it merged with the 'picturesque', made fashionable by Nash, particularly with his villa, Cronkhill, in Shropshire, of 1802. This was a country house designed to look like one of those vernacular farmhouse-villas in the paintings of Salvator Rosa, Claude, Gaspar Poussin and others. Many well-to-do clients commissioned villas similar to Cronkhill in the first quarter of the 19th century. Thus when the 15th century Italian Renascence style was brought into fashion by Barry and others in the late 1820's, it started a trend for 'Italian' in general 'polite' building. Many suburban villas were miniature versions of Cronkhill, and railway stations and public houses were often given the overhanging roofs, supported on consoles, that was one of the Italian Renascence features popularised.

22 *An American example of a typical 'Italian Renascence' pair of villas of the mid-19th century.*

Restauration/Restoration. In the French spelling, the late neo-classical style of 1814-15 to 1830, of the restored Bourbon monarchy after Bonaparte's fall and exile — coming between 'Empire' and 'Louis-Phillippe' and like both of them. In the English spelling 'Restoration' refers to the arts and literature of after 1660, the restoration of the Stuart monarchy.

Romanesque Originally the style of churches built in western Europe from *c*900 A.D. until the spread of the Gothic fashion *c*1200. Some secular buildings survive too. Thomas Rickman in his division of English medieval architecture uses the word 'Norman' for the period 1066-*c*1200.

Romanesque-revived is the great 'other' style of the 19th century — the main one being baroque classical. The sudden 'emergence' of a full-scale Romanesque building, the Natural History Museum, designed by a leading Gothic Revivalist, Alfred Waterhouse, and built 1873-81, is inexplicable without an understanding of this continuing Romanesque tradition in the U.S.A. and in Europe. The development of Romanesque-revived, can be set out like this:
1 *Rundbogenstil*, a German art-historical term, meaning 'round-arch style'. A development from 'Roman' Neo-classicism as in some ways Romanesque itself had been a development of some aspects of Roman architecture. As the name suggests, fashionable in Germany where the actual detailing of Pisa Cathedral (a late Romanesque Italian building of *c*1100) seems the inspiration for, amongst other buildings, Persius' Friedenskirche in Potsdam, 1845-8. In England there was the 'Nationalist' revival, 'neo-norman' (after Rickman's classification) which lasted for some years. One of the best examples is a small parish church in Cheltenham, St. Peter, by Dawkes, 1847-9. The Italian Romanesque style was also imported from Italy, as the Germans had done. The best example of this is the Wilton, Wiltshire, parish church by Wyatt and Brandon 1840-6. A more original variation on the style is by Wilde — Christchurch, Streatham, London (alongside the South Circular Road) of 1840-2. Up to this time there were only churches, but in 1851-2 Cubitt's design for King's Cross Station had no facade other than two huge ridged but otherwise unornamented arches which formed the ends of the train-sheds. These could be seen as either neo-classical (St. Petersburg gone industrial) or as Romanesque. In the middle there is an 'Italian' small clock tower which suggests that the architectural inspiration is *Rundbogenstil*. In America, *Rundbogenstil* is the style of Tefft's Union Station in Providence, R.I. (begun 1848) and of Upjohn's Utica City Hall (1852-3).
2 The influential figure in the second half of the century was the French architect J. A. E. Vaudremer (1829-1914), designer of Romanesque buildings in Paris, especially the church of St. Pierre de Montrouge of 1864-70 and Notre Dame in the Rue d'Auteuil of 1876. The Sacré Coeur (by Abadie) was also begun in 1876 in a somewhat Romanesque style. The young American architect Henry Hobson Richardson (1838-86) studied at the Ecole des Beaux-Arts and worked in Paris from 1859 to about 1870, with an interruption for service in the Civil War. He almost certainly saw and admired Vaudremer's work. Richardson's library at Quincy, Massachusetts (1880-3)

is in a kind of arts-and-crafts Romanesque. His better-known (but now demolished) Marshall Field warehouse in Chicago (1885-7) was in a massive Romanesque style applied to the design of an eight storey city block. Adler and Sullivan's Auditorium Building in Chicago (1887-9) seems in some ways a variation on Marshall Field, as does their Walker warehouse of 1888-9. The Romanesque of Richardson was one of the 'ingredients' of the first CHICAGO SCHOOL of tall office blocks; some (e.g. Burnham and Root's Rockery Building of 1866) are clearly in the same mode. Grand Central Station, Chicago (Merman, 1890) and the Newbury Library (Cobb, 1892) are 'smaller' examples of Richardsonian Romanesque.

3 In England most of the warehouses and mills were firmly in the classical 'polite' style. A few warehouses in Manchester and Bristol could be said to be more like Marshall Field, though earlier. E. W. Godwin's 104 Stoke's Croft, Bristol, of c1862 (illustrated in Hitchcock's *Architecture, 19th and 20th centuries*) is a good example. When the style came back into fashion in England with the Natural History Museum, there was a small revival of interest. Two buildings by Harrison Townsend, the Whitechapel Art Gallery of 1897-9 and the Horniman Museum, Forest Hill, of 1902 (both in London) are in a free Romanesque, as is the L.C.C. Central School of Arts and Crafts of 1907, by the County Architect W. E. Riley, but clearly influenced by the first Principal of the School, W. R. Lethaby.

In Scandinavia, Romanesque was the style chosen for the Norwegian Parliament House, the Storting, in Oslo (Langlet; built in the 1860's).

In Europe, Bonatza and Scholer's Stuttgart Railway Station, 1911-14, and 1919-27 was Romanesque; and the early work of the Amsterdam School (see EXPRESSIONISM) was in a Romanesque style too.

As has been said earlier, Classical has limitations for really large buildings. Some of the 'classical' Chicago blocks look ridiculous, probably even from the sidewalk. Adler and Sullivan did better than that even when they were using load-bearing walls, and they did it with Romanesque. As a style for grand buildings, Romanesque had practically no influence on 'polite' building. It is essentially a large style.

Rundbogenstil — see ROMANESQUE.

Satellite Towns A kind of outer suburb, given an identity by comprehensive planning and a geographical location, with a town centre and the amenities of a medium-sized town. The best-known examples are the satellite towns around Stockholm, beginning with Vällingby to the west of the city, planned in the 1940's and built in the '50's and '60's. It is about half an hour's ride on the underground from the centre of Stockholm. Apart from the fact that it was all designed and built in one go, there is not much to differentiate Vällingby from an outer suburb of say, London. Croydon also has a town centre, shops, and even a concert hall of international standing, but at eighteen minutes away from Victoria Station is still within reach of metropolitan amenities. So a satellite town is a conscious attempt to give outer suburbs of a large city an identity rather than leaving it to chance. The New Towns built in Britain after

1945 are significantly further out than satellite towns. From Harlow in Essex, for instance, people do commute every day into London, but it is a longer journey than from Vällingby to Stockholm. The towns like Harlow were sited as near to London as they are to make it more attractive for Londoners to move out not too far from relations.

Second Empire The French empire of Louis Napoleon, 1852-1870; see NEO-BAROQUE.

Shakers An English Non-Conformist community which emigrated to America in 1774. Their most famous settlements are in New York State near the Massachusetts border, e.g. New Lebanon. A severe sect, they designed austere buildings and furniture for themselves, much like plain 18th century English and New England designs. From the early 19th century they began to sell furniture in this plain style, chairs, tables, etc. There are little quirks in the designs, like extra finials on the tops of the back of rocking-chairs, but otherwise the plainness of the design shows the excellence of the craftsmanship. Morris and Co.'s Sussex chairs, for example, straightforward though they are on the whole, look fussy beside a Shaker chair, and inelegant too. There are many collections of Shaker work including, in England, the Shaker room at Claverton Manor (the American Museum) near Bath (the very quiet Shaker music should not be missed). New Lebanon itself can be visited.

READING:
E. D. and F. Andrews, *Shaker furniture.*

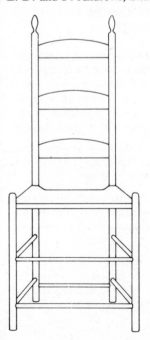

23 A Shaker chair.

Shingle Style Title of a book by Vincent Scully (1955), about large private houses in the U.S.A. built from about 1880 to 1900, and often designed by some of the best architects of the time — Richardson, McKim, Mead and White, etc. The walls are covered with shingles, rather than clapboard, that is, with split wooden tiles or 'shakes' (usually Cedar wood, which weathers to a silvery grey) rather than wooden boards. There is an obvious affinity with the work of architects like R. Norman Shaw and Philip Webb in England, who were reviving vernacular materials and practices like tile-hanging. (This has the same effect as shingles, but clay tiles are used instead of wood; it is a Weald — Surrey, Sussex and Kent — tradition.) The 'Shingle' houses themselves inside were a stage further in the development of open plan — in the late 19th century this meant having a number of rooms opening off a large central hall, which might also be the staircase hall (this was adopted as a 'lounge hall' in many English houses of about 1930); the plan does away with dark corridors.

READING:
H-R. Hitchcock, Architecture, 19th and 20th centuries (the chapter on the development of the small house in England and America).
Vincent Scully, *The Shingle style.*
Mark Girouard, *Sweetness and light* (a chapter on 'Queen Anne in America').

Slurb American word for urban and suburban mess, somewhat the same meaning as the British-English 'SUBTOPIA'.

S.O.A.B. Society for the Protection of Ancient Buildings founded in 1877 by amongst others, William Morris; see CONSERVATION.

Style of 1930 One of the terms for the style of the INTERNATIONAL MODERN MOVEMENT, the BAUHAUS and C.I.A.M., see entries in this guide for these. As labels go, 'The Style of 1930' has an increasing disadvantage as 1930 is further and further away in time — it will soon be its fiftieth anniversary. Those who coined the term did not think of it as a potentially historical style like any other. In Nikolaus Pevsner's radio talk at the end of 1966, he said:

> Here was the one and only style which fitted all those aspects which mattered, aspects of economics and sociology, of materials and functions. It seemed folly to think that anybody would wish to abandon it.

Pevsner claims that we are still living in the same 'time' as 1930, and this aspect of the phrase is discussed in the introduction to this book (and see also HISTORICISM). In a later part of the talk, he added that any Expressionist style is

> ... ill suited for most architecture now because the majority of buildings are built of industrially produced — i.e. impersonal — materials, because the majority of buildings are built for large numbers of anonymous clients and because the first concern of the architect must therefore be with their

practical and emotional needs, and not with the expression of his own personality.

It is significant that Pevsner sees only these as alternatives, and does not seem to realise that most people's emotional needs are unlikely to be satisfied in an 'impersonal' building. Bricks and tiles, too, were always 'impersonal' industrially produced materials. But perhaps the 'Style of 1930' is the right term for that kind of anonymous, impersonal office block, where 'practical needs' are paramount. Experience has shown that this industrial building is not satisfactory for houses.

READING:
The Pevsner talk was reprinted in *The listener* (see references under BRUTALISM.
Klaus Jurgen Sembach, *Stil 1930*, translated as *Into the thirties;* the illustrations are almost kitsch nostalgia.

Subtopia (American SLURB) A term given wide currency by Ian Nairn, is his article in the *Architectural review* for June 1955, entitled 'Outrage'. It is not only inter-city mess and neglect, but inappropriate design (rock gardens in city roundabouts) both in towns and in the countryside. The article was followed by a second, 'Counter attack'. Since then there has been, in England, the Civic Amenities Movement, strengthened by law, so that some of the neglect has been stopped. Similar movements have been started in other countries. However, in Britain the emphasis has tended to slip back to preserving 'outstanding works of art', especially when linked to events like European Architectural Heritage Year. Complete examples of certain periods stand a chance of sympathetic handling, but elsewhere the rockeries-on-the-roundabouts are flourishing again. In Nan Fairbrother's books there are photographs taken some fifteen to twenty years after Nairn's, showing many examples of the type of ugliness he was complaining about, especially the callous treatment of trees. Both Nairn's and Fairbrother's work can be linked to the Townscape writers.

EXAMPLES TO SEE:
The edges of most European and American cities seem to be the most neglected, whether it is in neat Holland or rough America. Predictably, Sweden is one of the few Western countries where the problem is least acute.

READING:
Ian Nairn, *Outrage* and *Counter-attack* were both issued as books.
Nan Fairbrother, *New lives, new landscapes* and *The nature of landscape design.*

Townscape Title of a book by Gordon Cullen (1961), but the ideas date from the late 1940's, the time of Thomas Sharp's books on three English towns: *Cathedral city* (Durham), 1945; *Exeter phoenix,* 1946; and *Oxford replanned,* 1948. All fall roughly under the heading of town planning, but unlike planners, the townscape writers start by trying to understand what it is that makes towns attractive, irrespective of shopping facilities, transport, industry, and all the rest, though of course, when it comes to making recommendations, these are given the importance they deserve. The approach is totally different from say, Corbusier's *Voisin Plan* for Paris, which would have involved simply knocking down a large part of the city. Because of the acceptance of what is already there, Townscape as an idea does not find much favour with modern critics (there is a particuarly unfeeling attack by Charles Jencks in *Modern movements in architecture*, chapter 7). The reason for this is not so much the 'indifference towards excellence',which was a common response of most Welfare States,as that the idea of Townscape removes altogether the architect-planner as formgiver. 'Keeping in keeping' is almost the worst thing some critics can say about a modern building which exemplifies the sacrifice of artistic egotism in favour of harmony with its neighbours.

Utility The name for designs (furniture, furnishings and clothing) under Government control in Britain during and after the '39-45 war. The main aim was to save materials, but the opportunity was taken by many designers to make general an attitude to design they had been preaching for many years. Furniture under their leadership, became solid, well-made, with little or no ornament; a kind of Cotswold BAUHAUS style, wholesome but a bit dull. When the time came for restrictions to be lifted, those who could afford to bought 'Scandinavian', and the rest went for High Street Art Deco. Not until the 'ethnic' movement in the late 1960's, fostered by, among others, Conran at Habitat, did a taste for solid, wooden furniture come back into fashion, and this was often traditional in design.

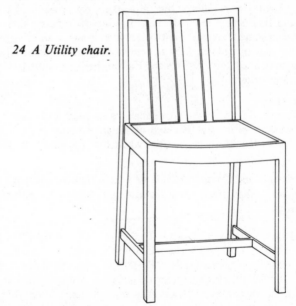

24 A Utility chair.

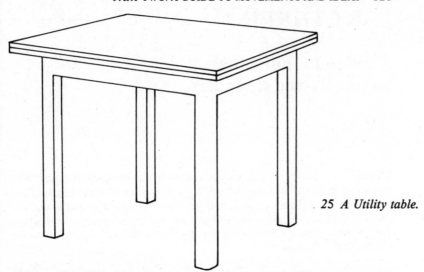

25 A Utility table.

Vienna Secession Viennese artists who 'seceded' from the official
Academy: painters, sculptors, architects and designers. They held exhibitions
of their own, and J.M. Olbrich designed a gallery for them in 1897-8. Much of
the Secession work was influenced, especially in the early years, by
Jugendstil, but some designers notably Hoffman and Otto Wagner, began to
design in a severer style, without reacting as badly to ornament as Loos did.
Mackintosh and Walton exhibited in the Vienna Secession in 1900 and may
have influenced some of the members towards a less exuberant *Jugendstil.*

PART THREE

A guide to individual architects and designers.

This is a list of architects and designers whose work can be seen, together with a note on books and articles on them. Only a selection of works is given, and 'small' crafts — glass, ceramics and jewellery — are not in this list, partly because they are mostly objects of private choice. Large cities, especially capital cities, have museums of 'decorative' or 'industrial' arts, covering the whole range of design.

.Alvar Aalto (1898-1976) Finnish architect and designer, one of those who adapted the INTERNATIONAL MODERN style to Scandinavian culture (by, for example, using natural materials, especially wood). Most of his buildings are in Finland, but in the U.S.A. there is the Baker Hall of Residence at M.I.T. in Cambridge, Mass. (1947) and in Germany the Cultural Centre at Wolfsburg (1959-62). In 1935 Aalto and his wife founded Artek, a company to promote his and other Finn's work. Aalto himself designed bentwood armchairs, stacking stools and glass vases with a 'wave' contour like his wooden ceilings.

READING:
F. Gutheim, *Alvar Aalto;* many photographs of his buildings.
C. Jencks, *Modern movements in architecture.* A section discusses Aalto's work.
Ulf Hård af Segerstad, *Modern Finnish design.*

C.R. Ashbee (1863-1942) English architect and designer, and a leading member of the ARTS & CRAFTS movement. He designed several houses in Chelsea, London, including 37-9 Cheyne Walk. Pieces by him, and made by his GUILD, can be seen in the V. and A.

Gunnar Asplund (1885-1940) Swedish architect. His early work was a 'modern' version of NEO-CLASSICAL, notably his Stockholm City Library of 1924-7. In 1930 he was architect-in-chief for the Stockholm EXHIBITION, and himself designed the café, etc. These Exhibition buildings were the first in an INTERNATIONAL MODERN style which were as attractive to the public as they were to other architects. Asplund himself seems to have worked through the International Modern Style very quickly: his last building, the Stockholm Crematorium Chapels, together with their landscape park (1935-40) is unlike C.I.A.M. or the Bauhaus.

M.H. Baillie-Scott(1865-1945) Best known for the furnishings he did for the Grand Duke of Hesse's palace at Darmstadt in 1895 (often illustrated). The Darmstadt pieces were made by the Guild of Handicrafts. Although coming from the world of Arts and Crafts, the furniture seems to owe much to Art Furniture and the Aesthetic Movement — painting and inlays on flat surfaces with siightly Art-Nouveau patterns. The chairs look particularly uncomfortable.

READING:
James D. Kornwolf, *M.H. Baillie-Scott and the Arts and Crafts Movement.*

Herbert Baker (1862-1946) Outstanding example of the kind of architect patronised by officialdom in the 1920's and 1930's. His designs are in a baroque style,then standard for big official buildings, but his taste seems to have been for something more mannerist — compare Baker's South Africa House (1935; he had spent many years in South Africa) on one side of Trafalgar Square with Aston Webb's Admirality Arch(1911) on the other — a more satisfying design. Baker rebuilt the Bank of England over the years 1921-37, destroying most of Soane's work, and boldy displaying his competence for everyone to see, where Soane had hidden his genius behind a screen wall (left by Baker as a ground floor for his building). Baker's most interesting work in England is perhaps his Rhodes House in Oxford(1929): a 'cotswold' manor house, with the Baker model of Bramante's domed Tempietto in the front courtyard. Baker designed several houses in Cape Province, South Africa.

Charles Barry(1795-1860). See ECLECTIC for a list of some of his buildings. Barry was not committed to any of the architectural dogmas fashionable in his lifetime. He is a good example of the 19th century professional architect, with a large office, pupils and assistants to cope with the many commissions he undertook. The largest of these was the new Palace of Westminster for the Houses of Parliament, which was built during the last 20 years of his life. His work has always been loved and cherished, so that a surprising number of his buildings are still standing. The work of many more original architects, contemporaries of Barry, has not been so well cared for. Most of Soane's remarkable buildings were allowed to be pulled down without much protest.

READING:
H-R. Hitchcock, *Early Victorian architecture in Britain.*
P. Fleetwood-Hesketh, 'Barry' in P. Ferriday (ed), *Victorian architecture.*

George Basevi (1794-1845) A pupil of Soane and later surveyor of Ely cathedral, where he fell to his death from a tower. A designer in the NEO-CLASSICAL style and interesting for two reasons: (1) his Fitzwilliam Museum in Cambridge, England, while broadly neo-classical in detail has an overall baroque quality. It was built in 1836-48, at the same time as Smirke's south front of the British Museum, which also uses neo-classical detail in a baroque way. Both buildings are examples of the return to baroque from neo-classical for public buildings; (2) Basevi designed several terraces of houses in Kensington, London, — Pelham Crescent (1840), Sydney Place, Thurloe Square (1843) — in a style which is still that of the Regency, and is like the late-Regency terraces in Brighton being built at the same time: white or cream painted stucco, with classical proportions and classical details confined to cornice and portico.

Peter Behrens (1868-1940) German architect and designer, one of the founders of the DEUTSCHE WERKBUND. In 1899 he joined a group of designers in Darmstadt where (in 1901) he designed a house for himself. In 1907 (the year the *Werkbund* was founded) he was appointed architect and consultant to A.E.G. (General Electric Co.) for whom he designed electrical goods in an elegant, plain — almost classical — style. His architecture is in the style of the NEO-CLASSICAL revival of the early 20th century. His A.E.G. turbine factory of 1909 is like a Roman temple (so much less 'modern' than, for example, the iron frame factories and warehouses of the early 19th century, that it is surprising that so many books include it as a modern 'pioneer'). Behrens designed the new German Embassy building for St. Petersburg (Leningrad) in 1911-12 to fit in well with its neo-classical neighbours. Behrens's work is a good example of the irrelevance of style'; what is more important is his contribution to the development of mass-production, for which Behrens's neo-classical is every much as appropriate as the later Bauhaus's De Stijl angularity.

READING:
R. Banham, *Theory and design in the first machine age;* and the same author's *Architecture of the well-tempered environment* discusses the question of 'appropriate style' and function.

J.H. Belter (1804-63) German immigrant furniture-maker in New York from 1844. His work is in the same vein as ART FURNITURE, and is a florid version of the mid-19th century revival of rococo — Biedermeyer-rococo, perhaps. There are examples of his work in the Metropolitan Museum in New York.

J.F. Bentley (1839-1902) English church architect. A Catholic convert, he designed most of his buildings for them. Although Gothic Revival was never a very popular style with Catholics (even in England, and in spite of A.W.N. Pugin), Bentley's early designs were Gothic. However, his best known design is that for the cathedral for the new Roman Catholic diocese of Westminster (1895-1903). It was built in the same way as cathedrals were built in the Middle Ages, and in a Byzantine style which is also not unlike the 'Rundbogenstil' variety of Italian romanesque as at St. Mary, Wilton of 1842-3. Although iron had been used in many otherwise traditional buildings in the 19th century (e.g. in the King's Library of the British Museum in 1823), Bentley did not use it in the construction of Westminster Cathedral: he called it 'that curse of modern construction'. The Cathedral now faces a new piazza open to Victoria Street.

READING:

There is a very good description of Westminster Cathedral in Nikolaus Pevsner's *London: the cities of London & Westminster* in the 'Buildings of England' series.

H.P. Berlage(1856-1934) Dutch architect: the Amsterdam Stock Exchange is his best-known building — see EXPRESSIONISM. He also designed some Insurance offices in Holland and an office block in the City of London, 23, Bury Street (1914).

Samuel Bing(1838-1919) He opened a shop in the Rue de Provence in Paris, France, in 1895 called L'Art Nouveau, selling goods designed in the style which then took its name from the shop. Bing was a Hamburg art dealer who had already travelled all over the world, first to Paris in 1871 and then to the Far East in 1875, after which he opened a shop back in Paris, *La Porte Chinoise*. This had a branch in New York, and Bing travelled to the U.S.A. in 1893 on behalf of the French Government. Impressed by the work of Richardson and Sullivan, he wrote *Artistic America* on his return.

READING:

Artistic America has recently been reissued, together with other essays, edited by R. Koch.

G.F. Bodley(1827-1907) A good example of a Gothic Revival architect in the later phases of the movement when commissions in a Gothic style were for churches and little else. The influence of the Ecclesiological Society, with its emphasis on historical correctness, had waned, and architects were freer to 'develop' Gothic. Some of the best examples of this 'development' are the churches designed by Bodley and his partner (from 1869),Thomas Garner (1839-1906): Holy Angels, Hoar Cross, Staffordshire (1871) and (in 1871-4) St. Augustine, Pendelbury, Lancashire — about five miles north-west of Manchester. On his own, Bodley designed Clumber Church, Nottinghamshire in 1886 and the chapel of Queens' College, Cambridge in 1890.

Marcel Breuer (b.1902) Educated at the Bauhaus from 1920; in charge of joinery and cabinet workshop there from 1925. He designed a very successful version of Mart Stam's cantilevered steel chair; Breuer's has a cane seat and back and is still in production. Breuer was a partner with Gropius in America from 1937 to 1940. Architect of UNESCO Secretariat in Paris, and St. John's Monastery at Collegeville, Minn. (both in 1953); the new De Bijenkorp store in Rotterdam (1953-7), and the U.S. Embassy in the Hague. Most of his buildings are in a standard International Modern Style, but the belfry of St. John's Monastery has a grand sculptural form which Peter Collins sees as a development from furniture forms.

READING:

P. Collins, *Changing ideals in modern architecture.*

P. Blake, *Marcel Breuer, architect and designer.*

Cuthbert Brodrick (1822-1905) English architect, most of whose work is in Yorkshire, and is an outstanding example of mid-19th century baroque. Leeds Town Hall, 1853-8 is the most famous, and he also designed the Leeds Corn Exchange (1861-3). Both these buildings are in an exhilarating baroque style. The Grand Hotel at Scarborough of 1863-7 is in a more 'Second Empire' variety of baroque, like a secular Melk perched on a cliff overlooking the sea.

James Brooks (1825-1901) English Gothic Revival architect, and so a designer almost solely of churches. His buildings tend towards the 'noble austere' rather than the 'rich ornamental' late Gothic Revival — like Pearson's buildings, unlike Burges's. Amongst Brooks's fine churches are a group in London — Ascension, Lavender Hill, near Clapham Junction (1874); Transfiguration, Lewisham (1880); and All Hallows, Gospel Oak (1889). None of these are dedicated to a saint — an interesting late-Gothic-Revival habit.

Isambard Kingdom Brunel (1806-59) An archetype of engineering genius and drive, though not included by Samuel Smiles in *Self help* as a model for the ambitious young, because Brunel was not self-made, being the son of the emigré French engineer who designed the Rotherhithe tunnel under the Thames. I.K. Brunel's greatest monument is the Great Western Railway (now British Rail, Western Region), with its bridges and tunnels, Paddington Station and Bristol Temple Meads Station. The *Great Britain*, now being restored in its dock in Bristol, was an extension even further westwards, to America. Among Brunel's bridges are the railway bridge at Saltash and the road bridge across the Avon gorge below Bristol — the Clifton Suspension Bridge. This was intended by Brunel to have Egyptian decoration on the towers holding the chains — they are in the shape of pylons (gateways) of Egyptian temples; however money ran out and they were left plain.

READING:

L.T.C. Rolt, *Isambard Kingdom Brunel.*
H-R. Hitchcock, *Early Victorian architecture in England.*

Colin Buchanan (b.1907) His report *Traffic in towns* (1963) was a very great influence on town-planning, and especially road-planning, for the next ten years. Many ring roads were planned, if not always built, in pursuance of the idea of separating through-traffic from local traffic. This had been argued before, but Buchanan gave many practical examples in his book. The oil crisis and fears about pollution have recently undermined one of Buchanan's main points — that the private automobile is the inevitable as well as the uniquely convenient means of transport. Perhaps his most lasting minor contribution is the classification of roads in the centre of cities by their function, so that if it is decided that a road's main function is shopping, then traffic is restricted — as in Oxford Street in London; or if the road's main function is through-traffic, then other functions are restricted — as with Gower Street, London.

READING:
The original Buchanan Report was published by H.M.S.O. in 1963; a shortened version, *Traffic in towns*, intended for the general public, was published by Penguins in 1964.

William Burges (1827-81) English Gothic Revival architect; an individualist, but also an early example of one of the trends of the later Gothic Revival — rich decoration. Burges designed interiors for Lord Bute in Cardiff Castle (1865) and Castel Coch nearby (almost rebuilt, as Viollet-le-Duc had 'realised' the Chateau of Pierrefonds in 1858-79), completed c1875. Burges's churches were very ornate: Cork Cathedral, Ireland (1862-76) and Studley Royal Church in Yorkshire (1871-8). His work for academics included the Harrow School Speech Room in 1872, and designs for Trinity College, Hartford, Conn., in 1873, part of which was built (1880). He designed his own house at 9, Melbury Road, Kensington (1875-80) and Knightshayes Court in Devon, now owned by the National Trust; built in 1870-3 and furnished by the firm J.D. Crace. Burges's work seems to have a similar relationship to his native Gothic as Gaudí's had to his; both architects seem forerunners of Expressionism.

READING:
Charles Handley-Read, 'Burges' in P. Ferriday (ed.), *Victorian architecture*.

D.H. Burnham (1846-1912) and **J.W. Root** (1850-91) Architectural partnership of the CHICAGO SCHOOL. Their best known buildings are : Rookery Building (1886); St. Gabriel's Church, (4501 South Lowe (1887); Monadnock Building (1891). The Reliance Building was begun to Root's design in 1890; the foundations and first storey being built *underneath* an existing four-storey building; this was taken off in 1894, and thirteen further storeys (steel-frame) were added to the design of Charles Attwood, of what had now become D.H. Burnham & Co. Burnham himself also designed the Flatiron Building in New York (1902) and was consultant for Selfridge's department store in London (begun 1908). He drew up a grandiose master plan for Chicago, mostly unrealized, but influential on the designs of parks and boulevards.

READING:
See CHICAGO SCHOOL.

Decimus Burton (1800-81) Like Charles Barry, he was a professional architect with a huge practice, but unlike Barry, Burton kept mostly to a refined neo-classical style. Colvin lists 83 private houses by Burton in the *Biographical dictionary*. Among his public buildings are: Hyde Park Screen and Constitution Arch (1825); the Athenaeum Club (1829-30); Charing Cross Hospital (1831-4) — altered in the 1870's; The Palm House in Kew

128 A CHOICE OVER OUR HEADS

Gardens (1844-8, with Richard Turner of Dublin as engineer). Among his housing estates are: Claverley Estate, Tunbridge Wells (1828 onwards); Adelaide Crescent, Hove, Sussex (1830-34). He designed whole towns, too: St. Leonard's-on-Sea, Hastings, Sussex (1828 onwards), and Fleetwood, Lancashire (1835 onwards).

William Butterfield (1814-1900) An architect who attracted a great deal of hero-worship in his lifetime (Philip Webb seems to have spoken of him in awed tones), but whose work has been regarded by many people since his death as an interesting monstrosity. Christopher Hobhouse's comments on Keble in his *Oxford* (1939) — mild compared with his remarks on Balliol — are typical — 'Butterfield's choice of materials is unspeakable' — 'Only a crank could like his work, but it is a mistake not to admire it.' Keble College was built in 1867-75, and is characteristic Butterfield, with Jacobean blue brick diapering patterns on red brick facades. The chapel is very high, and its grandeur is cancelled out by the bright colours, inside and out, of the surface decoration. It is interesting to compare the Keble chapel with the church of St. Alban, Holborn, London, designed by Butterfield in 1863. It was bombed in the 1939-45 war, and has been rebuilt with little of Butterfield's original decoration. The result is a superb interior, austere and moving, worthy of the imposing exterior. A further contrast can be made with a complete Butterfield church, All Saints', Margaret St., London (a block north of the eastern half of Oxford St.), built and decorated in 1849-59, an exemplar of what Butterfield, and the Ecclesiological Society who admired his work — and his upright character too — thought a church should be — a dazzle of competing bright colours and gold inside, half obscured by the clouds of incense. The exterior, and the clergy houses, that flank the church are not in medieval stone, but in diapered brick — the houses being Jacobean in style, with sash windows — a characteristic eclectic touch in Butterfield's work. This can also be seen in his house,s like the vicarage of Coalpitheath north of Bristol (1844), the grandfather of all later Victorian large upper-middle-class houses, especially those of Philip Webb. Fittingly, Butterfield designed the buildings of Rugby School in Warwickshire (1870-86).

READING:
Paul Thompson, *William Butterfield;* a massive, definitive work.
H-R. Hitchcock, *Architecture, 19th and 20th centuries.*

Chamberlain, Powell and Bon A leading British architectural firm in the twenty years after 1945; they have since then broken up into other partnerships, and Chamberlain has died (1978). Their work was basically in a moderate International Modern style, but often with quirky (and frowned upon by the orthodox) details. In the Golden Lane Housing Estate north of Smithfield in London, begun in 1952, the water tank on top of the highest slab of flats was given projecting, curved wind baffles, so that from afar it looks like a large gondola sitting on top of the building. Corbusier's hanging concrete arches were used in some of the later blocks, including the attractive curved facade to the main road. New Hall, Cambridge, England, begun in 1960, is one of their most notable academic buildings.

Wells Coates (1895-1958) A Canadian architect who practised in England from the 1930's until the 1950's. He was chairman of M.A.R.S. in April 1933 and their delegate to the C.I.A.M. meeting which produced the 'Athens Charter' in that year — a manifesto for housing. Coates was most respected for his design of the Lawn Road Flats in Hampstead, London, which were built in 1933-5, an early example of the International Modern style in England. Anthony Jackson, in *The politics of architecture*, reminds us that Cyril Connolly's *Horizon* awarded the Lawn Road Flats second prize in 1946 in a competition for ugly buildings. Apart from the heaviness of the design, the Flats were finished in cement which needs repainting every year to keep the intention of the design; Lawn Road had no doubt not been painted for many years. Coates was the designer of the theatre in the South Bank Exhibition in London in 1951 (since demolished along with most of the other Exhibition buildings). After 1951, Coates went back to Canada.

READING:
Anthony Jackson, *The politics of architecture.*

T. J. Cobden-Sanderson (1840-1922) A disciple of William Morris. Cobden-Sanderson was a barrister, but left the law for crafts. He became a book-binder in 1884, and founded the Doves Press. His work is characterized by limp parchment covers with gold patterns, much imitated in the decades before the First World War.

READING:
F.B. Adams edited the catalogue for an exhibition of the work in New York in 1968 — *Bookbindings by T.J. Cobden-Sanderson.*

C.R. Cockerell (1788-1863) The outstanding classical architect in England in the 19th century. Unlike Soane, Cockerell was content to design with a more conventional classical vocabulary, but like Decimus Burton, he adapted the classical proportions to the needs of office blocks, using 'Italian' features — heavy bracket-supported eaves, for example — to swell the number of motifs available to him. Among the buildings he designed which are nearest to a neo-classical style are the Ashmolean Museum and Taylorean Institute in Oxford (1841-5) and the Cambridge University Library (1837-40; now the Squire Law Library). His design for the new Royal Exchange is often illustrated and seems now to be a better design than the one that was built. Cockerell was architect to the Bank of England (which had been Soane's job, during which he rebuilt the London Bank), and designed several of its branch offices — Plymouth (1835), Bristol (1844), Liverpool (1845-8) and Manchester (1845-6). His Sun Insurance Building (1863) at the corner of Threadneedle St. and Bartholomew St. was a remarkable example of a classical Italian style adapted for an office block, with the corner particularly satisfying. It was altered in the 19th century, and demolished in the 1960's to make way for the new Stock Exchange. Cockerell was Professor of Architecture at the Royal Academy and one of the main targets of Gothic Revival hatred.

READING:
David Watkin, *Charles Robert Cockerell.*
E.M. Dodd, 'C.R. Cockerell' in P. Ferriday (ed.), *Victorian architecture.*

Henry Cole (1808-82) A British bureaucrat whose great influence over 19th century British design has been acknowledged only in recent years; he is not mentioned in, for example, Woodward's *Age of reform,* in the Oxford *History of England,* even in the second edition of 1961. Cole became interested in design, and won a competition for a tea set, using the pseudonym Christopher Summerley. As with much 'reforming' design of the 19th century, Cole/Summerley's crockery is clumsy when compared with 18th century tableware. Cole ran a firm, Summerley's Art Manufacture, from 1847 to 1850, and commissioned designs from painters, John Linnell, Richard Redgrave among them. Cole was active in the Society of Arts and worked with Prince Albert to put on the Great Exhibition of 1851. Then he was much involved in the Government Schools of Design controversies. He was first director of what was to become the Victoria and Albert Museum, and in the 1860's active in the plans for the Royal Albert Hall.

READING:
Cole wrote his own account, *Fifty years of public work.*
John Steegman, *Consort of taste.*
Quentin Bell, *Schools of design.*

'Le Corbusier' (Charles-Edouard Jeanneret-Gris) (1887-1966) The artist-hero of the Modern Movement, and the most influential of its architects; when he changed style, so did all the others. His books, *Vers une architecture* (1923) and *Urbanisme* (1925) were translated a few years later into English by Frederick Etchells, and are worth reading as a jumble of declamatory *non-sequiturs,* poetic insights and outright nonsense. Architects have delighted in his arrogance.

Although the whole range of his work is foreshadowed in his manifestoes of early years, the buildings fall roughly into three successive groups:— smooth-surfaced, 'machine' small houses; tall slabs standing over free-form podiums; and sculptural, reinforced concrete monuments. The early, 'machine' Corbusier was mostly private houses. The Villa Savoye at Poissy (1929) has been restored as a national monument.

Middle period Corbusier can be seen in the Swiss House in the Cité Universitaire in the south of Paris, France, and in the U.N. Secretariat and Assembly Hall in New York, for which he was consultant (1930-2, and 1947 respectively). In both these buildings, the 'repetitive' sections of the buildings — students' rooms, offices — are enclosed in a smooth 'glass box', while the 'exceptional' sections — common room, assembly hall — are in a free-form, rough-finished group of shapes. This differentiation of function and form had, of course been foreshadowed by Sullivan in, for example, the Carson Pirie Scott store, Chicago, of *c* 1900.

Late Corbusier has the almost purely sculptural religious buildings, the pilgrimage chapel at Ronchamp (1950-4), and the Monastery of La Tourette (1957-60), now abandoned by the friars; the huge concrete blocks, like the Unités d'Habitation at Marseilles (1947-52), and elsewhere, and the Law Courts at Chandigarh (1951-6) where the function — flats or courtrooms and office — is now all contained in one sculptured concrete-finished block (unlike the middle-period). His Jaoul Houses (private villas) of 1954-6 had shallow concrete arches in their facades, and these were imitated very quickly.

Corbusier did not confine his plans to buildings, but proposed designs for cities as well, partly influenced by the proposals of Tony Garnier. Plans for Algiers and Paris (Voisin Plan) were early examples, which would have meant destroying large parts of these towns. Corbusier claimed kinship with the minds of the past, but only with the minds of past *artists*; the accumulated experience and treasures of ordinary people must fall in his schemes before the vision of the artist. The one city Corbusier did plan and partly carry out was the new city of Chandigarh in India. The monumental buildings which he also designed (see above) are dramatic, but the city plan is bad in a very elementary way — the lowest-paid workers in the monumental complex have the furthest to go to work from their homes, etc.

READING:
Since Corbusier can easily be made out to be 'the great artist', his work has attracted a huge adulatory literature. Amongst the most sycophantic are:
P. Blake in *The master builders*; the section on Corbusier was issued separately by Pelican.
Charles Jencks, *Modern Movements in architecture*.

Lucio Costa (b.1902) The Brazilian architect and planner who won the competition for the new capital city of Brazil, Brasilia, in 1957. The plan is like a symbolic bird, with the government offices and Presidential Palace at the head, a grand avenue forming the 'backbone', etc. Like many such plans, the overall symbolism necessitates much of the detailed architecture to be monotonous so that it does not detract from the overall idea. The two houses of the Brazilian congress are designed (by Niemeyer) as a domed shape and a saucer shape, complementary. Much care has gone into this democratic symbolism. It is interesting that, since Brasilia was built, Brazil has become a military dictatorship.

Walter Crane (1845-1915) English artist. A good example of the restrained, English arts-and-crafts variety of Art Nouveau — compare his line illustrations with Beardsley's. He designed many children's books, wallpapers and ceramics; and several socialist posters around 1900.

Many of his books are being reproduced, in the current revival of the the Aesthetic and Art-Nouveau movements; and for reading, there is Isobel Spencer's *Walter Crane*.

W.H. Crossland (?1823-1909) was probably the architect for Ackroyden (see GARDEN CITIES) in Yorkshire in the 1850's. He designed Rochdale Town Hall in a Gothic style (1866-71), but is better known for the two buildings he designed in north-west Surrey for the industrialist Thomas Holloway, founder of the Royal Holloway College (built 1879-87) and the Holloway Sanatorium (1884). The College is one of the most remarkable of Victorian buildings, a huge (550 by 376 feet) paraphrase of Chambord, Francois I's palace on the Loire, but built in 'Queen Anne' materials — red brick and white stone. The Sanatorium is in a Flemish late-Gothic style (Bruges/Ypres). Both are near Egham, Surrey; the College fronts the A.30 road, and its picture gallery is sometimes open.

READING:
Very little: H-R. Hitchcock in *Early Victorian architecture* has a few paragraphs about Copley and Ackroyden.

P.J.H. Cuijpers (1827-1911) Dutch architect, the equivalent of the 'second generation' of English Gothic Revivalists, who used Gothic for churches only. Cuijpers designed many churches in the Netherlands Gothic style (similar to Perp.), especially in Amsterdam: Sacred Heart (Vondelkerk, near the Vondel Park) in 1873-80, and the Maria Magdalenakerk, outside the Haarlemerpoort, and near the Eigen Haard housing estate, in 1887. For his public buildings, however, Cuijpers revived another Netherlands style, the Renascence style of architects like Lieven de Key (who designed the Meat Hall in Haarlem, next to the Groote Kerk). Two of Amsterdam's grandest 19th century monuments were built to Cuijper's Renascence designs — the Rijksmuseum in 1877-85 and the Central Station in 1881-9.

John Darbourne and **Geoffrey Darke** English architectural partnership which has won many awards for housing estates. Their buildings are outstanding examples of a new 'humane' design, in reaction to the art-work of Corbusier and his followers. The use of brick in pleasant colours; the smaller scale, grouping and landscaping of the apartment blocks have all been welcomed. One of their earliest successes was the Lillington Gardens estate, on the west side of Vauxhall Bridge Road, London (1964-72, in three phases). They have also designed: housing estate in Marquess Road, Islington (begun 1970), housing in Camden Road, Holloway (1971-3), housing at Pershore in Worcestershire (1973-5), the East Stand of Chelsea Football Ground, London (1972-4), Children's Day Centre, Eddington Road, Islington (1974-5).

READING:
The architecture of Darbourne and Darke, R.I.B.A. Publications, 1977.

Alexander Jackson Davis (1803-1902) designed many State Capitols, and Colonnade Row, Lafayette St., New York City (1832), all in a Greek Revival style (see NEO-CLASSICISM), of which Davis was one of the best exponents.

He also designed a number of gothick villas, in partnership with Ithiel Town.

Wilhelm van Debschitz(1871-1948) A disciple of William Morris. He was an officer in the Prussian army who resigned to take up painting. Then, influenced by Morris's example, he turned to the crafts. He founded an arts-and-crafts school with Obrist in Munich in 1902. Work by him can be seen in German museums (e.g. Stuttgart).

Andrew Jackson Downing (1815-1852) American architect who was a publicist for the picturesque in architecture, gardens and planning. He was influenced by J.C. Loudon, the leading English exponent of the picturesque in the 1830's. Downing published *Landscape gardening* in 1841, *Cottage residences* in 1842, *Buildings in the country* in 1849 and *Architecture of country houses* in 1850. All these were widely read in America, and served as pattern books, much as their 18th century predecessors had done. Downing's influence lasted until the last quarter of the 19th century.

Christopher Dresser (1834-1904) A botanist, after training in a school of design. He travelled to Japan in 1872 (less than 20 years after the country opened its doors to Western visitors, but at a time when Japanese design was strongly influencing the Aesthetic Movement in England and elsewhere). Dresser, too, was much influenced by Japanese design. He published *Principles of design* in 1872, an early example of its kind. There are examples of his work in the V. and A. and in other museums. There was an exhibition of his work at the Fine Art Society in London in 1972, and the *Catalogue* of that exhibition is by R. Dennis and J. Jesse.

Henry Dreyfus (1904-72) American industrial designer, author of *Designing for people* (1955) and *Industrial design: a pictorial record* (1957), both of which were written for a wider public than his professional colleagues. Dreyfus himself is best known for this telephone designs for the Bell Company, especially 'Model 500', which has been much imitated throughout the world. His designs are good examples of undogmatic 'functionalism' — related to the Bauhaus, but without that school's extremism.

W.M. Dudok(b.1884) Dutch architect, city architect for Hilversum, where he designed a number of buildings, including the Town Hall (1928-30). Double influences on him from the work of Frank Lloyd Wright and of De Stijl, and he in turn influenced Charles Holden and other architects in England in the 1930's. His (and his followers') buildings are composed of tastefully arranged interlocking brick cubes with a sparing use of long bands of low windows. The use of brick in the 1920's was exceptional in an architect sympathetic with C.I.A.M. and undoubtedly designing in a variety of the International Modern style. As fashion has turned away from the smooth stucco surfaces of C.I.A.M. and even from the rough concrete surfaces of late Corbusier, the brick finish of Dudok's buildings has come back into favour, and is acceptable to the orthodox because of Dudok's links with De Stijl. Dudok's sparing use of windows is not yet back in fashion, but fuel costs may help that too.

Charles Eames (1907-78) American architect and designer. His own house at Santa Monica was built in 1949 from standard industrial components, and is the subject of a film, *House,* which gives a tantalising picture of the building. The film is spoiled by being put together from still photographs, none of them held long enough for a good look. The house looks Miesian, but much more imaginative in its arrangement of interior space than Mies's Tugendhat or Farnsworth houses — Eames's house has a double-height central hall. The house is surrounded by trees, which add a lot to its charm. Unlike Philip Johnson's own house at New Canaan, the Santa Monica house has walls only partially of glass, which therefore give a more interesting picture of the world outside.

Eames is world-famous for his much imitated chair designs, particularly a polyester/fibreglass shell resting on steel legs, and an armchair in bent rosewood and black cushions with a footstool to match, which is luxurious, even if it looks like a dentist's chair.

Charles Eastlake (1836-1906) Namesake and nephew of the President of the Royal Academy, the younger Eastlake was a designer and publicist for architecture and interior design. His books were widely read, especially *Hints on household taste,* first published in 1868, and often reissued in his lifetime. Eastlake was probably more responsible than anyone for the overcrowded late 19th century middle class interiors in England (and elsewhere). His overmantel with shelves was meant for a 'drawing-room museum'.

READING:
Charles Eastlake, *The Gothic revival in England* (edited by J. M. Crook), *Hints on household taste* (edited by J. Gloag).

Egon Eiermann (b.1904) German architect, who designed the German pavilion at the Brussels Expo 58, the rebuilt Kaiser-Wilhelm Gedächtnis-kirche in Berlin, 1959-62, and the German Embassy in Washington, D.C., in 1961-3. His style is the development of International Modern which emphasises whole walls composed of sheets of glass — an exaggeration of the 'structure' aesthetic.

Gustave Eiffel (1832-1923) Apart from his tower (for the Paris International Exhibition of 1889), he was a bridge builder: Douro, 1876-7; Garebit, 1880-4.

Harvey Lonsdale Elmes (1813-47) His major work was the St. George's Hall, Liverpool, the result of combining his winning designs in competitions for a concert hall (1839) and an assize court (1840). Liverpool Corporation decided to amalgamate the buildings, and Elmes made fresh plans which were agreed in 1841. After Elmes's death, the hall was completed by C. R. Cockerell (many of the interiors are his), with R. Rawlinson as engineer. The Hall was finished in 1856. Elmes had travelled in Germany and seen the work of Schinkel in Berlin and von Klenze in Munich. His own building is the crown of the Neo-classical Movement.

G.J. Frampton(1860-1928) Sculptor and designer of silverware. His work is in the spirit of the arts and crafts, and there are examples of it in the V. and A.

Maxwell Fry(b.1899) His early work was either classical, as in the plan for Birmingham Civic Centre (1927), and Kelmerly Village Club House, Kent (1929), or 'cottage vernacular', as in Ridge End, a house in Wentworth, Surrey (1930). Then he was converted to the International Modern style, to which he has remained faithful, on the Miesian side. His early work in London included blocks of workers' flats — Sassoon House in Peckham (1934) and Kensal House, Ladbrook Grove, Paddington (1936), which has a kindergarten and community rooms designed in a half circle in the place of a former gasometer, overlooking the G.W.R. line from Paddington. In the style of Corbusier's early period, Fry designed Sun House in Frognal Way, Hampstead (1936) and a private house in Kingston, Surrey, both of which are among the finest of their type. Fry was Gropius's partner in England in 1934-6 and they designed a house in Church St., Chelsea, and Impington Village College in Cambridgeshire (completed 1938). Previous village colleges commissioned by the Cambridgeshire council had been rambling buildings in a neo-Wren style; Impington is in a *rambling* International Modern style, quite unlike Gropius's own Bauhaus of ten years earlier, but more like his Harvard buildings of a few years later.

After 1945, Fry, Drew and partners designed housing at Chandigarh, Corbusier's new city in India, in 1951-4; a restaurant in the South Bank Exhibition (1951); several buildings for Ibadan University in Nigeria (1947-61), and the Co-op Bank there; and their most distinguished post-war building, the Pilkington glass works at St. Helen's, Lancashire (begun 1956), where the Miesian, Skidmore-Owings-and-Merril style, all walls made of glass panels, seems for once quite appropriate.

READING:
M. Fry, *Fine building*. Published in 1944, it gives an interesting picture of architecture and design ideas in wartime England.

Richard Buckminster Fuller (b.1895) An American inventor who has become one of the gurus of young designers. He pioneered the geodesic dome as a simple, and relatively cheap, method of covering large areas (he proposed it to cover cities too). It has been used for sports arenas in the U.S.A. and as the basis of the design of the U.S. pavilion at the Montreal Expo 67. Fuller's designs for houses (e.g. the Wichita and the Dymaxion) were really too much like engineering for the taste of the International Modern Movement, until the 1960's, when space technology, the film *2001*, the 'daring' work of groups like Archigram, and the craze of young architects for designing 'pods' made Fuller's designs suddenly seem fashionable, even conservative. The Geodesic Dome is the '20th century's' Crystal Palace: good for covering a large space, but perhaps for not much else, although on a small scale useful for greenhouses, and a hazard in children's playgrounds when used as a climbing frame.

Tony Garnier (1869-1948) One of the earliest of 20th century architects who thought that because some people have to work in factories, everyone should live in a city which looks as though it came off the assembly line. During the years 1899-1904 he worked on a plan for a *Cité Industrielle*: all buildings of concrete and unmistakably industrial. Garnier was appointed city architect for Lyons in 1905 (the newly elected Socialist mayor was an admirer), and designed the city's slaughter-house (1908-19) and the stadium (1913-16). Both these are massive buildings in exposed concrete, and interesting as examples of 'engineering' architecture, which were an inspiration for Corbusier and others.

Antoni Gaudí (1852-1926) A near contemporary of Lethaby, Sullivan, McKim Mead and White, Ebenezer Howard, Geddes, Holabird, and Roche, Harrison Townsend and George Jack; an individualist generation. His work is all in or near Barcelona: apartment blocks — Casa Milá and Casa Battló, both 1905; the Parque Güell, begun 1904 (concrete walls and seats with broken crockery pressed into the concrete while still wet — a bright idea for a public park); the church of the Holy Family, begun 1884 (crypt), 1891 (transepts), 1903 (transept towers), and unfinished at Gaudí's death, it is now being built from his drawings. Outside Barcelona is the chapel of Sta Colomá de Cervelló, with its unexpected but quite functional pillars. Although there has been a great revival in interest in Gaudí and his designs in the last dozen years, it is hard to see whether he is having any influence; he remains unique.

READING:
G. Collins, *Antonio Gaudí.*
J.Ll. Sert. *Antoni Gaudí.*
Nikolaus Pevsner and J.M. Richards (eds.), *The anti-rationalists;* it has an essay on Catalan contemporaries of Gaudí.

Patrick Geddes (1854-1932) A scientist turned planner, and almost the only non-designer to have had a great influence on architecture in this century — another is his near contemporary Howard. Geddes was Professor of Botany at Dundee from 1889 to 1918, and Professor of Sociology at Bombay from 1920 to 1923. He published *City development* in 1904 and *Cities in evolution* in 1915, which had an influence on Lewis Mumford. Geddes thus stands at the head of the large and distinguished modern discussion of the nature of cities since the Industrial Revolution, which has had to revise so many ideas on 'the city' based on Athens, Florence or Bath. Geddes coined the term 'conurbation'.

Frederick Gibberd (b.1908) His early work was in the International Modern style, like Fry's in the 1930's. Gibberd designed Pulman Court Flats, Streatham Hill in London in 1934-5. After the war he popularised a blend of tradition (brick, low-rise buildings, garden-city layouts) with modernism (horizontal windows, some tower blocks — it is these which distinguish him from the Dudok tradition), which became standard, especially for British local authority housing and some of the new towns. This blend lasted until the mid-'60's, and the influence of Spain. Some examples of this Gibberd style are: Lansbury Estate, Poplar (for the Festival of Britain), 1951; Harlow New Town in Essex — layout and some of the buildings, 1948 onwards; London Airport (Heathrow), 1950 onwards. In a quite different style, Gibberd is the designer of Liverpool Roman Catholic Cathedral (competition won in 1960), built 1962-7, where the funnel-shaped concrete framework owes more to the work of engineer-architects (Nervi and others) than to English tradition.

E.W. Gimson (1864-1919) Arts and crafts furniture designer. He founded a firm, Kenton and Co., in partnership with Sidney and Ernest Barnsley and W.R. Lethaby, designing and making furniture. In 1895 Gimson and the Barnsleys moved to Sappington, Gloucestershire, beginning a general movement of arts and crafts designers into the Cotswolds. Leicester Museum and Art Gallery has a permanent exhibition of Gimson's work, since Leicester was his home town. The furniture is characteristic of the 'cotswold classical' that the Arts and Crafts favoured: designs not so rigid that they excluded cabinet-maker's invention — inlays are important in this.

E.W. Godwin (1833-1886) Architect and designer. As an architect he designed Northampton Town Hall in 1860-4 in a Ruskinian Venetian Gothic style — a large commission for so young an architect. Later, he designed a number of houses in Tite Street, Chelsea, London, in what was intended to become an artistic, if not an artists' quarter: No 35, the White House, for Whistler (who had to sell it almost straight away to pay for the costs of his libel action against Ruskin); nos. 29 and 33; no. 44 (1880) and the Tower House (1885). Godwin was one of those architects who took the lead in designing Art Furniture and was partly influenced by Japanese design, one of the main influences in the Aesthetic Movement. Godwin and Ellen Terry were the parents (in 1872) of Edward Gordon Craig, the theatre designer.

Charles Sumner Greene (1868-1957) and his brother **Henry Mather Greene)** (1870-1954) were American architects and furniture designers, best known for their very luxurious houses in California, of which the Gamble House in Pasadena of 1908-9 is the richest. It is now owned by the University of California and used as a guest house, preserved also as a kind of museum. The Greenes, like F.L. Wright, admired Japanese design and craftsmanship; the Greenes also admired the crafts of China. Their houses are related to the 'Stick style' — wooden, verandah'd houses, in more or less Second Empire style, popular in Rhode Island in the 1870's. The Gamble house, however, if freer in its motifs, seems to owe as much to Swiss Chalets as it does to France — but most to the Greene's invention.

READING:
H-R. Hitchcock, *Architecture, 19th and 20th centuries*, chapters 15 and 19.

Hector Guimard (1867-1942) French architect in the late 19th century. His buildings are famous for their Art Nouveau ironwork, as on the Castel Béranger apartment block in the Rue de la Fontaine of 1894-8. Even more famous are the Métro station entrances, some of the finest examples of architectural Art Nouveau ironwork, entirely appropriate to their function, but also graceful and charming. They date from 1899-1904.

Walter Gropius (1882-1969) see BAUHAUS, etc. Gropius's work falls roughly into four phases —
1 before 1914: a mixture of neo-classical and factory functionalism — an apparent preview of the Bauhaus, and seen in his Fagus factory at Ahlfeld, 1911, and in the *Deutsche Werkbund* Exhibition factory offices at Cologne in 1914.
2 1919-23: Expressionism — the Monument to the March dead of 1919, and projects for houses.
3 Having attacked functionalism in an expressionist manifesto in 1919, he did an about-turn some time in 1922 or 1923. This third phase lasted until the 1950's, and his buildings (the bulk of his work) include the Bauhaus at Dessau; Siemenstadt and other houses (1929 etc.), much of which was illustrated in *The new architecture and the Bauhaus*. During 1934-6 he worked in England with Fry; he also designed the Rank Laboratories in Denham, Buckinghamshire, in 1936. He became Professor of Architecture at Harvard in 1937 and designed a number of houses for staff and for himself as well as the Harvard Graduate Center (1950). He worked through a group he formed called The Architects Collaborative (TAC); they designed the Pan-Am building on Park Avenue, New York City.
4 After the mid-1950's, he seems to have given up the International Modern style, and its successors, for a semi-expressionist style, as in his Temple Oheb Shalom in Baltimore, Md. (1957) and the Baghdad University project of 1958.

Gropius was regretfully excluded by Peter Blake from his survey *The master builders* (in favour of Corbusier, Mies and Wright), because he did not create sufficiently pregnant forms. On the other hand, Gropius is the hero of Nikolaus Pevsner's *Pioneers of modern design*, and this figures, because Pevsner was praising an anonymous, functional style, which Gropius's Bauhaus phase could certainly claim to be — anonymous if not in the end functional.

READING:
Charles Jencks, *Movements in modern architecture* (he is hard on Gropius).
H-R. Hitchcock, *Architecture, 19th and 20th centuries* and see BAUHAUS books.

Philip Hardwick (1792-1870) He designed in both the standard late neo-classical of the 1830's — Euston Arch, 1836, and the station, in London (both fine examples of different aspects of neo-Greek, and both demolished: although the demolition firm numbered the stones of the arch, it ended up as rubble for the M.1 motorway); the City Club, 1837 — and in the 'Jacobethan' (c1600) style — Lincoln's Inn new hall and library, designed by Hardwick in 1842 and carried out by his son, **Philip Charles** (1822-92), who designed several blocks of offices in the City of London in the 1850's and 1860's, in an Italian Renascence style, following Cockerell — 4, Threadneedle St., (1854), 54 Lombard St., (1854-5), and 15 Lombard St., (1864).

Georges-Eugene Haussmann (1809-91) See 'Town planning' in the introduction. He was prefect of the Seine Department from 1853 to 1870 and responsible for many of the Grand Boulevards in Paris.

Ambrose Heal (1872-1959) The best known member of the family which has the famous shop in Tottenham Court Road, London (and branches). The shop itself is by Smith and Brewer (1916) and by Maufe — the architect of Guildford Cathedral (1937). Under A. Heal's direction, the firm made and sold oak furniture in a plain arts and crafts style (*Plain oak catalogue*, 1898) which became very popular and much imitated up to 1939. Heal's now commission textile designs as well as selling house furnishings. They were notable propagandists for Scandinavian furniture in London in the 1950's and '60's.

Poul Henningsen (b.1894) Danish designer and writer, editor of the magazine *Kritisk Revy* from 1926 to 1928, in which he attacked fussy furniture. His polemics had an important part to play in the development of Danish design in the 1920's and he himself was a designer of light fittings, etc.

Jacob Ignez Hittorf (1792-1867) Architect of the church of St. Vincent de Paul in Paris, France (1824-44) and of the Gare du Nord (about half a mile north of St. Vincent) in 1861-5. A town planner as well as an architect, he was also an archaeologist — he discovered that the Greeks had painted their buildings. The style of Hittorf's own buildings is a late neo-classical with some Renascence details: the scale of the Gare du Nord edges its style towards the baroque, a similar development to those in England of about twenty years before.

Charles Holden (1875-1960) English architect, most of whose work is in or near London. In the years before 1914 his style is part of the Neo-classical Movement which was strong in America and Scandinavia; Holden's is heavier and slightly more baroque than contemporary work in, for example, Denmark. Holden designed — in 1904, the Law Society in Chancery Lane at Carey St., and 127-9 High Holborn at Southampton Place (offices over shop); in 1907 the British Medical Association offices in the Strand — the building was adorned with Jacob Epstein statues — it later became Rhodesia

House; in 1909 62 Oxford Street at Rathbone Place.

In the 1920's he was commissioned by Frank Pick of the London Passenger Transport to design a number of buildings, beginning with the L.P.T.B. headquarters in Broadway, south of St. James Park, (1927-9). Holden designed a number of railway furnishings and bus shelters at this time (the bus shelters are almost pure De Stijl — perhaps the most appropriate role for that style). His greatest achievement for Frank Pick was the series of underground stations he designed for the Northern and especially the Piccadilly Lines, mostly dating from the early 1930's. These stations are the best examples in England of the influence of Dudok, and through him F.L. Wright. At the same time, Holden began designs for the new University of London buildings, which have risen in Bloomsbury during the last 30-40 years — Senate House, with its tower, being faced in stone, the rest in brick (Birkbeck, Students Union, etc.).

William Holford (b.1907) Town planner and architect. He was on the jury for Brasilia in 1957. Charles Holden and Holford brought out *The City of London, a record of destruction and survival* in 1951 for the City Corporation. Their plans included 'rebuilding' the Mansion House on a site near the Guildhall and, apparently, knocking down Hawksmoor's St. Mary Woolnoth altogether, amongst other improvements. Holford's own plan for the precinct for St. Paul's Cathedral was not carried out wholly to his designs, but the idea of contrasting Wren's baroque with Miesian glass boxes arranged round piazzas is generally his. It has not proved to be popular, largely because of the gusts of wind that the layout produces.

Josef Hoffman (1870-1956) One of the founders of the Vienna Werkstätten in 1903, and so one of the Europeans influenced by design from Britain, first by Morris and the Arts and Crafts and then by Mackintosh and Walton whose work was shown at the eighth Vienna Secession Exhibition in 1900. Hoffman was the architect and interior designer of the Palais Stoclet in Brussels (1905-11) one of the outstanding Art Nouveau buildings of its time — a lavish private house with detailing including a mural by the Viennese painter Gustav Klimt. There are examples of Hoffman's furniture in Paris museums.

William Holabird (1854-1923) and **Martin Roche** (1855-1927) An architectural partnership in the 'first' Chicago School. Both trained in the office of W. LeB. Jenney. Their Tacoma Building of 1886-7 in Chicago was iron frame but not free standing (it has since been demolished); their classic was the Marquette Building of 1895, which still stands, though the top couple of floors have been altered, spoiling the 'lid' effect. They designed the Gage building (1898 — part by Sullivan), and the Crown Building, 218 South Wabash (1900).

READING:
Chicago's famous buildings.
C. Condit, *The Chicago school of architecture.*

Thomas Hope(1769-1831) He designed his own furniture after a close study of Greek and Egyptian models. He published *Household furniture and interior decoration* in 1807, illustrated with very unappealing, but characterically neo-classical, line drawings. His work was taken up by cabinet-makers and had a great influence on Regency design generally. There is a table designed by Hope himself in the V. and A.

READING:
David Watkin, *Thomas Hope and the neo-classical idea.*

Victor Horta (1861-1947) An Art Nouveau designer (especially of light fittings) and an architect. He designed the Maison du Peuple in Brussels, Belgium in 1896-99, and the department store L'Innovation in 1901. Both of these were in an art nouveau style; L'Innovation had an ironwork facade which was like the contemporary facade of Samaritaine in Paris; both have gone now — L'Innovation in a recent fire. Horta also designed the Palais des Beaux-Arts in Brussels in 1922-9 in a classical style.

Ebenezer Howard (1850-1928) A shorthand-writer in the City of London who was deeply concerned with the state of civilization as he saw it in England, and published *Tomorrow* in 1898, later republished as *Garden cities of tomorrow*, after the first edition had stimulated the founding of the Garden City Movement.

Elbert Hubbard(1856-1915) An American designer influenced by William Morris. He founded a kind of 'Guild' called the Rycrofters in East Aurora, N.Y., which lasted until 1938. Several European craftsmen came and worked in East Aurora. Hubbard's own work seems square and uncomfortable. There is an example of it in Princeton.

Richard Morris Hunt (1827-1895) He was educated in France and he designed in a Beaux-Arts style. His best-known works are the Tribune Building (1893) and the Metropolitan Museum (1900-1902), both in New York City, and Biltmore, a very late example of a Grand French-Renascence style country house (1890-2), in North Carolina. His work is a good example of the Beaux-Arts influence — not always tied to a particular style, though classical was the most popular, but efficiently using the chosen style to produce a convincing and functional building. This 'method' proved in the end more fashionable — because, perhaps, it was more superficially varied — than the (also partly French inspired) Romanesque of Richardson and the Chicago School.

George Jack (1855-1932) He worked with Philip Webb in the 1880's and then became chief furniture designer for Morris and Co. from the early 1890's. His work, like Gimson's, is in an arts-and-crafts classical, but allowing much more scope for craftsmanship than had been allowed in the 18th century. There are examples of his work in the V. and A.

Arne Jacobsen (1902-1971) Danish architect and designer. His are the town halls of Aalborg (1938-42, with Eric Møller), Søllerud (1939-42) and Rødovre (1955-6), the last two being in the suburbs of Copenhagen. These buildings are in a typically Scandinavian revision of the International Modern style — using brick, etc. to produce a more humane environment, and Jacobsen's Munkegaard School in Copenhagen (1952-6) is also on a humane scale. The S.A.S. Hotel in Copenhagen (1960), however, is an essay in the Miesian glass shoe-box, like the Lever Building in New York, though even this is elegant and unobtrusive in a charactieristic Danish manner — the glass is smoke-grey, so that the building tends to merge with the colour of the sky. One of his last buildings was the new St. Catherine's College, Oxford (1960-64). For many of his buildings Jacobsen also designed the furnishings, and some of these — for example the 'Swan' chair for the S.A.S. Hotel — have become well known in their own right. An earlier chair design was the 'Egg', and he also designed cutlery. He designed the garden for his own house near the Sound, north of Copenhagen, and the gardens of St. Catherine's College.

William LeBaron Jenney (1832-1907) A Chicago architect, the 'inventor' of the characteristic Chicago office tower, using iron frame construction. See CHICAGO SCHOOL. He also designed 'Stick style' houses in Riverside.

Georg Jensen (1866-1935) Danish silversmith, founder of the famous firm. It has produced a wide range of silverware, including cutlery. The early work, including Jensen's own, was influenced by Art Nouveau; the later work, especially cutlery, is more in line with Scandinavian 'ergonomic' design. There are examples of Jensen's work in the V. and A., the Kunstindustrimuseum in Copenhagen, and in other museums and on sale in shops.

Philip Johnson (b. 1906) Together with Henry-Russell Hitchcock, he arranged an exhibition at the Museum of Modern Art in New York City in 1932 called *The international style: architecture since 1922,* the title of their book in the same year. They included Swedish architecture, unlike the Smithsons later. Johnson himself went on to study architecture, graduating from Harvard (where Gropius was Professor) in 1943. Apart from his own house at New Canaan (1946, very Miesian; the guest house of 1952 is in a different style — a species of International Modern Moorish), his best known buildings are: the Synagogue at Fort Chester, N.Y. (1956); Fort Worth Museum, Texas, (1961), the Art Gallery for the University of Nebraska at Lincoln (1962); and the New York State Theater at the Lincoln Center in New York City (1962-4). He has recently proposed a 'Chippendale' skyscraper for A.T. & T. in New York City.

READING:
Philip Johnson, *Mies van der Rohe,* published in 1947.
Charles Jencks, *Modern movements in architecture*; he discusses Johnson under 'American camp'.

Owen Jones (1809-74) Designer of wallpapers and textiles. His book, *The grammar of ornament* (1856 and many reprints),became the standard 19th century textbook on the subject, not only in England. It included examples of Egyptian, Maori and other 'exotic' decorative forms as well as Renascence, Tudor, etc. Jones admired Islamic art, and there are some splendid plates of it in his book. Much English 19th century design based on styles from 'the past' had been irritatingly incorrect to connoisseurs, and there is no doubt that Jones's book did much to improve this state of affairs, even if it did not encourage originality. There are examples of Jones's work in the V. and A.

READING:

Alf Bøe, *From Gothic Revival to functional form.* He discusses Jones's work and its importance, and reprints 'General principles of the arrangement of form and colour in architecture and the decorative arts', an essay in Jones's *Grammar.*

Louis Kahn (1901-1974) American architect in a Brutalist style. Among his buildings are the Yale Art Gallery (1951-3), the Richards Medical Research Building in the University of Pennsylvania, Philadelphia (1957-60); Trenton Bath House, N.J. (1958); the Dacca Assembly Building, in what is now Bangladesh (begun 1962); the First Unitarian Church, Rochester, N.Y. (1964); and the Salk Institute Laboratories at La Jolla, Cal. (1965).

READING:

Charles Jencks, *Modern Movements in architecture*; he discusses Kahn under 'American non-camp'.

Leo von Klenze (1784-1864) German neo-classical /rundbogenstil architect. He designed for Munich the Glyptothek (Sculpture Gallery), 1816-34, a part of the Royal Palace, the Königsbau, 1826 and the All Saints Church, 1827 (this last in a Byzantine style). These buildings are among the best examples of their type — neo-classical architecture adapted from the antique only very slightly but imaginatively, for uses not so far removed from those of ancient buildings.

Jensen Klint (1853-1930) Danish architect best known for his Grundtvig Church in Copenhagen, begun in 1921, built in brick to a design developed from traditional Danish parish churches. The building, in honour of the 19th century founder of the Danish Folk High Schools, is an interesting example of the Arts and Crafts tradition serving a late Nationalist Revival.

Kaare Klint (1888-1954) Jensen's son; a furniture designer, who worked with cabinet-makers in the 1920's and designed furniture partly inspired by a study of plain English 18th century furniture. He was the first Professor of Furniture at the Royal Academy in Copenhagen. His work is an interesting contrast with the contemporary developments at the Bauhaus, where the principle of ignoring all earlier designs was being set up.

Richard Payne Knight (1750-1824) His book *An analytical enquiry into* *the principles of taste* (1805) was the most important work in the English Picturesque Movement — which encouraged designers, especially of parks, but also of new housing estates — to create 'pictures' out of their arrangments of buildings in landscapes, the 'pictures' being derived from the favourite landscape paintings of the fashionable élite of the late 18th century. John Nash's layouts of Regent's Park, with its terraces and villas in parkland, and St. James's Park with Buckingham Palace in the background, are good examples of this Picturesque design.

Henri Labrouste (1801-1875) Architect of the St. Geneviève Library near the Sorbonne and the Pantheon in Paris, designed and built 1843-50, with a Renascence exterior, but the interior made wide by having a row of thin iron columns down the centre of the main room, supporting an iron roof. Labrouste also designed the reading room of the National Library in Paris (1862-8). The style of the St. Geneviève ironwork is classical, of the National Library, romanesque. They make an interesting comparison with the reading room of the British Museum, an iron dome, designed by S. Smirke, and built in 1854-7; like the National Library, an 'infill' into an existing building.

Denys Lasdun (b.1914) Outstanding architect in Britain of the Brutalist 'Movement'. All his buildings stand out from the surroundings. All have been acclaimed by the critics on completion. The most outstanding are:—
Flats in Bethnal Green (1959-9) arranged in a 'cluster' pattern to recreate vertically the old street pattern; each floor has four flats opening off a common walkway, on the inside of the building.
St. James's Place flats, facing Green Park next door to Spencer House, and built 1957-61; the design allows for the reception rooms to be higher than the service rooms.
The Royal College of Physicians in Regent's Park (1960-4), next to Nash's terraces (the view of the terraces had been wrecked already by a high block of council flats in the street behind).
University of East Anglia, near Norwich, begun in 1963 — rows of about a dozen pyramids of concrete horizontal bands;
A new building for Christ's College, Cambridge, which glares across at the old buildings, also with stepped bands of windows.
The National Theatre on the South Bank, finished in 1976, the most prominent of all his buildings; architecture meant to recall a rocky landscape (also made up with horizontal bands of concrete and glass, with taller glass panels at the river entrance).

READING:
William Curtis, *A language and a theme: the architecture of Denys Lasdun and Partners.*

Hector M. Lefuel (1810-80) with **Louis Visconti** (d.1853) designed the new north wing of the Louvre, Paris in 1852-57. It is in a distinctly baroque style, and marks the transition in France from the revival of French Renascence to a more florid style known as Second Empire, the time of its construction. The style had been anticipated in London in Paddington Station Hotel (1851-2). The new Louvre wing now houses the Museum of Decorative Arts.

William Richard Lethaby (1857-1931) English architect and propagandist for the Arts and Crafts Movement. He designed only a few buildings himself; among them are the Orion Insurance Building, Colmore Row, Birmingham, England (1900), and Brockhampton Church, Herefordshire (1900-1902). There are examples of his furniture in the V. and A. He founded the Central School of Arts and Crafts in 1896, and was Professor of Design at the Royal College of Art from 1900. He was the author of a number of books, including *Form and civilization* and *Architecture*, written in 1911 for the Home University Library. Lethaby's love of Gothic architecture and dislike of classical made him an impassioned guide to his subjects and he had a great influence on a whole generation of young architects, most of whom became adherents of the International Modern style, which Lethaby himself never was.

READING:
Robert Macleod, *Style and society;* it contains a most sympathetic appreciation of Lethaby's ideas, and of his relationship with Philip Webb, whose life Lethaby wrote.

Arthur Liberty (1843-1907) He founded the shop which still bears his name, from which came the Italian term for Art Nouveau. Liberty's originally imported oriental textiles and goods; later they sold arts and crafts fabrics, metalware and ceramics. Unlike Heal's, they have not made a point of pushing any particular modern movement.

READING:
Alison Adburgham, *Liberty's, a biography of a shop.*

Lippincote and Marguiles An American industrial design consultancy, founded by these two in 1946. Their portfolio includes Eastern Airlines, Chrysler, Esso Service Stations, Decca Radio and Philips. See INDUSTRIAL DESIGN.

Raymond Loewy (b.1893) American industrial designer. He became art director for Westinghouse in 1929. Then he started his own design firm and designed the Coldspot refrigerator for Sears Roebuck in 1932 — there was work for some in the slump. He has published books explaining his kind of design to the general public. The company is now Raymond Loewy-William Smith, Inc. (1961), one of the largest consultancies. See INDUSTRIAL DESIGN.

READING:
R. Loewy, *Never leave well alone: the personal record of an industrial designer from lipsticks to locomotives.*

Adolf Loos (1870-1933) Austrian architect. In 1908 he published an article entitled 'ornament and crime' and carried this neurosis into his actual designs, especially the often-illustrated Steiner House in Vienna (1910). For his interiors he favoured English 18th century furniture and photographs of his rooms look surprisingly Edwardian for someone who undoubtedly was one of the godfathers of the Bauhaus aesthetic. In 1922 Loos entered the competition for the *Chicago Tribune* tower block. His design was a many-storied Doric column — perhaps this was a joke.

READING:

Vincent Scully's *American architecture and urbanism* has a photograph of Loos's *Chicago Tribune* entry.

John Claudius Loudon (1733-1843) An English writer on architecture, interior design and garden design. His most influential book was the *Encyclopaedia of cottage, farm and villa architecture*, first published in 1833 and with several editions after this, ending with one prepared by his widow in 1844. Many of Loudon's designs were illustrated in his books, and he also commissioned designs from other architects. It is chiefly as a popularizer of various styles that he is important, and most of all for a kind of Italian villa style for suburban houses. In gardens, he more than anyone else was the advocate of 'gardenesque', which is roughly a scaled-down landscape garden with island flower beds, a style which settled in British public gardens for a hundred years. His influence (Italian villas set in shrubberies and flower beds) spread to America, where his chief disciple was A.J. Downing.

READING:

John Gloag, *Mr. Loudon's England.*

Edwin Lutyens (1869-1944) English architect who designed many country houses, but also a number of churches and other public buildings. David Watkin in his *Morality and architecture* claims Lutyens as the greatest English architect after Wren and — even if one is not worried about this kind of ranking — shrewdly points out that Lutyens is a kind of touchstone for general attitudes of writers and art historians, their appreciation of Lutyens showing their bias (so that the 'claim' may be a challenge rather than a pecking order). Lutyens was born in the same decade as several Arts and Crafts architects and designers, and there are houses by him in this tradition: Munstead Wood (1896), Deanery Gardens, Sonning (1898), Orchards, Godalming (1899); some of these can be seen, even if only from the road. Many of Lutyens's early houses in the hills around Godalming had gardens designed by Gertrude Jekyll. Then, like Norman Shaw before him, Lutyens turned to the various classical styles that were fashionable around the turn of the century. Among Lutyens' buildings in a Queen-Anne or Wren-Baroque style are the Liberal Club of Farnham, Surrey (1894), Tigbourne Court, also in Surrey (1894) and the Midland Bank in Piccadilly, next door to St. James's Church (1922). Lutyens also designed in a 'Tudor' castle style, 'realising' Lindisfarne Castle, off the coast of Northumberland, in 1903, and building a completely new one on the edge of Dartmoor in Devon,

Castle Drogo (1910-30, now owned by the National Trust).

Lutyen's religious buildings are in a more personal style — the church for Hampstead Garden Suburb, St. Jude, is in a very individual style related to Gothic (1909-11), and the Cenotaph in Whitehall (1919-20) is indebted to no other style.

The fashionable style throughout most of Lutyens's lifetime for large public buildings was baroque, and Lutyens was given commissions for these in the later stages of his career. In London he designed Britannic House, a large office block in the City (1920), but the most spectacular commission was for the layout of New Delhi as the capital of British India. At the new King George V's durbah in 1911, it was announced that the capital would be transferred from Calcutta to Delhi, the old capital of the Mughal empire, and new buildings were required. Some of them were designed by Herbert Baker, but Lutyens himself designed the Viceroy's Palace (now the Presidential Palace). It is one of the grandest baroque buildings anywhere.

As well as being the near-contemporary of several Arts and Crafts designers, it is interesting to note that Lutyens was born in the same year as the Art-Nouveau designer Alphonse Mucha, and as Frank Lloyd Wright. Lutyens's work seems not to have been influenced at all by either Art Nouveau, nor by any of the concerns that mark Wright's work out from others'. This seems to have been too much for art historians, especially those with historicist leanings. Thus there are few good short accounts of Lutyens's work. H-R. Hitchcock is easily the most useful, in *Architecture, 19th and 20th centuries.*

Charles Rennie Mackintosh (1868-1928) Scottish architect and designer. His most famous building is the Glasgow School of Art, designed in 1896 (the Library extension in 1907-9), in an individual style which has clear affinities with *Jugendstil,* if not quite with Art Nouveau. Also in Glasgow is his Scotland Road School of 1906. He designed a number of private houses in the countryside near Glasgow. Although he entered for competitions (for example, for the new Anglican Cathedral for Liverpool), he had no success abroad except in Vienna, where his work was admired, and was influential, but where he was not offered any commissions. Some of his furniture can be seen in Glasgow — see GLASGOW SCHOOL.

READING:

Robert Macleod, *Charles Rennie Mackintosh*.

Thomas Haworth, *Charles Rennie Mackintosh and the modern movement. Glasgow at a glance.*

Arthur Mackmurdo (1851-1942) English architect and designer. His early work is a prefiguration of Art Nouveau — the title page of a book on Wren's City churches and a design for the back of a chair; both these can be seen at the William Morris Gallery in Walthamstow in East London. Mackmurdo founded the Century Guild in 1882 and published a magazine *Hobby Horse* for the Guild from 1884 onwards. Some of his buildings are unexpected from a follower of Morris — Charterhouse Cold Storage Co., Charterhouse St., London (1900); the Savoy Hotel, river front, c1890. Among his houses is 12, Hans Road, London (1894).

READING:
Nikolaus Pevsner, *Studies in art, architecture and design,* Volume 2.

Sven Markelius (1889-1972) He was the chief architect and planner for the City of Stockholm from 1944 to 1954, and so responsible for overall planning of the Arsta suburban centre, and of the satellite town of Vällingby, for which he also was the designer of the town centre (begun 1953).

Leslie Martin (b.1908) Architect to the London County Council from 1953 to 1956, and so in charge of the Roehampton development, at the time of the change-over from 'Swedish' to 'Corbusier' — see BRUTALISM. Working as a private architect, Martin later designed the new Harvey Court for Caius College, Cambridge (beyond the Backs, 1960-2), and the Law Library at Oxford (1961-4). The Caius building has rooms in stepped galleries looking inwards to a central dining room; the Law Library is a good example of International Modern emphasis on dominant horizontal lines, stressed not only by the bands of windows, but the shapes of the blocks, steps, etc.

Robert Matthew (1906-1975) Architect to the London County Council from 1946 to 1953, the time of the Festival of Britain and the South Bank Exhibition. He was architect-in-chief for the Royal Festival Hall (in its first form, finished in 1951; the exterior and some parts of the interior — restaurants, for example — altered in the 1960's: the hall itself is largely unchanged). With Johnson-Marshall, Matthew designed New Zealand House (Pall Mall at Haymarket) in 1958-63, and the Commonwealth Institute in Kensington in 1959-62. New Zealand House is an orthodox Miesian glass-walled block, but the Institute is a bold design all under one parabolic roof, with a free arrangement of levels and compartments inside

McKim, Mead and White American architectural partnership, in the front of fashion in the last quarter of the 19th century, representing the triumph in America of the Beaux-Arts principles of organisation and competence. Charles Follen McKim (1847-1909) and Stamford White (1853-1906) were the chief partners. In the Italian Renascence style they designed the Villard Houses in Madison Avenue, New York City, in 1882, and the Boston Public Library, 1888-92. In a classical style, one of their finest buildings was the Pennsylvania Railway Station, also in New York, of 1904-10, now demolished. The firm also designed a number of houses in the Shingle Style, especially in Rhode Island. The W.G. Low house, famous from photographs, built 1887 has now been demolished.

READING:
H-R. Hitchcock, *Architecture, 19th and 20th centuries.*
Theo Crosby, *The necessary monument* (a section on the Pennsylvania Station).

Eric Mendelsohn (1887-1953) After leaving Germany in the 1930's, Mendelsohn came to England at first, where he worked with Chermayeff, designing a house in Church Street, Chelsea, next to the one designed by Gropius and Fry, and the De La Warre Pavilion at Bexhill-on-Sea, Sussex (1935-6). Then in Palestine Mendelsohn designed the Hadrassah University Medical Centre (1936-8). Finally, in the U.S.A., he designed the Maimonides Hospital in San Francisco, Cal. (1946-50). He is best known for his work in Germany in the 1920's, for which see EXPRESSIONISM.

Ludwig Mies van der Rohe (1876-1969) A German (until 1938) and American architect. One of the leaders of the International Modern Movement, both before and after the war of 1939-45, his buildings are more consistently 'pure' (and certainly more consistently cubic) then either Corbusier's or Gropius's. Mies's early work was neo-classical (he was a pupil of Behrens); then, along with many other German architects, he had an Expressionist phase (Rosa Luxemburg Monument). From the mid-1920's onwards he settled down into International Modern, designing housing in Berlin (1924). He organised the *Deutsche Werkbund* exhibition at Stuttgart in 1927, himself designing a small apartment block on the Weissenhof site. His German Pavilion at the Barcelona Exhibition (which had the Barcelona chairs in it, designed for the exhibition by Mies), in 1929, and the Tugendhat house in Brno, Checkoslovakia in 1930 — basically a flat roof held up by widely spaced steel columns, with plate-glass outer walls — became a formula which Mies used again for the Farnsworth House at Plano, Illinois, in 1950, and which his admirer Philip Johnson used for his own house at New Canaan in 1946.

In 1938 Mies was appointed Professor of Architecture at the Armour Institute in Chicago (since renamed the Illinois Institute of Technology). In 1939 he designed the campus for the Institute, and over the next decades also designed several of the buildings. All these buildings are in the same Tugendhat-Farnsworth style, so that they have to carry labels to avoid confusion. They are among the world's most imitated buildings — the Smithson's Hunstanton School in Norfolk is a cheap version of them.

Mies had designed a 'glass skyscraper' in the 1920's, and in the 1950's he built several towers which look as though they are iron-frame, but are of reinforced concrete construction. They are uniformly faced with glass panels, for windows or for walls. The Seagram Building in Park Avenue, New York City (1956-9), is the most famous of these towers, but it was preceded by apartment blocks alongside Lake Michigan, including the Lake Shore Drive apartments of 1951. These glass towers have been imitated *ad nauseam*; the most distinguished early essay in the style by other architects was the Lever Building, also in New York City, by Gordon Bunshaft of S.O.M. (also 1952) — its particular variation, a tall thin slab rising out of a podium which covers the whole site, usually leaving a courtyard open to the sky, was also soon imitated, as at Castrol House in Marylebone Road in London.

READING:
Philip Johnson, *Mies van der Rohe.*
Werner Blaser, *Mies van der Rohe.*

Peter Blake, *The master builders*; the section on Mies has been issued separately by Pelican.

William Morris (1834-1896) Poet; then architectural student (in Street's office); then head of a group making stained glass and furniture. Morris designed wallpapers in the 1860's, then chintzes and tapestries, and finally books in the late 1880's. He learnt all about the crafts as he went along — dyeing, papers, inks, etc. Ruskin influenced his ideas on art and, partly also under Ruskin's influence, and partly acting on his own experience, he turned to political questions, joining the Social Democratic Federation. As a medievalist, Morris travelled from outright copying and fantasising to an attempt to draw out a 'medieval' — or even 'Gothic' — *spirit* in social and artistic life; something which could have become quite different from what we know of actual medieval art and life. This was an intellectual journey made by many of his contemporaries. However, Morris's legacy was to the Arts and Crafts designers who, by withdrawing to the Cotswolds, in a sense admitted defeat.

Morris has been quite wrongly claimed as the forerunner of the modern movements in design. Even his European and American followers stood out against mass-production as much as his English followers did, and as he himself had done. The desire to 'serve' the needs of one's fellow men often conceals a desire to control one's fellow men. The market system, with all its faults — more glaring in Morris's England than in ours — acted then as a check on ambitions; Morris never convincingly put forward any suggestions for the system of checks which would replace the market which he so rightly hated; *News from Nowhere,* his report from a bright future, seems to describe an England with a much smaller population then even in Morris's time. Perhaps the kernel of his message, taking into account his work for the preservation of old buildings as well as his original designs, is that designers should avoid *mannerisms* (past, present and future), and should study the whole of design and architecture, and ensure they learn from it. What the Bauhaus did was to reject the past; and contemporary fashions for 'change', allowing new techniques to dominate design, reject Morris's message even more harshly.

His designs can be seen in two museums. The V. and A. has a bay in the later 19th century galleries devoted to the early (1860's) work of Morris and his friends. The William Morris Museum at Walthamstow in East London is in the house the Morris family owned during his boyhood. It has examples of his work — textiles, papers, furniture and books — from all periods of his life.

READING:
Paul Thompson, *William Morris and his work.* This is by far the best survey of all sides of his remarkable career.
William Morris: selected writings and designs; edited by Asa Briggs (text) and Graeme Shankland (illustrations).
G.D.H. Cole's edition of William Morris's writings for the Nonesuch Press

has a selection of his verse, and the whole of *News from Nowhere*.

Alphonse Mucha (1869-1939) A Bohemian Art Nouveau graphic designer, who drew some famous theatre posters (for Bernhardt, especially). He also designed some of the first postage stamps for the new independent Czechoslovakian republic in 1918-19. His posters have been reprinted in the Art Nouveau revival in the 1960's, for which he has been one of the main inspirations.

READING:
Brian Reade, *Art Nouveau and Alphonse Mucha*.

Herman Muthesius (1861-1927) German art and design propagandist. He came to England in the late 1890's to study English design and architecture of behalf of the Prussian government, from which he gathered material for his book *Das Englische Haus* which encouraged European house design away from 'Second Empire'. Muthesius was the presiding genius of the *Deutsche Werkbund*, which he helped to found in 1907. At the 1914 *Werkbund* Exhibition in Cologne, he spoke in favour of industrial standardisation in a debate against Van der Velde and craftsmanship.

John Nash (1752-1835) Prolific Anglo-Welsh architect and planner. He laid out London's best picturesque sequence, from Carlton House Terrace through Regent Street and Portland Place to Regent's Park, of which only the outline remains, for the starting point (the Prince Regent's Carlton House) was pulled down when the Regent became George IV, and most of the buildings between that and Park Crescent have been replaced. The terraces around Regent's Park, and the picturesque layout of the Park itself, are still there. Nash landscaped St. James's Park in time for the peace celebrations after the defeat of Bonaparte and he designed Buckingham Palace — now obscured by Aston Webb's front building. Of Nash's other buildings, the most accessible is the Brighton Pavilion (1815, etc.).

READING:
Terence Davis, *The architecture of John Nash* (many photographs and plans).
Terence Davis, *John Nash, the Prince Regent's architect*.
John Summerson, *John Nash, architect to George IV*. (In spite of their titles, the last two books cover the whole of Nash's career.)

Pier Luigi Nervi (b.1891) Italian engineer-architect, whose concrete structures have excited much admiration:
Stadium in Florence, 1930-32.
Exhibitions Halls in Turin, 1948, 1950 and 1961.
An exhibition hall in the *rond-point* of the Défense in Paris, 1958.
Sports Palaces in Rome (for the Olympic Games of 1960).

Richard Neutra (1892-1970) Austrian architect who worked with Loos in Vienna in 1912-14, and eventually emigrated to America (Chicago 1923, Los Angeles 1925). His style is a Bauhaus squareness not unlike Mies's house style of 1930-50. Most of Neutra's work after 1925 was private houses, and most of them were in California.

READING:

Richard Neutra, *Building and projects;* there are now two volumes — (1) 1925-50, and (2) 1950-60.

Richard Neutra, *Survival through design* (a collection of his thoughts, given in lectures and speeches).

Rupert Spade, *Richard Neutra* (photographs by Yukio Futagewa, and a commentary).

Oscar Niemeyer (b.1907) Brazilian architect, whose later designs, especially for the public buildings of the new city of Brasilia, have exploited the sculptural possibilities of reinforced concrete more than most other contemporary architects — his work having a freer form (partly because of the freer functional demands) than, for example, Nervi's structures. In 1936 Niemeyer collaborated with Corbusier and others in the Ministry of Education Buildings in Rio de Janeiro; in 1958 he designed for Brasilia its Cathedral, the law courts, the President's Palace and a hotel. Niemeyer's work is the outstanding example of what might be called International Modern Baroque, especially the Cathedral, a hugh funnel-shaped building with concrete spokes.

READING:

Rupert Spade, *Oscar Niemeyer.*

Joseph Maria Olbrich (1867-1908) Austrian architect who designed the Secession Building in Vienna in 1897-98, and was with the group of artists and designers in Darmstadt in the early years of the 20th century, where he designed some houses, and the Hochzeit tower (1907), all in a kind of cleaned-up Art Nouveau leaning towards the currently fashionable revival of neo-classicism.

Frederick Law Olmstead (1822-1903) American landscape designer who laid out Riverside, Illinois (an early prototype of the Garden Suburb), Central Park, New York City, the gardens of Biltmore, North Carolina and the Palo Alto campus of Stamford University, California. He is the most notable exponent in the second half of the 19th century of the English landscape garden tradition in its later, picturesque, phase.

Omega workshops Founded by Roger Fry in 1913; closed in 1919. Vanessa Bell and Duncan Grant were among those who made designs for pottery, rugs and fabrics. They were among the first English designers to use Fauvist colours and patterns for such fabrics as curtain material, colours such as purples and oranges set in light grounds. These fabrics were printed in France.

Because of its Bloomsbury connections, Omega had a wider influence among educated people than its short life would lead one to expect.

READING:
Quentin Bell, *Bloomsbury.*
Richard Shone, *Bloomsbury portraits.*

Ragnar Östberg (1866-1945) Famous for his Stockholm City Hall, 1909-23. The design has echoes of the Swedish Renascence and of Venice (it is sited alongside a lake). The fabric of the building reflects Arts and Crafts ideals — the bricks are hand-made. The interior is lavishly fitted up in a typical Swedish mixture of 18th century elegance and folk traditions and colours, though the Golden Hall is perhaps a bit too much like Hollywood. The Blue Hall (a large and high glass-roofed hall used now for exhibitions) is interesting as an example of Ruskin-Morris principles in action — Östberg asked the workmen laying the tiled floor to design their own patterns for it.

J.J.P. Oud (1890-1963) Dutch architect, one of the founders of De Stijl. His Hook-of-Holland estate of low-cost housing of 1927 made him famous. He designed a terrace of houses for the Weissenhof at Stuttgart in the Deutsche *Werkbund* Exhibition of 1927, and these had an influence on Corbusier. He was a typical exponent of De Stijl and Bauhaus architectural ideals — his buildings in the 1920's were bleak and cubic. His later work disappointed those who admired his ruthlessness — his Shell Building in the Hague of 1938-1942 is more conventionally modern.

Joseph Paxton (1801-65) Designer first of greenhouses for the Duke of Devonshire, and then of the Crystal Palace for the Great Exhibition (designed in 1850 and erected in a few months at the beginning of 1851). Paxton also designed the alterations for the rebuilding of the Crystal Palace in a grander manner at Sydenham in 1852. With his son-in-law, Stokes, he was the architect of Mentmore Towers for one of the Rothschild family (1852-4), the first country house in England to be built with central heating. As well as designing greenhouses, Paxton designed the layout of gardens, especially the layout of the new centre of Birkenhead in Cheshire, including the plan of Birkenhead Park, which remains today.

READING:
G.F. Chadwick, *The works of Sir Joseph Paxton.*

Auguste Perret (1974-1954) The main subject of Peter Collins's book *Concrete, the search for a new architecture,* though there are many 'traditional' aspects of Perret's work — enough to allow John Summerson to include him at the end of *The classical language of architecture.* The classical side of Perret is most apparent in his later work, particularly in the rebuilding of the port of Le Havre in Normandy after the 1939-45 war. Perret's earlier buildings were 'pioneers' in the use of exposed concrete for smart commissions: the apartment block at 25b, Rue Franklin, of 1905, the

Champs-Elysées theatre, of 1911-14, a commission which Perret took over from Van der Velde, and the church of Our Lady at Raincy, of 1922-3, a reinterpretation of late Gothic in terms of exposed concrete.

Duncan Phyfe (1768-1854) Originally the family name was Fife, and Duncan is thought to have changed the spelling to match the influx of French cabinet-makers into New York after the Revolution; *French 'flu* arrived early in America too. Phyfe was the leading cabinet-maker of the Federal period (late neo-classical). His furniture is in the same tradition as the pattern-books of Hepplewhite and Sheraton. There are examples of his work in the Museum of the City of New York, and in the Du Pont Winterthur Museum, Delaware.

READING:
The Du Pont Museum has published catalogues of its collections — that for the Federal period is by C.F. Montgomery, 1967.

Hans Poelzig (1869-1936) His industrial buildings before 1914 in eastern Germany have become famous as a kind of pre-Brutalist Expressionism, particularly the chemical factory of 1911-12 at Luban near Posen (Poznan since 1945). After 1918 he made designs for theatres in Berlin and Salzburg which are good examples of the high period of Expressionism.

READING:
Nikolaus Pevsner and J.M. Richards, *The anti-rationalists.*

George Browne Post (1837-1913) Of the generation of W. LeBaron Jenney rather than the leaders of the Chicago School, he designed 'eclectic' office towers in New York at the same time as they were designing towers in a developed form of Romanesque in Chicago. Post's best known buildings are the Equitable Building of 1869, the New York Times Building and the Pulitzer Building, both of 1889, and the St. Paul Building of 1897-9. Post also pioneered the large, hygienic American hotel.

Powell and Moya A leading English architectural partnership, formed by A.J.P. Powell (b.1921) and J.H. Moya (b.1920). Their first success was the commission to build what became the Churchill Gardens housing estate in Pimlico, up-river from Westminster. It is a large estate of slab blocks of different heights, the predominant colours being pale yellow (brick) and green-grey (concrete and glass). It was begun in 1946 and was completed slowly over the next 20 years. Other notable buildings of theirs are the Mayfield School in Putney (1956, etc.), a 'model' comprehensive school for girls, and the Festival Theatre at Chichester, Sussex (1962), which has a more 'sculptural' exterior, and an open-stage plan inside. Although Chichester Theatre has a leaning towards the fashionable Brutalism, their work generally is in a sensitive, glass-panelled cubism, mid-way between Bauhaus anonymity and Miesian graph-paper.

A.W.N. Pugin (1812-52) Son of an emigré French artist, who collaborated with Rowlandson for Ackermann's books. Pugin's polemical importance stems from his conversion to Catholicism and simultaneous conversion to the idea that Gothic was the only true Christian style. This is against historical evidence, as was witheringly pointed out at the time, but it was the driving force behind his work. He wrote two books: *Contrasts* (1836), with drawings of early 19th century buildings carefully chosen so that they could be shown up to maximum disadvantage against drawings of (romanticised) 14th century buildings; and *True principles of Christian or pointed architecture* (1841), much plagiarised by his successors. Of his vast number of designs over a short working life, few could be realised with the costly materials they needed: only the Palace of Westminster, where he collaborated with Barry in two spurts of activity — this design is in a 15th century style; Scarisbrick Hall, Lancashire (1838-42); Alton Towers, Staffordshire (1849 — now an impressive ruin); St. Giles, Cheadle, Staffordshire (1841-6), and St. Augustine, Ramsgate (1846-51), next door to his own house, and which he paid for himself. Most of his other buildings (e.g. St. Chad's Cathedral at Birmingham) do not show him at his best.

READING:
Phoebe Stanton, *Pugin.*

James Renwick (1818-95) Good example of an American mid-19th century eclectic architect. St. Patrick's Cathedral, New York (1853-87) is in a Gothic style; the Smithsonian Institute in Washington (1946) in Romanesque; and Vassar (1865) in Renascence.

Henry Hobson Richardson (1838-86) See ROMANESQUE, in which style Richardson designed most of his public buildings — Brattle Sq. (1870) and Trinity (1872) churches in Boston; Quincy Library, 1880 (south of Boston — a much 'freer' style, more like the English Arts and Crafts); two halls of residence at Harvard, Sever (1878) and Austin (1881); and, most influential of all, the Marshall Field Warehouse in Chicago in 1885, now demolished). His only remaining building in Chicago is the former Glessner House, 1800 South Prairie, of 1886. Before then, on the east coast, Richardson had been one of the pioneers of the Shingle style — of which his best known example is the Stoughton House in Cambridge, Mass., of 1882-3. See SHINGLE STYLE.

READING:
Marianna Griswold van Rensselaer, *Henry Hobson Richardson and his works.*

Gerrit Thomas Rietveld (1898-1964) Dutch architect and furniture designer, one of the founder members of De Stijl. The most committed of them all to design in terms of separated, distinct planes, preferably at right angles to each other. This principle is most evident in his design for the Schroeder House in Utrecht, built in 1925, where the insistence on little flat square surfaces dodging in and out all over the place gives a fussy rather than a spiritual look to the house. His frightening furniture looks like prototypes for some of the nastier devices in medieval Nuremburg, in fact the famous chair of *c*1917 is more a piece of abstract sculpture than a seat — or even a sitting function.

READING:
Theodore M. Brown, *The work of G. Rietveld, architect.*

Karl Ivanovich Rossi (1775-1849) Architect of some of the grandest neo-classical buildings of St. Petersburg (Leningrad): the General Staff Arches leading into Alexander Square (1819-20), and the Senate and Synod (1829-34). It is the scale of these buildings which is (and was meant to be) intimidating; they are the outstanding examples of the 'Roman imperial' variety of neo-classical architecture.

Paul Rudolph (b.1918) American architect in an International Brutalist style. He has designed a number of townscape-wrecking housing projects, and his buildings are characterised by the use of powerful blocks of exposed concrete. The two best known are academic complexes: the Art and Architecture Building at Yale University of 1958-64, and the Southeastern Massachussetts Technological Institute at North Dartmouth, Mass, begun in 1963.

READING:
The works of Paul Rudolph, with an introduction by Sybil Moholoy-Nagy. Charles Jencks discusses Rudolph under 'Middle Camp' in *Modern movements in architecture.*

J.E. Ruhlmann (1879-1933) A designer of expensive French furniture in the 1920's: neo-classical with very costly materials. There are examples in the V. and A., the Louvre, and the Museum of Decorative Arts in Paris.

John Ruskin (1819-1900) English art critic, and profoundly influential writer on architecture and on society. He was also a very good draughtsman; his drawings and water-colours seem to have been relatively neglected, and not given their rightful place in English 19th century art. There is a collection of them in the Ashmolean Museum in Oxford, and some of them are on view. Kenneth Clark's selection of his writings, with commentary, *Ruskin today,* is an excellent introduction to his work.

Gordon Russell (b.1892) English furniture designer, whose work is a development from the Cotswold Art and Crafts tradition. He was a leading designer of Utility furniture in the 1940's. He has written an autobiography, *Designer's trade,* and there is an essay on his work by N. Pevsner in *Studies in art, architecture and design,* Volume 2.

Eero Saarinen (1910-61) He emigrated with his father, Eliel, to the U.S.A., as a boy. He has designed in a number of different 'styles', which has troubled the orthodox:

Miesian glass box graph-paper: General Motors Technical Center, Warren, Mich., 1948-56.
Expressionist Brutalism: airport buildings — T.W.A. terminal at Kennedy Airport, New York, 1955-62, and the Dulles Airport departure lounges, etc. (Washington D.C.), 1958-63.
Perret classicism: U.S. Embassies in Grosvenor Sq., London, 1955-61, and in Oslo, 1959.
Nervi concrete: Yale University Hockey Rink, 1953-9.
His chapel at M.I.T. was derived from Finnish castles.

READING:
Allan Temko, *Eero Saarinen*.

Eliel Saarinen (1873-1950) (Eero's father) The leading Finnish architect of his generation. He designed Helsinki Railway Station (1905-14), one of the great transport monuments of the early 20th century (see Stuttgart Station, and Pennsylvania, New York City). Saarinen emigrated to the U.S.A. in the 1920's and designed there, amongst other buildings, Christ Church, Minneapolis (1949).

Anthony Salvin (1799-1880) English country-house architect, specializing in 'Elizabethan' or 'Jacobean' styles (see NATIONALIST REVIVALS). His best known houses are Harlaxton Hall in Lincolnshire (1834 — one of the earliest examples of the revived Elizabethan style), and Thoresby Hall in Nottinghamshire (1864), which is open to the public.

READING:
H-R. Hitchcock, *Early Victorian architecture in England*.

Timo Sarpaneva (b.1926) A Finnish designer who is an outstanding example of the Scandinavian who designs in many fields — glass, lithography, cast-iron, kitchenware, and textiles. He is also an exhibition designer. He started with needlework design.

READING:
Segersted, *Modern Finnish design*.
Sarpaneva's work is occasionally discussed in magazines — for example in the Danish magazine *Mobilia*.

Hans Scharoun (1893-1972) An Expressionist architect who did not button everything down in the 1920's as the Bauhaus men did. The most notable of his later buildings is a concert hall, the Berlin Philharmonie of 1956-63.

Karl Friedrich Schinkel (1781-1841) The great neo-classical architect of Prussia. Before he designed buildings he was a wildly romantic painter of imaginary Gothic cathedrals standing in misty forests. He also designed theatre sets (for example, some famous sets for the *Magic Flute*). Among his buildings are:

The Theatre in Berlin of 1818-21.
Altes Museum, Berlin, 1823-30 (Neues Museum when first built; it has a long colonnaded front like the British Museum, only straight, concealing steps up to what turns out to be second storey inside the colonnade — Smirke did not commit this solecism.

George Gilbert Scott — the first (1811-78) One of the most vicious of church 'restorers', worse than Wyatt had been, and disingenuously claiming to preserve what he found. His chapels at Exeter College Oxford (1856) and St. John's College (1863-9) both involved the demolition of chapels already there (Exeter's had to be blown up, when the excuse for rebuilding had been that it was unsafe — a characteristic piece of Gothic Revival deceit). Both these chapels are out of scale with their colleges, and both disrupt the quadrangle or court they stand in, like cuckoos.

Scott surprisingly designed one or two fine buildings — Doncaster parish church, in Yorkshire (1854), the Albert Memorial (1864) and St. Pancras Station Hotel (1865) stand out from the mass of dull buildings he designed. They are in a variety of Gothic styles. He wrote *Remarks on secular and domestic architecture* in 1858, but his attempts in this sphere were not a success — Broad Sanctuary, outside Westminster Abbey (1854) and Kelham Hall, near Newark, Nottinghamshire (1857 — it became a college and is now council offices). Perhaps his most satisfactory building is the Foreign Office in London (1861) which, thanks to Lord Palmerston, Scott was compelled (at the risk of losing the commission) to design in an Italian style. There is an essay on Scott by David Cole in P. Ferriday (ed.), *Victorian architecture.*

George Gilbert Scott — the second (1839-97), and **John Oldrid Scott** (1842-1913), sons of G.G. the first, both designed churches, and collaborated in the design of the Roman Catholic Cathedral in Norwich, Norfolk, 1884-1910.

Giles Gilbert Scott (1880-1960), grandson of G.G. the first. He secured the commission for Liverpool Anglican Cathedral in 1904, against entries by many distinguished architects, including C.R. Mackintosh. The cathedral is due to be finished by the late 1970's, but most of it was in use by 1939. Scott was also the architect of Battersea Power Station (begun 1932), Waterloo Bridge (1939-45) in London, and the New Bodleian in Oxford (1936-46). This library is generally agreed to be of dismal design, and it replaced some charming 17th century houses. The industrial buildings however have a grandeur lacking from many modern buildings. The loss of Rennie's Waterloo Bridge, though, is to be regretted, especially by anyone struggling across the gritty open space of the present bridge.

Richard Norman Shaw (1831-1912) Most fashionable architect and acknowledged leader of the QUEEN ANNE style in the mid-1870's. He began as a Goth; and designed churches (Bingley in Yorkshire, 1864-8); then Tudoresque country houses (e.g. Cragside, Northumberland, 1870 onwards — now owned by the National Trust). Shaw turned towards a classical style in the 1870's, with his work at Bedford Park, London (see GARDEN CITIES), and buildings like Lowther Lodge, Kensington (now Royal Geographical Society), 1873, and Swan House, on Chelsea Embankment, 1876. His style turned more Wren-Baroque, notably with Bryanston House in Dorset (now a school), 1890, etc.; and the Piccadilly Hotel, fronting on to both Piccadilly and Regent Street, wrecking Nash's quadrant in the process (1905), though both it and Blomfield's additions towards Piccadilly Circus — particularly the arches over side-streets — are very confident swagger Edwardian Baroque. Blomfield, who admired Shaw, wrote a life of him; and there is a new life/architecture book on him by Andrew Saint — both are called *Richard Norman Shaw.*

Camillo Sitte (1843-1903) Austrian architect of several buildings, but best known for his book *Der Stadtbau* translated as *City planning according to artistic principles* by G.R. and C.C. Collins. His views are an early example of what came to be known as the Townscape Movement.

READING:
G.R. & C.C. Collins, *Camillo Sitte and the birth of modern city planning.*

Skidmore, Owings and Merril, American architectural partnership of the mid-20th century, well-known for their Lever Building in New York, designed in 1952 by Gordon Bunshaft, a partner; and the U.S. Air Force Academy at Colorado Springs, 1955, etc.

READING:
Christopher Woodward, *Skidmore, Owings and Merril,* photos by Yukio Futagawa.

Robert Smirke (1780-1867) Although the outstanding 'correct' neo-classical architect in England in the early 19th century, his early buildings were in a romantic castle style — Eastnor Castle in Herefordshire (near Ledbury) of 1814. His most famous buildings are the British Museum (built from 1823 — King's Library — to 1847, when the south colonnade was finished); and the block on the west side of Trafalgar Square, now added to, and now all Canada House, but originally the Royal College of Physicians (north) and Union Club (south) — 1824-7). His churches, also correct neo-classical, include St. Anne, Wandsworth (1824) and St. Mary, Wyndham Place (1823), both in London.

Sidney Smirke (1798-1877), younger brother of Robert, designed the iron-frame domed reading room which was built inside the courtyard of the British Museum in 1854-7.

John Soane (1758-1837) Few of his buildings survive unaltered. Only his own house, 13, Lincoln's Inn Fields, London, built 1812-13, but much altered afterwards into a kind of museum (and now the Soane Museum) which he established by Act of Parliament. His Bank of England was destroyed by Baker in the 1920's, but the screen on the street level is for the most part still there. His *villa surburbana* at Ealing is now the public library. The Dulwich

College picture gallery was damaged in the war, but has been rebuilt. Some of Soane's mannerisms — vertical grooves instead of pilasters, to mark divisions — were taken up by builders.

READING:
Dorothy Stroud, *The architecture of Sir John Soane.*

'Span' The name of an English building development firm, which had Eric Lyons as chief architect. They produced a very fashionable type of middle-class housing in the 1950's and '60's, beginning in Blackheath in south-east London, and then continuing with other estates in e.g. Petersham, in south-west London. These estates are a mixture of two storey blocks of flats and two storey terrace houses, in a generally International Modern style (wall to wall horizontal strakes of windows), but using traditional materials (brick, tile-hanging) which would not have been allowed by the Bauhaus (or the Smithsons). The grouping of the blocks is in a 'collegiate' rather than a 'picturesque' manner. The dwellings are arranged in series of interlocking quadrangles. Many other estates have been designed in the same way; local authority housing in the '60's also followed suit. Span/Eric Lyons turned to an even more vernacular style with their New Ash Green 'village' in North Kent, begun in the late 1960's as a kind of 'private' new town.

Mart Stam (b.1899) Dutch furniture designer, the inventor of the cantilevered steel chair; designed 1924, but without the means of making it properly until 1926. The design has remained almost unchanged ever since; Breuer designed a chic version of it in 1928.

Gustav Stickley (1857-1942) American furniture designer, who manufactured quite plain furniture in the tradition of the English Arts and Crafts, though cheaper than them, and more aimed at a general market. His work became known as Mission furniture.

James Stirling (b.1926) Architect (with James Gowan, b.1924) of Leicester University engineering department laboratories (1959-63); the Cambridge University History Library (1961-8); the Florey building for Queen's College, Oxford (1968-70). One of the objects of N. Pevsner's attack in 1966-7.

George Edmund Street (1824-81) Gothic revival architect. He designed St. James the Less, off Vauxhall Bridge Road, London (1860-1); St. Philip the Less, in North Oxford (1860-2) and St. Mary Magdalen, Paddington (1868-78); these are all heavy, serious and worthy buildings. In 1866 Street won the competition for the new Law Courts to be built in the Strand, London; they were not finished until after his death. Lawyers have complained about them almost since the day they were opened; Peter Collins has some very interesting things to say about the competition and the judging in his *Architectural judgement* (London 1971). Philip Webb was a pupil of Street's and it was in Street's office (at the time in Oxford) that Webb and Morris met.

Second Empire
17 The "New Louvre": north wing of the Louvre, Paris (Visconti and Lefuel, 1852-71). Now the *Musée des Arts Décoratifs.*

18 Remote "Second Empire" influence in Rhode Island, U.S.A., c.1880.

Neo-Baroque
19 'Edwardian Baroque
Admiralty Arch,
London (Aston Webb, 1911).

20 National Provincial
Bank, Bishopsgate,
London (Gibson, 1865).

'Edwardian Baroque' Planning: Aldwych, London (laid out c.1900).
21 The western half of Aldwych, with, on the right, Bush House (Helmle and Corbett, 1923-35).

22 The western half of Aldwych, with the Waldorf Hotel (Mackenzie, 1907-8).

Neo-Classical
23 Greek Revival: Oslo Stock Exchange (Grosch, 1820).

24 (opposite page, top) Mixture of sources: Ashmolean Museum and Taylorian Institute,
Oxford, England (C. R. Cockerell).

25 (opposite page, bottom) American Greek Revival: 186 Main St., Concord, Mass.
A 'federal style' house of c.1813 by Josiah Davis, with a Greek Revival portico
added by David Loring in the middle of the 19th century.

26 (left) Nationalist Revival: Central Station, Amsterdam, in a Dutch Renascence style by Cuijpers (1881-89).

The 'Romanesque' tradition in the Nineteenth Century
27 The Natural History Museum, London (Waterhouse, 1868).

28 King's Cross Station, London (Cubitt, 1850).

The 'Romanesque' Tradition
29 Central School of Arts and Crafts, Holborn, London (Riley, 1901).

30 Rookery Building, Chicago (Burnham and Root, 1883-86).

William Strickland (1788-1854) American neo-classical architect. His most famous building is the Merchants' Exchange in Philadelphia (1834), and he also designed the U.S. Mint (1829-33) in Washington, D.C., and the State Capitol at Nashville, Tennessee (1845-9).

Louis Sullivan (1856-1924) Worked with W. LeBaron Jenney in Chicago, and then with Vaudremer in Paris (Richardson had done no more than *admire* the work of Vaudremer). In 1879 Sullivan joined the firm of Dankmar Adler, which became Adler and Sullivan. Their first success was the Auditorium Building in Chicago (1886-9), in the Romanesque style established by Richardson in America (Marshall Field Store, 1885). Sullivan's other masterpieces are the Wainwright building in St. Louis, (1890); the Guaranty Building in Buffalo (1894) — both rare examples of Chicago School work outside Chicago; and the Carson Pirie Store in Chicago, of 1899 and 1904. *Chicago's famous buildings* lists several other works by Sullivan, including houses; in his later years he was joined in his office (on top of the Auditorium Building) by the young Frank Lloyd Wright. Louis Sullivan was the great decorator of the Chicago School, rather than in any way a structural innovator.

Bruce James Talbert (1838-81) Furniture designer in England, author of *Gothic forms applied to furniture, metal work and decoration for domestic purposes,* but designing himself in a mixed style; his later *Examples of ancient and modern furniture* (1876) was even more popular. The V. and A. has his 'Pet' sideboard; and his work is discussed by E. Aslin in *English 19th century furniture.*

Kenzo Tange (b.1913) Leading Japanese architect in a modern 'Expressionist' style, using reinforced concrete in a sculptural way, like Niemeyer and the later Corbusier. It was especially remarked on at the Osaka Exhibition in 1960; see also his Tokyo City Hall (1966) and Memorial Hall at Hiroshima (1950).

Alexander Thompson (1817-75) — 'Greek' Thompson; Glasgow architect; his buildings are described in *Glasgow at a glance,* and include Moray Place of 1859 and other terraces of a remarkably severe (especially for their late date) neo-classical style; and three churches — Caledonian Road, 1856; Vincent Street, 1859; and Queen's Park, 1867; only Vincent Street is in a good state of repair now. Thompson wrote a very spirited attack on the Gothic style of architecture, with particular reference to Scott's getting the commission for the new Glasgow University Building (and one can sympathise with Thompson on many counts). This attack is reprinted in part by R. Macleod in *Style and society.* Thompson's building has more in common with contemporary Greek Revival buildings in America than with contemporary work in England and Europe.

Michael Thonet (1796-1871) perfected his process for bentwood furniture, with successful designs by 1850; his bentwood is in 'tubes', unlike Aalto's in the 1930's, which is in flat 'strips'. The designs of his dining (café) chair were finalised in 1859 and are still in production — one of the most successful of all 19th century designs, having become almost identified with cafés; the other lasting design was the bentwood rocking chair, simple but with graceful curls also still in production, usually with a cane seat and back.

Harrison Townsend (1851-1928) English architect who designed in the Romanesque style of the 19th century, somewhat in the manner of Richardson in America. In London, Townsend's three buildings are the Bishopsgate Institute (1894), the Whitechapel Art Gallery (1897-9) and the Horniman Museum in Forest Hill in South London. These buildings are in a similar style to that of Riley's Central School of Arts and Crafts of 1907, though the two museums gave Townsend greater freedom in the design of their facades than Riley had with C.S.A.C.

Raymond Unwin (1863-1940) Together with Barry Parker (1867-1947), his partner until 1914, designed the layout of Letchworth Garden City, Hampstead Garden Suburb and Wythenshaw near Manchester. See GARDEN CITIES. Unwin wrote *Town planning in practice* in 1909, which was influential.

J.A.E. Vaudremer (1824-1914) Leading French 19th century Romanesque architect who had Sullivan as a pupil and who also seems to have influenced Richardson — see ROMANESQUE. He designed St. Pierre de Montrouge, Avenue de Maine at the Avenue d'Orleans (1864-70); the Santé Prison, Boulevard Arago (1865-85), and Notre Dame, Rue d'Auteuil (1876-83), all in Paris. There is a brief note on him in H-R. Hitchcock, *Architecture, 19th and 20th centuries.*

Calvert Vaux (1824-95) Partner of A.J. Downing for architecture and with F.L. Olmstead for the layout of Central Park, New York City, and Riverside, Illinois. His 'Olana', Hudson, N.Y, is a house in a moorish style.

Henri Van der Velde (1863-1957) Belgian architect and designer. A painter, who, like many others, turned to design under the influence of William Morris. His early work was typography; then interiors (including Samuel Bing's shop L'Art Nouveau in Paris in 1895). In the late 1890's he settled in Germany. In 1904-7 he designed the School of Arts and Crafts at Weimar, later being appointed as Director, a post he kept until war broke out in 1914. He recommended Gropius as his successor, and this was the institution that became the Bauhaus. In the 1914 debates at the *Deutsche Werkbund* Exhibition, in Cologne, Van der Velde defended individual craftsmanship against Muthesius's advocacy for designing for industrial production. In the years before the First World War, Van der Velde designed furniture, much of which has found its way into museums, in Karlsruhe, Nuremburg, and Hagen in Germany, in Zurich, and in Trondheim. One of his later buildings was the Kröller-Müller Museum at Otterloo in the Netherlands (1937-54).

E.E. Viollet-le-Duc (1814-79) The only considerable propagandist in France for the Gothic Revival. He restored many churches and castles, including Pierrefonds. He designed one church which is well-known: St. Denys-de-Estrée in St. Denis, Seine (1864-7). His book *Entretiens* (vol 1 in 1863 and vol 2 in 1872) ingeniously but rebarbatively sets out ways in which Gothic structural devices once carried out in stone could be done with iron pipes. His ideas are discussed in Peter Collins's *Changing ideals in modern architecture*.

C.F.A. Voysey (1857-1941) Father of the suburban semi-detached, pebble-dashed, slightly Cotswoldy house. He also advocated low ceilings, a structural change which speculative builders were glad to take up. Most of Voysey's architecture is private houses and few of them can be seen (none is open to the public). Broadleys and Moor Crag overlook Lake Windermere (both 1898); Annesley Lodge (1895) is in Platts Lane, Hampstead, London; and Voysey also designed a house for the Bedford Park estate (see GARDEN CITIES), no. 14, South Parade, facing over Acton Green. From 1883 onwards, Voysey designed wallpapers which are midway in style between Morris and Art Nouveau (some of them can be seen in the V. and A.).

READING:
David Gebbard, *C.F.A. Voysey, architect.* A selection of Voysey's writings, with a commentary.
N. Pevsner, *Studies in art, architecture and design.* Vol. 2.
John Brandon Jones, 'C.F.A. Voysey' in *Victorian architecture*, ed. P. Ferriday.

Otto Wagner (1841-1918) Designer of the Vienna Underground station entrances in a *Jugendstil* (Art Nouveau) manner, contemporary with Guimard's Métro Station entrances in Paris. Wagner's Post Office Savings Bank in Vienna of 1904 is a plain building which, while it reflects the fashion for cutting out ornament, does not look at all like the International Modern of the 1920's.

Thomas U. Walter (1804-1887) added the wings and dome to the Capitol, Washington D.C., in 1851-65, transforming it from a neo-classical into a Baroque building.

Alfred Waterhouse (1830-1905) A very rare example of an architect who was more or less in the Gothic Revival tradition, but was not primarily a church builder. His Manchester Town Hall (1868-77) was one of the last great commissions in Gothic; his Natural History Museum in London, begun in 1868, was in a Romanesque style. The National Liberal Club of 1884 — completing the Whitehall Court apartments, which are in a French Renascence style — is in a kind of French late Gothic which matches the Renascence but leaves out the Italian trimmings. His Prudential Buildings (main office in Holborn, London, 1876) are unmistakable with their hot red brick faces; they are in a possibly Flemish late-Gothic town-hall style, considerably simplified. There are many smaller versions of the main office in cities in Britain. Waterhouse also designed a number of unloved buildings in Oxford and Cambridge in the late 1860's and early '70's.

Aston Webb (1849-1930) Architect of many of the grandest buildings of late Victorian and Edwardian England, most of them in a Baroque style of one variety or another. Among them are the Royal Naval College, Dartmouth, 1894-1904 (red brick with white stone trimmings); Royal College of Science and Imperial College, 1900-6 and 1911, both stone; Admiralty Arch, the refacing of Buckingham Palace, and the *rond-point* of the Palace all finished 1911, all stone; and Birmingham University — in a more Romanesque style, 1906-9. The south front of the Victoria and Albert Museum is in a style of its own, with suggestions of Renascence and of Newcastle and Edinburgh cathedrals in its tower, and should be studied from the safety of the other side of the road.

Philip Webb (1831-1915) Two namesakes could not be more contrasted architects. Philip Webb was the subject of one of Lethaby's more important books, as both Webb and Lethaby are the main subject of R. Macleod's *Style and society*. Webb designed houses for well-to-do clients (and one office block in Middlesbrough); few of them remain standing, let alone unaltered. The famous Red House in Bexleyheath of 1859 for William Morris is well looked after now; it is an interesting variation on the type of house Butterfield was designing in the 1840's for clergymen — only in Kent and in brick rather than Gloucester and stone. Otherwise, of Webb's houses, only a comparatively late one, Standen, a mile or so out of East Grinstead in Sussex, survives intact. It was given to the National Trust by the last surviving member of the family for whom it was built (in 1891-4) and is a remarkable example of the whole Webb-Morris ideal of a country house, with carpets, wallpapers, curtains, furniture, etc., all in the same mood. There is a nice description of Standen in Mark Girouard's *Victorian country houses*. R.W. Lethaby's *Philip Webb and his work* is the only full-scale study.

William Wilkins (1778-1839) Refined 'neo-Greek' variety of neo-classical architecture, best seen in Downing College, Cambridge (begun 1806), though the original design was spoiled by Baker (of the Bank of England) when he added to it in the 20th century. Wilkins was also the designer of the National Gallery (re-using columns from Carlton House) in 1834-8; and of St. George's Hospital at Hyde Park Corner, 1828-9. However, he could also design a competent Gothic, quite early for that — the screen and lodge of King's, Cambridge, is 1823-7.

Tapio Wirkkala (b.1915) One of the leading Finnish designers, over a wide field. Artistic director of Ittala since 1947. Prizewinner at Milan Triennale for glassware, light fittings and exhibition design. He has also designed silverware, porcelain and furniture.

J.L. Wormersley (b.1910) City architect of Sheffield; and the designer in charge of the huge estate of flats on the east side of the City, Parkhill Housing, 1955-60. The blocks walk down a hill, starting off with only a few storeys at the top and several at the bottom, so that 'streets' for milk floats, removal trucks and people run right along the blocks. These were intended to recreate in a 'modern' setting the old streets, but like most of these schemes for 'streets in the sky', they haven't.

Frank Lloyd Wright (1869-1959) The best way of getting to know Wright's work (without actually going to see it — and much of it is private) is to get hold of a copy of Henry-Russell Hitchcock's *In the nature of materials: the buildings of F. L. W. 1894-40* which has photographs of all his important work to that date. Apart from that, there is a revealing description of Wright's 'Prairie' houses and their ventilation and heating systems in Reyner Banham's *The architecture of the well-tempered environment.* These are some examples of his work, chosen to represent the various 'styles' he has worked in:

Prairie houses: Robie House, Chicago, 1908.
International Modern: Falling water, Bear Run, Pennsylvania, 1937-9.
Factories: Johnson Wax Co., Racine, Wis. Office block (with mushroom columns, and glass-tubing walls), 1936-9; Laboratory tower, 1944.
Museum: Guggenheim, (designed 1942, finished 1960).
Skyscraper: Bartlesville, Oklahoma (offices and flats), 1955.

Most of Wright's architecture differs greatly from the International Modern stylists who were his contemporaries; he had deep ideas about being in harmony with nature; the hearth as the centre of the home played a large part in determining his designs. Even his skyscraper projects were linked to the idea of a tree's growth. There is a good short survey of his work by Peter Blake, the best part of his *The master builders* (1963), also issued separately as a paperback.

Thomas Henry Wyatt (1807-80) Architect (with Raphael Brandon) of St. Mary, Wilton, 1842-3, one of the few outstanding examples of Italian Romanesque revival architecture in England. The church, about 5 miles west of Salisbury, is worth visiting. It is quite unlike any other parish church of the 1840's.

Mathew Digby Wyatt (1820-77) Brother of T.H.; architect of Paddington Station Hotel (1854-5), in a French Renascence style; and secretary of the Executive Committee for the Great Exhibition in 1851 — a leading protagonist in design discussions in mid-century.

Yorke, Rosenberg and Mardall English architectural partnership, best known for the design of Gatwick Airport, in a cool, Miesian style (begun 1957). Gatwick Airport is a good example of that species of 'impersonal', 'industrial' architecture which was the aim of the International Modern Movement. As a style it is perhaps most appropriate for a transit building, especially when it is carried out with some elegance of proportions, as at Gatwick.

PART FOUR

A guide to places and museums

Examples of architecture and design can be seen in a variety of settings. Many countries now have an open-air museum with buildings — usually rural — re-erected in the grounds, and some of these buildings are examples of 19th and even 20th century design. Many houses are preserved as the homes of famous people — those of Charles Dickens or Franklin D. Roosevelt, for example, — and incidentally serve as examples of the furniture and design of their occupants' tastes. In museums, there are often 'period rooms'; although these are misleading, because most people, especially away from fashionable circles, have tended to have pieces from several periods in their rooms. However, the 'period room' is usually an improvement on having objects lined up behind ropes, or in glass cases, which is the museum alternative. Similar to the 'period room', and often in the same museums, is the 'period street' which contains reconstructions of shops, where the contents are fixed for a predetermined period.

The following are notes on different countries, with selections from their museums and galleries.

BRITAIN

Guides to museums:
Museums and galleries in Great Britain.
Historic houses, castles and gardens.
Both these are published annually by A.B.C., and give short descriptions, opening times and travel directions.
Museums in London:
The major national collections are in London:

Victoria and Albert Museum, South Kensington. Its collections lean towards 'design as art'. The 19th and 20th century galleries are more 'artistic' than the earlier ones. The Museum also has a room furnished by Morris and Co. as a dining room, now a small exhibition gallery.,
Geffrye Museum, Kingsland Road, Shoreditch. It has rooms furnished in periods up to 1939.
Bethnal Green Museum. The building was constructed around the re-erected Brompton Museum of the 1850's, which gave way to the V. and A. It now contains furniture, dolls' houses, etc.
William Morris Gallery, Walthamstow. Designs by him, and by some Arts and Crafts designers, including Mackmurdo.

Museums in large cities:
Brighton: the Museum and Art Gallery has exhibitions of furniture, etc. The Royal Pavilion has complete Regency furnishings.
Edinburgh: the Royal Scottish Museum.
Glasgow: the Art Gallery and Museum, and the collections of the University.
Leicester: the Museum and Art Gallery (Gimson collection); Newarke Houses Museum.
Manchester: the Whitworth Gallery has a large collection of textiles, including some by Morris.

Museums with 'streets' of period shops, and sequences of period rooms:
Leeds: Abbey House Museum, Kirkstall.
Northampton: Abington Museum.
Salford: Museum and Art Gallery.
Stockton-on-Tees: Preston Hall Museum, Preston Park.
York: Castle Museum.

Open air museums:
Beamish, County Durham.
St. Fagan's, near Cardiff: the Welsh Folk Museum.
Singleton, near Chichester: the Weald and Downland Museum.

Houses which have furnishings characteristic of periods:
GRAND HOUSES
Carlton Towers, near Goole, Yorkshire.
Castle Drogo, Devonshire (Lutyens's building and furnishings).
Hughenden Manor, Buckinghamshire (Disraeli's home).
Knebworth House, Hertfordshire (Lord Lytton's home).
Knightshayes Court, Devonshire (designed by Burges).
Polesden Lacey, near Dorking, Surrey — Edwardian Baroque interior.

LESS GRAND HOUSES
Carlyle's house, 24 Cheyne Row, Chelsea.
Dickens's house, 48 Doughty Street, Holborn.
Standen near East Grinstead (designed by Philip Webb).
Haworth, the Brönte Museum.
Sir John Soane's Museum (his own house), Lincoln's Inn Fields.
Wightwick Manor, Wolverhampton (furnishings by Morris and Co.).

Books useful as guides:
'THE BUILDINGS OF ENGLAND'
Edited and mostly written by Nikolaus Pevsner; an invaluable record. The volumes are arranged county by county, on the old divisions, with some counties in two volumes. There is a concentration on 'art' buildings, especially medieval churches. The earlier volumes have relatively little on townscape.

THE SHELL GUIDES
These now cover about half of England, county by county, and Wales (groups of counties). Many photographs, less detailed descriptions of individual buildings than *The buildings of England,* but often better accounts of town building.

MURRAY'S ARCHITECTURAL GUIDES
Only for Berkshire, Buckinghamshire and Lancashire. Similar to the Shell guides.

CITY BUILDINGS SERIES
Published by Studio Vista. More detailed, and with more photographs, than any of the above books (covering much smaller areas). The list is:
Birmingham by D. Hickman.
Bristol by T.H.B. Burrough.
Liverpool by Q. Hughes.
Manchester by D. Sharp.
Portsmouth by A. Balfour.
York by P. Nuttgens.

David Piper, *The companion guide to London.*
Ian Nairn, *Nairn's London;* highly selective and always illuminating.

FRANCE

Books:

The French *Office du Livre* publish a *Guide des Musées de France,* which has a subject index (e.g. *'arts décoratifs'*), and their Tourist Office publishes *Parks and Châteaux of France.*
Ian Nairn, *Nairn's Paris*; the same kind of book as his *London.*
World cultural guides: Paris.

Museums:

Many of the major cities have museums of decorative arts — Bordeaux, Nancy and Tours being among the best-known — but, as with England, the collections are in the capital:

Musée des arts décoratifs; in the north wing of the Louvre building, opposite the Louvre Museum. Staffing shortages mean that only parts of the museum are open on any one day.
The Louvre itself has some furniture, etc.
Musée Carnavalet has furniture.

THE GERMAN-SPEAKING COUNTRIES

For West Germany, the general guide for museums is:
Museen in der Bundesrepublik Deutschland, published by Heinz Moos Verlag in Munich. It has a list of *Kunstgewerbliche Museen.*
Each of the Länder (provinces) has a *Landsmuseum;* among the better-known are:

Darmstadt: Hesse Land Museum.
Karlsruhe: Baden Land Museum.
Munich: Bavarian Land Museum.
Stuttgart: Württenberg Land Museum.
Several cities have a *Kunstgewerbemuseum,* among them Berlin, Cologne and Hamburg. Cologne also has a *Stadtmuseum,* which has exhibits of design interest.

In Austria, the major museum is the Kunsthistorisches Museum in Vienna.

In Switzerland, there is the Kunstgewerbemuseum in Zurich.

ITALY

The guide *Museums, galleries, monuments and archaeological complexes* is unfortunately for official use only; visitors are advised to apply to city and regional tourist offices for guides to museums.

NETHERLANDS

Museum guide: Ian M. Keown, *K.L.M.'s guide to Holland's museums,* published by the airline. A most informative guide. Amongst the useful museums are:
Amsterdam: Stedelijk Museum (furniture, designs, as well as paintings).
The Rijksmuseum also has some furniture.
Museum of architecture.
Arnhem: the Netherlands Open Air Museum (rebuilt houses, etc.).
Groningen: Town and Country Museum.
Gouda: Stedelijk Museum Het Catharina-Gasthuis.
The Hague: Gemeentemauseum (Municipal Museum).
Leiden: Lakenhal Museum (has period rooms).
Rotterdam: Historical Museum of the City of Rotterdam.
Bouwcentrum (Building Centre; it has exhibitions).
Utrecht: Central Museum.

For Belgium, see Jean-Pierre Vanden Branden, *Musées de Belgique: une guide.*

SCANDINAVIA

The Scandinavians were among the first to pioneer museums of domestic design, especially the open-air museums with re-erected buildings from the various regions. These parks with buildings are called *'Skansen'.*

Guides to museums:
Danish Museums, published by the Danish Embassy in London.

Peter Michelsen, *Frilands Museet: the Danish museum village at Sorgenfri;* a history as well as a guide; beautiful illustrations; a useful guide in itself to Danish vernacular building.

Danish Journal; issue no.77 was devoted to museums, and has lists (1974).

Museums in Norway, published for the Ministry of Foreign Affairs by Grøndahl, Oslo.

A key to the museums of Sweden, published by the Swedish Institute.

Traveller's guide to Denmark, published by the Danish Tourist Board; it has list of museums, by town and region.

Some interesting museums:
Copenhagen: Kunstindustrimuseum, Bredgade 68. Variously translated as 'Museum of decorative/industrial arts'. The museum is housed in the former Frederick Hospital, a building of 1752-3, in the Danish rococo style.
Oslo: Kunstindustrimuseum. Norwegian Folk Museum, Bygdøy.
Stockholm: National Museum. Nordic Museum. State Historical Museum.
Trondheim: Kunstindustrimuseum.
Books:
G.E. Kidder Smith, *Sweden builds;* one of the best introductions to a country's architecture, unfortunately now out of print, but worth borrowing.
The architecture of Denmark, a special number of the London *Architectural Review,* published as a book in 1949; a general survey.
S.A.R.'s Stockholm Guide to modern architecture in the city; revised every few years; each entry has a tiny photograph.
Thomas Paulsson, *Scandinavian architecture.* A general survey.
Ulf Härd af Segerstad's books (see list of books cited).

U.S.A.

The *Official Museum Directory* (ed. by the American Assn. of Museums, and published by the National Register Pub. Co.) is a massive volume which can be consulted in a library in the U.S. State capitals have museums with exhibitions illustrating the history of the state. Here are notes on some special kinds of museum, all of which are on interest for design or architecture:

National Public Collections:
Smithsonian Institute, Washington, D.C.
Metropolitan Museum, New York.
Museum of Modern Art (M.O.M.A.), New York.
Art Institute, Chicago.
Philadelphia Museum of Art.
Museum of the City of New York.

Museums Funded by Private Wealth:
Henry Ford Museum, Dearborn, Michigan.
Henry Francis Du Pont Winterthur Museum, Delaware.
Huntingdon Hartley Museum, California.

Museums of Educational Institutions:

Harvard, Princeton and Yale Universities have galleries for art and design.
Rhode Island School of Design, Museum of Art.

In England:

American Museum, Claverton Manor, on the south-eastern outskirts of Bath.
It has period rooms from the 17th to the 19th centuries (including a Shaker.
room) and collections of textiles, folk art, etc., together with a garden laid out
on the model of George Washington's at Mount Vernon.

Sites:

Colonial Williamsburg by definition is 54 years before 1830. Several New
England towns are well-preserved examples of the 19th century, especially
some of the ports, like Mystic, Conn. Outstanding among preserved
settlements is the Shaker community at New Lebanon in New York State.

Books:

The world's cultural centres: New York.
Arthur Siegel (ed.), *Chicago's famous buildings.*
Thomas Aidala, *The great houses of San Francisco.*
Reyner Banham, *Los Angeles, the architecture of four ecologies.*
H.L. and O. Williams, *Guide to old American houses.*

PART FIVE

A guide to further reading

At the end of this section of the guide there is a list of books
cited in the earlier sections. These books range from readable
introductions to authoritative monographs, and most of them contain
information which is valuable. If one wants to explore a certain topic
further, they are often the only available resource. As a critique of this
list, here are some notes on certain types of books.

Books that are a good read for beginners:

Some authors are a pleasure to read whatever topic they choose to
write on. These are among the most readable:

REYNER BANHAM.
His *Guide to modern architecture* is the best short guide available.
Committed to the Modern Movement, but not dogmatic about it. Not
surprisingly, because his *Architecture of the well-tempered environment*
undermines many of the key dogmas of the Modern Movement, as well
as being perhaps the best single book on modern architecture. His *Los
Angeles* is also a fascinating book.

NAN FAIRBROTHER
Her last two books, *New Life, new landscapes* and *The Nature of
landscape design,* are very readable and important discussions of their
topics. Her early death was a sad blow.

MARK GIROUARD
His talks on the radio, and his T.V. programmes, are a delight. The two
books on 19th century architecture which he has recently published are
splended examples of wit and scholarship — *Victorian country houses,*
and *Sweetness and light.*

OSBERT LANCASTER
His series of brilliant drawings with commentaries are one of the best
possible introductions to British design and architecture. They have now
all been gathered together and augmented in *A cartoon history of
architecture,* a title which does less than justice to the accuracy of his
descriptions. Some of his labels have become the standard terms — 'Pont
St. Dutch'; 'Wimbledon transitional'; 'By-pass variegated'; there is
nothing to replace them, even if one wanted to.

IAN NAIRN

His articles in *The Sunday Times* have been worth following over the years. He wrote much of *Surrey* and *West Sussex* for *The buildings of England*, as well as *Outrage; Nairn's London* and *Nairn's Paris*.

STEEN-EILER RASMUSSEN

Although he is a little influenced by the prevailing Historicist fashion, his books are among the best ever written about architecture. *Experiencing architecture* is perhaps the best introduction to building, past or present; *Towns and buildings* is a quite unusual approach to its subject; and *London, the unique city* has been the inspiration for a whole school of thought about city designs, and about London in particular.

Books which are reliable and readable surveys of their subjects:

Julian Barnard, *The decorative tradition* (ornament on buildings).

Colin and Rose Bell, *City fathers, the early history of town planning in Britain*.

Leonardo Benevolo, *The origins of modern town planning*.

T.S.R. Boase, *English Art, 1800-1870*. This is a book which seems more impressive every time one opens it. He combines a judicious survey with an interesting and readable style.

R.W. Brunskill, *Illustrated handbook of vernacular architecture*.

Kenneth Clark, *The Gothic Revival*.

Carl Condit, *The Chicago School of Architecture*.

Henry-Russell Hitchcock, *Architecture, 19th and 20th centuries*. The most comprehensive survey of its subject. It would be hard to try to read it straight through. With a few exceptions (like 'Architecture in iron and glass'), the earlier chapters are very dense with information, espcially about French architects with multiple Christian names; the later chapters are easier to read, and some of them, for example those on the development of office blocks, and of smaller private houses, are little books in their own right. Hitchcock is always readable; his other work is more particular, but *Early Victorian Architecture in Britain* is as interesting as it is authoritative.

Alan A. Jackson, *Semi-detached*; almost the only account of the development and the styles of London suburban houses in the first 40 years of the 20th century, and fortunately an excellent book.

Anthony Jackson, *The politics of architecture*. A superb account of the buildings of the International Modern Movement in Britain since the 1920's. One of the best books on modern architecture.

Charles Jencks, *Modern movements in architecture*. Lively, and apart from a terrible diagram at the beginning, clear. Inexplicably he admires Giedion's *Space, time and architecture*, which many people find the most unreadable of all the Historicist tracts.

Peter Kidson, Peter Murray and Paul Thompson, *A history of English architecture.* A great achievement to be interesting and thought-provoking in a relatively short survey.
Robert Macleod, *Style and society.* The best account of architectural ideas in England in the 19th and early 20th centuries.
Gillian Naylor, *The Arts and Crafts Movement.* A good account of the Arts and Crafts, and also the best available short introduction to English 19th century design.
Iona Plath, *The decorative arts of Sweden.* Traditional folk arts and modern developments from them.
David Pye, *The nature of design.*
Alistair Service, *Edwardian architecture.*
Robin Spencer, *The Aesthetic movement.*
John Summerson, *The classical language of architecture;* based on a series of radio talks; a wonderfully clear analysis of classical architecture; it is quite a short book, and essential reading. *Georgian London* is also a classic account.
Arnold Whittick, *European architecture in the 20th century.* A very detailed survey, paying much more attention than Hitchcock does to the various non-Bauhaus architectural movements. Many interesting photographs.
Doreen Yarwood, *The English home.* Excellent illustrations, and a clear text.

Reference books:

Graham Ashworth, *Encyclopaedia of town planning.* Good illustrations.
H.M. Colvin. *Biographical dictionary of English architects, 1660-1840.* The new edition starts in 1600, and is for *British* architects.
The Oxford companion to art (which includes architecture) and the *Oxford companion to the decorative arts.* They have longer general essays, and fewer personal entries, than the Penguin *Dictionaries,* of *Architecture,* and of *The decorative arts,* which in turn are much more Historicist than the Oxford *Companions.*
John Penoyre and Michael Ryan, *The observer's book of architecture.* Covers British architecture with good notes and very clever illustrations — line drawings with sparing colour codes.
John A. Walker, *Glossary of art, architecture and design since 1945.* The best of its kind.

Good authoritative monographs (not necessarily easy reading, and mostly narrow in range of interests):

Alison Adburgham, *Liberty's: a biography of a shop;* she has also written a *History of shopping.*
G.F. Chadwick, *The park and the town.*
G.F. Chadwick, *The work of Sir Joseph Paxton.*
Peter Collins, *Concrete, the search for a new architecture;* half of the book is an account of the work of Auguste Perret.
J.M. Crook, *The British Museum.*
J.M. Crook, *The Greek Revival* (in Britain).
Robert Macleod, *Charles Rennie Mackintosh* (a shorter but clearer account than Thomas Howarth's).
Nikolaus Pevsner, *Some architectural writers of the nineteenth century, Studies in art, architure and design.* These two volumes have many short essays on architects and designers — especially on Schinkel, Mackmurdo, Voysey — which cannot be matched elsewhere in English. There is also a very useful essay on Frank Pick, who masterminded London Transport's design in the 1920's and 1930's.
L.T.C. Rolt, *Isambard Kingdom Brunel.*
L.T.C. Rolt, *Victorian engineering.*
Gordon Russell, *Designer's trade;* an autobiography, but an account also of furniture design in the first half of the 20th century in England.
Andrew Saint, *R.N. Shaw.*
Isobel Spencer, *Walter Crane.*
Dorothy Stroud, *John Soane* (excellent photographs).
John Summerson, *John Nash, architect to George IV.*
Paul Thompson, *The work of William Morris.* Not only much the best introduction to Morris, but one of the best surveys of his work, covering all aspects.

Books on 'unusual' topics, which are of special interest or readability:

Boericke and Shapiro, *Hand-made houses.* Lovely colour photographs.
Boudon, *Lived-in architecture.* An interesting account of an early small housing estate by Corbusier at Pessac, revisited nearly half a century later. Many of the houses have been altered to look more 'traditional' — the cubic starkness of Corbusier's design has mostly gone. Told about this, Corbusier is said to have made the unexpected remark — 'People are right, architects are wrong'.
Theo Crosby, *How to play the environment game.*
Theo Crosby, *The necessary monument.* Amongst the monuments is Tower Bridge in London.
Jane Jacobs, *The death and life of great American cities.* An early and important challenge to many of the beliefs of town planners, which has had a very wide audience.

Carl Larsson: *Ett hem (Our home)*. Larsson was a Swedish painter active from the late 1880's until the First World War. He added to and decorated his house in Dalarna around the turn of the century. He illustrated it in a series of water colours published as a book then, and since reissued. The house itself is now preserved and can be seen; it is the subject of *Carl Larsson's home*, with a commentary by Segerstad.

John Prizeman, *Your house, the outside view;* principles of decoration of houses in Britain, with excellent colour illustrations — drawings and photographs.

Historicists:

All the books mentioned under the headings so far can be recommended. The books in this section, on the other hand, are mentioned by way of warning. Their authors all seem to subscribe to the Historicist picture of design and architecture, and to write about 'the style of our time', etc.

Anthony Bertram. His *House — a machine for living in,* and *Design,* both first published in the 1930's, are uncritical propaganda for the Bauhaus styles.

Peter Blake. Of the three sections of his *Master builders,* the Wright is the most useful, because least dogmatic; the Mies is dull (appropriately?) but the Corbusier is ridiculous, underpinned by naive Historicism.

Trevor Dannat, *Modern architecture in Britain;* as committed as the Smithsons, if less aggressively, to the International Modern style. It is probably true to say that the word 'modern' applied to architecture by British writers invariably means 'International Modern Movement', the Bauhaus, etc., which is of course a misleading use of the word 'modern', which should have a neutral, unattached meaning.

John Gloag. In some of his books (*Victorian comfort,* for example), his Historicist thought is not apparent, but it is in *Industrial art explained* and, oddly enough, in *Georgian grace.*

R. Furneaux Jordan, *Victorian architecture;* hardly a history of its subject at all.

Bernat Klein, *Design matters;* emphasizes change for its own sake, which is one of the supports for the Historicist position.

The Penguin *Dictionaries;* their Historicist bias is particularly misleading (for a reference work) on figures like Morris and Van der Velde.

Nikolaus Pevsner; the heart of his position can be seen in the *Listener* articles of 1966/7; his views are discussed by David Watkin in *Morality and architecture.*

J.M. Richards, *Introduction to modern architecture.*

J.M. Richards, *The functional tradition* (with Eric de Maré's lovely photographs).

J.M. Richards. *Castles on the ground* (about suburbia) is uncharacteristically without dogma.

The chief writers against Historicism, either directly or indirectly, have been:
Reyner Banham: though a supporter of the Modern Movement, his *Architecture of the well-tempered environment* disposes of, for example, the International Modern claim to be the 'only' functional style of 'our time'.
Peter Collins, *Changing ideals in modern architecture*, traces the beginning of the 'functional' fashion in modern architecture to the 18th century, thus disproving the Historicist argument that these ideals came out of the collapse of style, etc. in the 19th century.
David Watkin, *Morality in architecture.*

PART SIX

Select bibliography

F.B. Adams (ed.), *Bookbindings by T.J. Cobden-Sanderson*, Catalogue of exhibition, 1968.

Alison Adburgham, *Liberty's: a biography of a shop*, London, Allen & Unwin, 1975.

Thomas Aidala & Curt Bruce, *The great houses of San Francisco*, New York, Knopf; London, Thames & Hudson, 1974.

Bruce Allsop, *The study of architectural history*, London, Studio Vista, 1970.

Bruce Allsop, *Style in the visual arts*, London, Oriel Press, 1956.

Bruce Allsop, *Towards a humane architecture*, London, F. Muller, 1974.

John Allwood, *The great exhibitions*, London, Studio Vista, 1977.

(Anon), *The architecture of Darbourne and Darke*, London, R.I.B.A. Publications, 1977.

Graham Ashworth, *Encyclopaedia of town planning*, London, Barrie & Jenkins, 1973; New York, Beckman Publications.

William Ashworth, *The genesis of modern British town planning*, London, Routledge, 1954.

Elizabeth Aslin, *The Aesthetic Movement: prelude to Art Nouveau*, London, Elek, 1969.

Elizabeth Aslin, *Nineteenth-century English furniture*, London, Faber, 1962.

Kell Aström, *City planning in Sweden*, trans. Ruby Flichtner, published by the Swedish Institute. Swedish edition, *Svensk stadsplanering*, Stockholm, 1967.

Edmund N. Bacon, *Design of cities*, London, Thames & Hudson, 1967.

George Baird, *Alvar Aalto*, ('Masters of modern architecture' series), London, Thames & Hudson, 1970.

Alan Balfour, *Portsmouth*, ('City buildings' series), London, Studio Vista, 1970.

Mary Banham & Bevis Hillier (eds.), *A tonic to the nation*, London, Thames & Hudson, 1976.

Reyner Banham, *Guide to modern architecture*, London, Architectural Press, 1962.

Reyner Banham, *The architecture of the well-tempered environment*, Chicago University Press, 1969.

Reyner Banham, *Los Angeles: the architecture of the four ecologies,* New York, Harper & Row, 1971; London, Allen Lane, 1971; Harmondsworth, Penguin Books, 1973.

Reyner Banham, *Megastructures: urban futures of the recent past,* London, Thames & Hudson, 1976; New York, Harper & Row, 1977.

Reyner Banham, *The new brutalism: ethic or aesthetic?,* London, Architectural Press, 1966.

Reyner Banham, *Theory and design in the first machine age,* London, Architectural Press, 1960; New York, Praeger, 1967.

Reyner Banham, 'The Bauhaus gospel' in *The listener* for 26 September 1968.

Reyner Banham (ed.), *The Aspen papers,* London, Pall Mall, 1974.

Julian Barnard, *The decorative tradition,* London, Architectural Press, 1973.

Herbert Bayer & Walter Gropius, *Bauhaus 1918-28,* New York, M.O.M.A., 1976; London, Secker & Warburg, 1976.

Colin & Rose Bell, *City fathers: the early history of town planning in Britain,* London, Barrie & Rockliffe, 1969; Harmondsworth, Penguin, 1972.

Quentin Bell, *Bloomsbury,* London, Weidenfeld & Nicolson, 1968; Omega Books, 1974.

Quentin Bell, *Schools of design,* London Routledge, 1963.

Leonardo Benevolo, *The origins of modern town planning,* trans. Judith Landry, London, Routledge, 1967; Cambridge, Mass., M.I.T. Press, 1971.

Anthony Bertram, *Design,* Harmondsworth, Penguin, 1936.

Anthony Bertram, *The house: a machine for living in,* London, Black, 1935.

Gordon Biddle, *Victorian stations,* Newton Abbot, David & Charles, 1973.

Samuel Bing, *Artistic America,* edited by R. Kock, Cambridge, Mass., M.I.T. Press, and London, 1970.

Anthony Bird, *Paxton's palace,* London, Cassell, 1976.

John & Avril Blake, *The practical idealists: 25 years of designing for industry,* London, Lund Humphries, 1969.

Peter Blake, *Marcel Breuer: sun and shadow,* New York, Longmans, 1956.

Peter Blake, *The master builders,* New York, Norton Library, 1976; London, Gollancz, 1960. In 1963 this book was issued in three separate volumes: *Frank Lloyd Wright: architecture and space; Mies van der Rohe: architecture and structure; Le Corbusier: architecture and form,* published by Penguin, Harmondsworth.

Werner Blaser, *Mies van der Rohe,* London, Thames & Hudson, 1972; New York, Praeger, rev. edn., 1972.

Reginald Blomfield, *Richard Norman Shaw,* London, Batsford, 1940.

T.S.R. Boase, *English art, 1800-1870,* Oxford, Clarendon Press, 1959, (Oxford history of English art).

Alf Bøe, *From Gothic Revival to functional form,* Oslo, University Press; Oxford, Blackwell; New York, Humanities Press, 1957.

Art Boericke & Barry Shapiro, *Handmade houses: a guide to the woodbutcher's art,* San Francisco, Cal., Scrimshaw, 1975; London, Ideal Books International, 1975.

Margaret Bolsterli, *The early community at Bedford Park,* Ohio University Press, 1977; London, Routledge, 1977.

Victor Bonham-Carter, *Dartington Hall, the formative years, 1925-57,* London, Phoenix House, 1958, and Exmoor Press, 1970.

Phillippe Boudon, *Lived-in architecture: Le Corbusier's Pessac revisited,* trans. Gerald Onn, Cambridge, Mass., M.I.T. Press, 1969; London, Lund Humphries, 1972.

Asa Briggs, *Victorian cities,* London, Odhams, 1963; New York, McCosh, 1965; Harmondsworth, Penguin, 1968.

Asa Briggs, *William Morris: selected writing and designs,* Harmondsworth, Penguin, 1962; New York, Peter Smith, 1962.

Brent C. Brolin, *The failure of modern architecture,* New York, Macmillan Company; London, Studio Vista and Collier-Macmillan, 1975.

Theodore M. Brown, *The work of Gerrit Rietveld, architect,* Utrecht, A.W. Broonalz, 1958.

R.W. Brunskill, *Illustrated handbook of vernacular architecture,* London, Faber, 1971.

Colin Buchanan, *Bath, a study in conservation,* London, H.M.S.O., 1968.

Colin Buchanan, *Traffic in towns,* London, H.M.S.O., 1963; *Traffic in towns: the specially shortened edition of the Buchanan Report,* Harmondsworth, Penguin, 1964.

John Burchard & Albert Bush-Brown, *The architecture of America: a social and cultural history,* Waltham, Mass., Little, 1961; Abridged edn., London, Gollancz, 1966.

T.H.B. Burrough, *Bristol* ('City buildings' series), London, Studio Vista, 1970.

G.F. Chadwick, *The park and the town,* London, Architectural Press, 1966.

G.F. Chadwick, *The works of Sir Joseph Paxton,* London, Architectural Press, 1961.

Stanley D. Chapman (ed.), *The history of working-class housing,* Newton Abbot, David & Charles, 1971.

Ivan Chermayeff, *Observations on American architecture,* photographs by Elliott Erwith, London, Thames & Hudson, 1972.

Serge Chermayeff and Christopher Alexander, *community and privacy: toward a new architecture of humanism,* New York, Doubleday, 1963; Harmondsworth, Pelican, 1966.

Gordon E. Cherry, *Town planning in its social context*, London, Leonard Hill, 1970.
R. Judson Clark (ed.), *The Arts and Crafts Movement in America, 1876-1916*, Catalog of an exhibition at the Art Museum, Princeton and the Art Institute, Chicago, in 1972-3.
Kenneth Clark, *The Gothic Revival*, London, Murray, (new edn.), 1974; New York, Harper & Row, 1974.
Kenneth Clark, *Ruskin today*, London, Murray, 1964.
Basil F.L. Clarke, *Church builders of the 19th century*, London, S.P.C.K., 1938; Newton Abbot, David & Charles, 1969.
Alec Clifton-Taylor, *The pattern of English building*, (new edn.), London, Faber, 1972; Cincinnatti, Watson-Gupthill, 1973.
Council of Industrial Design (C.O.I.D.), *Design in the Festival*, London, H.M.S.O., 1951.
George R. Collins, *Antoni Gaudí*, ('Masters of world architecture' series), London, Mayflower, 1960; New York, Braziller, 1960.
George R. & C.C. Collins, *Camillo Sitte and the birth of modern city planning*, (Columbia University studies in art and architecture. no. 3), New York and London, Phaidon, 1965.
Peter Collins, *Architectural judgement*, London, Faber, 1971; Montreal, McGill-Queens University Press, 1971.
Peter Collins, *Changing ideals in modern architecture*, London, Faber, 1965; Montreal, McGill-Queens University Press, 1965.
Peter Collins, *Concrete: the vision of a new architecture; a study of Auguste Perret and his predecessors*, London, Faber, 1959
H.M. Colvin, *A biographical dictionary of English architects 1660-1840*, London, Murray, 1954.
H.M. Colvin, *A biographical dictionary of British architects, 1600-1840*, London, Murray, 1978.
Carl W. Condit, *The Chicago school of architecture*, Chicago University Press, 1973. This is a re-writing of — *The rise of the skyscraper*, 1952.
Ulrich Conrads, *Programmes and manifestos of 20th century architecture*, original edn., Frankfurt, 1964. Trans. Michael Bullock, Cambridge, Mass., M.I.T. Press, 1971; London, Lund Humphries, 1970.
Le Corbusier, *The city of tomorrow*, translated from the eighth French edition of *Urbanisme* by Frederick Etchells, London, John Rodker, 1929; London, Architectural Press, 1971.
Le Corbusier, *Towards a new architecture*, translated from the thirteenth French edition of *Vers une architecture* by Frederick Etchells, London, John Rodker, 1927; London, Architectural Press, 1970; New York, Praeger, 1970.
Harry B. Cresswell, *The Honeywood file*, London, Faber, 1929. (Reprinted 1964).

J. Mordaunt Crook, *The Greek revival : neo-classical attitudes in British architecture,* London, Murray, 1972.

Theo Crosby, *How to play the environment game,* Harmondsworth, Penguin, 1973.

Theo Crosby, *The necessary monument,* London, Studio Vista, 1970.

Dan Cruikshank & Peter Wyld, *London: the art of Georgian building,* London, Architectural Press, 1975; New York, Hastings, 1975.

Gordon Cullen, *Townscape,* London, Architectural Press, 1961.

Gordon Cullen, *Concise townscape,* New York, Van Nos. Reinhold, 1961; London, Architectural Press, 1971.

William Curtis, *A language and a theme: the achitecture of Denys Lasdun and Partners,* London R.I.B.A. Publications, 1976.

Trevor Dannat, *Modern architecture in Britain,* London, Batsford, 1959.

Dartington Hall and its work, (2nd edn. revised and edited by Nicolas Cottis) Totnes, Dartington Press Ltd., 1974.

Trevor Davis, *The architecture of John Nash,* London, Studio Vista, 1961.

Trevor Davis, *John Nash, the Prince Regent's architect,* London, Country Life, 1966; Newton Abbot, David & Charles, 1973.

R. Dennis & J. Jesse, *Catalogue of the exhibition of work by Christopher Dresser,* London, Fine Art Society, 1972.

Gill Dorfles, *Kitsch: an anthology of bad taste,* London, Studio Vista, 1969.

Henry Dreyfuss, *Designing for people,* (New edn.) New York, Crossmann, 1967.

H.J. Dyos, *Victorian suburb: a study of the growth of Camberwell,* Leicester University Press, 1961.

Charles Locke Eastlake, *The Gothic Revival in England,* (1872 edn.), (ed.), J. Mordaunt Crook, Leicester University Press, 1970.

Charles Locke Eastlake, Hints on household taste, 1868, (ed.), John Gloag, New York, Dover, 1970.

Ralph Edwards & L.G.G. Ramsey (eds.), *The connoisseur's complete period guides to the houses, decoration, furnishing, and chattels of the classic periods,* London, The Connoisseur, 1968.

Anthony Emery, *Dartington Hall,* Oxford University Press, 1970.

Norma Evenson, *Le Corbusier: the machine and the grand design,* New York, Braziller, 1969.

Nan Fairbrother, *The nature of landscape design,* London, Architectural Press, 1974.

Nan Fairbrother, *New lives, new landscapes,* London, Architectural Press, 1970; Harmondsworth, Penguin 1972.

Ann Ferebee, *A history of design from the Victorian era to the present,* New York, Van Nos. Reinhold, 1970.

Peter Ferriday (ed.), *Victorian architecture,* London, Cape, 1963.

Maxwell Fry, *Fine building,* London, Faber,1944.

J.K. Galbraith, *Economics and the public purpose,* New York, Houghton Miflin, 1973; London, Deutsch, 1974; Harmondsworth, Penguin, 1975.

David Gebhard, *C.F.A. Voysey, architect,* Los Angeles, Hennessy and Ingells Inc., 1975.

Patrick Geddes, *Cities in evolution,* New York, Fertig Howard, 1969.

Patrick Geddes, *City development,* Shannon, Irish Universities Press, 1973; New Brunswick, N.J., Rutgers University Press, 1973.

C.H. Gibbs Smith, *The Great Exhibition of 1851,* London, H.M.S.O. (Victorian and Albert Museum), 1950.

Mark Girouard, *Sweetness and light,* Oxford Clarendon Press, 1977.

Mark Girouard, *Victorian country houses,* Oxford, Clarendon Press, 1971.

Ludwig Glaeser, *The work of Frei Otto,* New York, M.O.M.A., 1972.

John Gloag, *The English tradition in design,* Harmondsworth, Penguin (King Penguin) 1947; enlarged 2nd edn., London, A. & C. Black, 1959.

John Gloag, *Industrial art explained,* London, Allen & Unwin (1934), (5th edn.) 1946.

John Gloag, *Mr. Loudon's England,* London, Oriel Press, 1970; New York, Routledge.

John Gloag, *Victorian comfort: a social history of design, 1830-1900,* London, A. & C. Black, 1961; Newton Abbot, David & Charles, 1976.

Harry S. Goodhart-Rendell, *English architecture since the Regency: an impression,* London, Constable, 1953; New York, Somerset Pubs.

Paul & Percival Goodman, *Communitas: means of livelihood and ways of life,* New York, Vintage Books, (2nd edn.), revised 1960.

Greater London Council, *G.L.C. architecture 1965-1970,* London, G.L.C., 1971.

T. Affleck Greeves, *Bedford Park: the first Garden Suburb,* London, Anne Bingley, 1975.

Marianna Griswold van Rensselaer, *Henry Hobson Richardson and his works,* New York, Dover Books, 1969.

Walter Gropius, *Apollo in the democracy,* New York, McGraw-Hill, 1968.

Walter Gropius, *The new architecture and the Bauhaus,* London, Faber, 1935; Cambridge, Mass., M.I.T. Press, 1965.

Frederick Gutheim, *Alvar Aalto* ('Masters of world architecture' series), New York, Braziller, 1960.

Ulf Hård af Segerstad, *Carl Larsson's home,* trans. Pearl Lömfors, Stockholm, Swedish Booksellers Assn., 1975.

Ulf Hård af Segerstad, *Modern Finnish design,* London, Weidenfeld and Nicolson, 1969.

Ulf Hård af Segerstad, *Modern Scandinavian furniture*, trans. Nancy & Edward Maze, London, Studio Books, 1963.

George Henderson, *Gothic*, Hardmondswoth, Penguin, 1967.

D. Hickman *Birmingham*, ('City buildings' series), London, Studio Vista, 1970.

Bevis Hillier, *Art Deco of the 20's and 30's*, London, Studio Vista, 1968; New York, Dutton, 1968.

Bevis Hillier, *Austerity binge: the decorative arts of the 40's and 50's*, London, Studio Vista, 1974.

Bevis Hillier, *The world of Art Deco*, New York, Dutton, 1971; London Studio Vista, 1971.

Georg Himmelheber, *Biedermeyer furniture*, London, Faber, 1974; New York, Scribner, 1974.

Henry-Russell Hitchcock, *Architecture, 19th and 20th centuries*, Harmondsworth, Penguin, 1958; (3rd edn.), 1969.

Henry-Russell Hitchcock, *Early Victorian architecture in Britain*, London, Architectural Press; New Haven, Yale University Press, 1954, vol. 1, text, vol. 2, plates; reprinted, New York, De Capo, 1972.

Henry-Russell Hitchcock, *In the nature of materials: the buildings of Frank Lloyd Wright, 1894-1940*, New York, De Capo, 1973.

Henry-Russell Hitchcock, and Philip Johnson, *The international style: architecture since 1922*. Original publication 1932. Reissued as *The international style*, with new foreword & appendix by H-R.H. New York, Norton Library, 1966.

Christopher Hobhouse, *1851 and the Crystal Palace*, London, Murray, (revised edn.), 1950.

Charles Holden and William Holford, *The City of London: a record of destruction and survival*, London, City of London Corporation, 1951.

Hugh Honour, *Neo-classicism*, Harmondsworth, Penguin, 1968.

Ebenezer Howard, *Garden Cities of tomorrow*, London, Faber, 1945; Cambridge, Mass., M.I.T. Press.

Thomas Howarth, *Charles Rennie Mackintosh and the Modern Movement*, London, Routledge, (1st edn. 1952, 2nd edn. 1977).

D. Hudson and K.W. Luckhurst, *The Royal Society of Arts, 1754-1954*, London, Murray, 1954.

Quentin Hughes, *Seaport: architecture and townscape of Liverpool*, London, Lund Humphries, 1964.

Alan A. Jackson, *Semi-detached London: suburban development, life and transport, 1900-1939*, London, Allen & Unwin, 1973.

Anthony Jackson, *The politics of architecture: a history of modern architecture in Britain*, London, Architectural Press, 1970; Toronto, University of Toronto Press, 1970.

Jane Jacobs, *The death and life of great American cities*, New York, Random House, 1961; Harmondsworth, Penguin, 1962.

Jane Jacobs, *The economy of cities*, New York, Random House, 1969; Harmondsworth, Penguin, 1969.

H.L.C. Jaffé, *De Stijl, 1917-31*, London, Tiranti, 1956.
Charles Jencks, *Modern movements in architecture*, Harmondsworth, Penguin, 1973.
Charles Jencks and Nathan Silver, *Adhocism: the case for improvisation*, London, Secker & Warburg, 1972.
Charles Jencks and G. Baird (ed.), *Meaning in architecture*, London, Barrie & Rockliffe/The Cresset Press, 1969.
Frank Jenkins, *Architect and patron: a survey of professional relations and practice in England from the 16th century to the present day*, Oxford University Press, 1961.
David Joel, *Furniture design set free*, London, Dent, 1969.
Philip C. Johnson, *Mies van der Rohe*, New York, M.O.M.A., 1947.
Percy Johnson-Marshall, *Rebuilding cities*, Edinburgh University Press, 1966.
Robert Furneaux Jordan, *Victorian architecture*, Harmondsworth, Penguin, 1966.
Barrington Kaye, *The development of the architectural profession in Britain*, London, Allen & Unwin, 1960.
Bryan Keogh and Melvyn Gill, *British domestic design through the ages*, London, Arthur Barker Ltd., 1970.
Peter Kidson, Peter Murray & Paul Thompson, *A history of English architecture*, Harmondsworth, Penguin, 1965. A revised edition of an an earlier book with the same title.
Bernat Klein, *Design matters*, London, Secker & Warburg, 1976.
James D. Kornwolf, *M.H. Baillie-Scott and the Arts and Crafts Movement*, Baltimore, Johns Hopkins University Press, 1972.
Osbert Lancaster, *A cartoon history of architecture*, London, Murray, 1975; Ipswich, Mass., Gambit, 1976. This is a revision of *Here of all places* (Murray, 1959), which was itself a combination of *Pillar to post* (Murray, first edn. 1938) and *Homes, sweet homes* (Murray, first edn. 1939), both re-edited and reprinted many times.
Royston Landau, *New directions in British architecture*, London, Studio Vista, 1968; New York, Braziller.
Carl Larsson, *Our home*, Stockholm, Bonniers, 1968 (*Ett Hem;* text by Lennart Rudström).
W.R. Lethaby, *Architecture*, London, Home University Library, 1911.
W.R. Lethaby, *Form and civilization*, London, Oxford University Press, 1922.
W.R. Lethaby, *Philip Webb and his work*, Oxford University Press. 1935.
Kenneth Lindley, *Seaside architecture*, London, Hugh Evelyn, 1973.
Kenneth W. Luckhurst, *The story of exhibitions*, London, Studio Books, 1951.
London County Council, *Hook, the planning of a new town*, London, L.C.C./G.L.C., 1961.
Fiona MacCarthy, *All things bright and beautiful*, London, Allen & Unwin, 1972.

Robert Macleod, *Charles Rennie Mackintosh,* London, Country Life, 1968.

Robert Macleod, *Style and society: architectural ideology in Britain, 1835-1914,* London, R.I.B.A., 1971.

Stephan Tschudi Madsen, *Art Nouveau,* London, Weidenfeld & Nicolson 1967; New York, McGraw-Hill.

Stephan Tschudi Madsen, *The sources of Art Nouveau,* Oslo, Aschehoug 1956; New York, De Capo, 1976.

Eric de Maré *The canals of England,* London, Architectural Press, 1950.

Eric de Maré *London 1851,* London, Folio/Dent, 1973.

Robert Maxwell, *New British architecture,* London, Thames & Hudson, 1972.

Ian McCallum, *Architecture U.S.A.,* London, Architectural Press, 1959/60.

Charles McKean & Tom Jestico, *Modern buildings in London: a guide,* London, Warehouse Pub., 1976.

Blake McKelvey, *The city in American history,* London, Allen & Unwin, 1969.

Peter Michelsen, *Frilands Museet* (the Danish Museum at Sorgengfri), Copenhagen, National Museum of Denmark, 1973.

William Morris, *On art and socialism,* lectures selected by Holbrook Jackson, London, John Lehmann, 1947.

William Morris, *Selected writings and designs,* edited by Asa Briggs (writings) and Graeme Shankland (designs), Harmondsworth, Penguin, 1962.

William Morris, *Stories in prose, stories in verse, shorter poems, lectures and essays,* edited by G.D.H. Cole for the Nonesuch Press, London, 1934; reissued 1948.

Murray's architectural guides, edited by John Betjeman and John Piper: *Berkshire,* London, Murray, 1949; *Buckinghamshire,* London, Murray, 1948; *Lancashire,* London, Murray, 1955.

Ian Nairn, *Nairn's London,* Harmondsworth, Penguin, 1966.

Ian Nairn, *Nairn's Paris,* Harmondsworth, Penguin.

Ian Nairn, *Outrage,* London, Architectural Press, 1955.

Ian Nairn, *Counter-attack,* London, Architectural Press, 1956.

Gillian Naylor, *The Arts and Crafts Movement,* London, Studio Vista 1971; Cambridge, Mass., M.I.T. Press, 1971.

Gillian Naylor, *The Bauhaus,* London, Studio Vista, 1968; New York, Dutton, 1968.

Arthur Negus and Max Robertson, *Going for a song: English furniture,* London, B.B.C., 1969; Collins/Fontana, 1971.

Eckhard Neumann (ed.), *Bauhaus and Bauhaus people,* New York, Van Nos. Reinhold, 1970.

Richard Neutra, *Buildings and projects,* Zurich, Editions Girsberger 1951. Reissued as: *Buildings and projects, Vol 1: 1925-50,* London, Thames & Hudson, 1964, together with *Vol 2: 1950-1960.*

Richard Neutra, *Survival through design*, New York, Oxford University Press, 1954.
Patrick Nuttgens, *York*, ('City buildings' series), London, Studio Vista, 1970.
F.J. Osborn & Arnold Whittick, *New towns, the answer to megalopolis*, London, Leonard Hill, 2nd edn., 1969; Cambridge, Mass., M.I.T. Press, 1970.
A.L. Osborn, *Country life guide to English domestic architecture*, London, Country Life, 1967.
The Oxford companion to art, (includes architecture), Oxford, Clarendon Press, 1970.
The Oxford companion to the decorative arts, (edited by Harold Osbourne) Oxford, Clarendon Press, 1975.
Thomas Paulsson, *Scandinavian architecture*, London, Leonard Hill, 1958.
Mark L. Peisch, *The Chicago School of architecture: early followers of Sullivan and Wright*, London, Phaidon, 1964; New York, Random House, 1965.
The Penguin dictionary of architecture (Fleming, Honour & Pevsner) (2nd edn.) 1972; enlarged edn. (hardcover) 1975.
The Penguin Dictionary of the decorative arts (Fleming and Honour), London, Allen Lane, Penguin Books, 1977.
John Penoyre & Michael Ryan, *The Observer's book of British architecture*, London, Warne, 1951, and subsequent edns.
Nikolaus Pevsner, *Academies of art, past and present*, Cambridge at the University Press, 1940; New York, De Capo.
Nikolaus Pevsner, (ed., and, for the most of them, author), *The buildings of England*, Harmondsworth, Penguin.
Nikolaus Pevsner, *An enquiry into industrial art in England*, Cambridge at the University Press, 1937.
Nikolaus Pevsner, *Pioneers of modern design*, Harmondsworth, Penguin, 1960, etc.; a reprint of the same title published in New York by M.O.M.A. in 1949, which was a revision of - *Pioneers of the Modern Movement*, London, Faber, 1936.
Nikolaus Pevsner, *Some architectural writers of the nineteenth century*, Oxford, Clarendon Press, 1972.
Nikolaus Pevsner, *Sources of modern architecture and design*, London, Thames & Hudson, 1968.
Nikolaus Pevsner, *Studies in art, architecture and design*, 2 volumes, London, Thames & Hudson, 1968; New York, Walker & Co.
Nikolaus Pevsner, 'The anti-pioneers', a talk published in *The listener* for 29 December 1966 and 5 January 1967.
Nikolaus Pevsner & J.M. Richards (eds.), *The anti-rationalists*, London, Architectural Press, 1973; New York, Harper & Row, 1976.
Donald Pilcher, *The Regency style, 1800-1837*, London, Batsford, 1947.
David Piper, *The companion guide to London*, London, Collins, 1974.
Iona Plath, *The decorative arts of Sweden*, New York, Dover

188   A CHOICE OVER OUR HEADS

Publications, 1966.
Karl R. Popper, *The poverty of Historicism*, London, Routledge, 1960.
John Prizeman, *Your house: the outside view*, London, Hutchinson, 1975.
A.W.N. Pugin, *Contrasts* (1836), (intro. by H-R. Hitchcock), Leicester University Press, 1969; New York, Humanities Press.
David Pye, *The nature of design*, London, Studio Vista, 1964.
Malcolm Quantrill, *Ritual and response in architecture*, London, Lund Humphries, 1974.
Stanley C. Ramsey & J.D.M. Harvey, *Small Georgian houses and their details*, London, Architectural Press; New York, Architectural Book Publishing Co., 1974 (originally published as two volumes in 1919 and 1923).
Amos Rapaport, *House form and culture*, Englewood Cliffs, N.J., Prentice Hall, 1969.
Steen-Eiler Rasmussen, *Experiencing architecture*, Cambridge, Mass., M.I.T. Press, first edn. 1959, 2nd. edn. 1962 (first edn., has colour photographs). First Danish edn. 1957.
Steen-Eiler Rasmussen, *London, the unique city*, London, Jonathan Cape, 1937; (first Danish edn. 1934) Abridged and revised edn., Harmondsworth, Penguin, 1960.
Steen-Eiler Rasmussen, *Towns and buildings*, Liverpool at the University Press, 1951, (first Danish edn. 1949); Cambridge, Mass., M.I.T. Press, 1969.
Herbert Read, *Art and industry*, London, Faber, 1934; 5th edn. 1956.
Brian Reade, *Art Nouveau and Alphonse Mucha*, London, H.M.S.O., 1963.
J.M. Richards, *The castles on the ground: the anatomy of suburbia*, London, Architectural Press, 1946. 2nd edn. (with drawings by John Piper), Murray, 1973.
J.M. Richards & Eric de Maré, *The functional tradition in early industrial buildings*, London, Architectural Press, 1958.
J.M. Richards, *Introduction to modern architecture*, Harmondsworth, Penguin, 1936 and subsequent edns.
L.T.C. Rolt, *Isambard Kingdom Brunel*, Harmondsworth, Penguin, 1970.
L.T.C. Rolt, *Victorian engineering*, London, Allen Lane, 1970; Harmondsworth, Penguin 1974.
Helen Rosenau, *The ideal city*, London, Studio Vista, 1974; New York, Harper & Row, 1975.
Bernard Rudolfsky, *Architecture without architects*, New York, M.O.M.A., 1964; London, Academy, 1977.
The architecture of Paul Rudolph; introduction by Sybil Moholy-Nagy; commentary by Paul Rudolph, London, Thames & Hudson, 1970.
John Ruskin, *Seven lamps of architecture*, 1849, Everyman/Dutton, 1906. *Stones of Venice* (3 volumes): 1851-3, Everyman, 1907. *Unto this last*, 1862, Everyman/Dutton, 1907. Ed. L.J. Hubenke,

Nebraska, University of Nebraska Press, 1967.

Gordon Russell, *Designer's trade,* London, Allen & Unwin, 1968.

Richard Saint, *Richard Norman Shaw,* New Haven and London, Yale University Press/Mellon Center, 1976.

S.A.R.'s Stockholm Guide, Stockholm Arkitekturs Riksforbund; editions published every few years.

Frank Schaffer, *The new town story,* London, MacGibbon & Kee, 1970; Paladin, 1972.

Robert Schmutzler, *Art Nouveau,* trans. Roditi, London, Thames & Hudson, 1964 (original edn., Stuttgart, 1962).

E.F. Schumacher, *Small is beautiful,* London, Blond & Briggs, 1973; New York, Harper & Row, 1976.

Richard Shone, *Bloomsbury portraits,* London, Phaidon; New York, Dutton, 1976.

Scientific American: cities (Various authors), New York, Knopf, 1965; Harmondsworth, Penguin, 1967.

Geoff Scott, *Building disasters and failures,* London, Construction Press, 1976.

Geoffrey Scott, *The architecture of humanism: a study in the history of taste,* London, Constable, first edn. 1914, 2nd edn. 1924.

Vincent Scully, *American architecture and urbanism,* New York, Praeger, 1968; London, Thames & Hudson, 1969.

Vincent Scully, *The Shingle Style and the Stick Style,* New Haven, Yale University Press, Revised edn., 1971.

Peter Self, *World cities,* London, Weidenfeld & Nicolson, 1956.

P. Selz & Mildred Constantine (eds.), *Art Nouveau,* London, Secker & Warburg, 1976.

Klaus-Jergen Sembach, *Into the thirties,* London, Thames & Hudson, 1972, (original title, *Stil 1930).*

Alistair Service, *Edwardian architecture,* London, Thames & Hudson, 1972.

John Seymour, *Bring me my bow,* London, Turnstone Books, 1978.

Dennis Sharp, *Manchester* ('City buildings' series), London Studio Vista, 1969.

Dennis Sharp, *Modern architecture and Expressionism,* London, Longmans, 1966.

Thomas Sharp, *Cathedral city,* (Durham), London, Architectural Press, 1945.

Thomas Sharp, *Exeter phoenix,* London, Architectural Press, 1946.

Thomas Sharp, *Oxford replanned,* London, Architectural Press, 1948.

Thomas Sharp, *Town planning,* Harmondsworth, Penguin, 1936.

Richard Sheppard, 'Monuments to the architect?' Talk printed in *The listener* for 8 June 1967.

Arthur Siegel (ed.), *Chicago's famous buildings,* Chicago at the University Press, 1965.

Jack Simmons, *St. Pancras Station,* London, Allen & Unwin, 1968.

Camillo Sitte, *City planning according to artistic principles (Der*

Stadtbau translated by G.R. & C.C. Collins), New York, Random House; London, Phaidon, 1965.

A.W. Skempton & H.R. Johnson, 'The first iron frames' in *The architectural review*, London, for March 1962 (vol CXXI, pp. 175-86).

G.R. Kidder Smith, *The new architecture of Europe*, New York, World Publishing Co., 1961; Prentice-Hall, 1962.

G.R. Kidder Smith, *Sweden builds*, Harmondsworth, Penguin, 1950.

Alison & Peter Smithson, *Without rhetoric: an architectural aesthetic*, London, Latimer, 1973.

Rupert Spade, *Richard Neutra*, London, Thames & Hudson, 1971.

Rupert Spade, *Oscar Niemeyer*, London, Thames & Hudson, 1969. .

Rupert Spade, *Paul Rudolph*, London, Thames & Hudson, 1971.

Isobel Spencer, *Walter Crane*, London, Studio Vista, 1975.

Robin Spencer, *The Aesthetic Movement*, London, Studio Vista: New York, Dutton, 1972.

Geoffrey Speyer, *Architect and community*, London, Peter Owen, 1971.

Phoebe Stanton, *Pugin*, London, Thames & Hudson, 1971.

Willy Stäubli, *Brasilia*, London, Leonard Hill Books, 1966.

John Steegman, *Consort of taste*, London, Sidgwick & Jackson, 1950.

Robert A.M. Stern, *George Howe: towards a modern American architecture*, London and New Haven, Yale University Press, 1975.

Robert A.M. Stern, *New directions in American architecture*, London, Studio Vista, 1969.

Jacques Sternberg, *Kitsch*, London, 1973.

Dorothy Stroud, *The architecture of Sir John Soane*, London, Studio Books, 1961.

John Summerson, *The Architectural Association, 1847-1947*, London, Pleiades for the A.A., 1947.

John Summerson, *The classical language of architecture*, London, Allen & Unwin, 1964; Cambridge, Mass., M.I.T. Press, 1966.

John Summerson, *Georgian London*, London, Pleiades, 1945, new edn.; Harmondsworth, Penguin, 1962.

John Summerson, *The London building world of the 1860's*, London, Thames & Hudson, 1973; Levittown, N.Y., Transatlantic, 1975.

John Summerson, *John Nash, architect to George IV*, London, Allen & Unwin, 2nd edn. 1949; New York, Somerset Pubs.

John Summerson (ed.), *Concerning architecture*, London, Allen Lane, Penguin Books, 1968.

R.W. Symonds & B.B. Whineray, *Victorian furniture*, London, Country Life, 1962.

Allan Temko, *Eero Saarinen*, ('Makers of modern architecture' series), London, Prentice-Hall; New York, Braziller, 1962.

John Tetlow & Anthony Goss, *Homes, towns and traffic*, London, Faber, 1968.

E.P. Thompson & Eileen Yeo (eds.), *The unknown Mayhew*, London,

Merlin Press, 1971; Harmondsworth, Penguin, 1973.

Paul Thompson, *William Butterfield,* London, Routledge, 1971; Cambridge, Mass., M.I.T. Press, 1972.

Paul Thompson, *The work of William Morris,* London, Heinemann, 1967.

David C. Thorns, *Suburbia,* London, MacGibbon & Kee, 1972.

John F.C. Turner & Robert Fichter, *Freedom to build,* New York, Macmillan Company, 1972.

Reginald Turnor, *Nineteenth-century architecture in Britain,* London, Batsford, 1950.

Guilia Veronesi, *Into the twenties,* trans. Diana Burran, London, Thames & Hudson, 1968.

Don Vlack, *Art Deco architecture in New York, 1920-1940,* New York, Harper & Row, 1974.

John A. Walker, *Glossary of art, architecture and design since 1945,* London, Clive Bingley; Hamden, Conn., Linnet Books, 1st edn. 1973, 2nd revised edn. 1977.

Barbara Ward, *The home of man,* Harmondsworth, Penguin, 1976; New York, Norton.

David Watkin, *The life and work of C.R. Cockerell,* London, Zwemmer, 1974; Montclair, N.J., Schram, 1975.

David Watkin, *Thomas Hope and the neo-classical idea,* London, Murray, 1968; Levittown, N.Y., Transatlantic, 1970.

David Watkin, *Morality and architecture,* Oxford, Clarendon Press, 1977.

J.F. White, *The Cambridge Movement,* Cambridge University Press, 1962.

Arnold Whittick, *European architecture in the twentieth century,* London, Crosby Lockwood (originally 5 parts in 3 volumes), 1953; Scranton, Pa., Abelard, 1974.

Henry Lionel Williams & Ottalie K. Williams, *A guide to old American houses, 1700-1900,* South Brunswick, N.Y., A.S. Barnes & Co, 1962; London, Thomas Yoseloff, Ltd., 1972.

H.M. Wingler, *The Bauhaus,* Cambridge, Mass., M.I.T. Press, 1969.

Christopher Woodward, *Skidmore, Owings and Merril,* London, Thames & Hudson, 1970.

Doreen Yarwood, *Robert Adam,* London, Dent, 1970.

Doreen Yarwood, *The English Home,* London, Batsford, 1956.

Andrew Maclaren Young & A.M. Doak, *Glasgow at a glance: an architectural handbook,* Glasgow, Collins, 1965.

192